MYCHAL WYNN

Empowering African-American Males

TEACHING, PARENTING, & MENTORING SUCCESSFUL BLACK MALES

RISING SUN
PUBLISHING

EMPOWERING AFRICAN-AMERICAN MALES

Teaching, Parenting, & Mentoring Successful Black Males
Formerly titled: *Empowering African-American Males to Succeed: A Ten-Step Approach for Parents and Teachers*
Original publication date, 1992

ISBN 1-880463-69-5
Copyright © 2005 Mychal Wynn
Copyright © 2005 Rising Sun Publishing, Inc.

The poems, *There's A New Day Coming* and *Born to Win,* are reprinted from the book, **Don't Quit – Inspirational Poetry** copyright 1990 by Mychal Wynn.

Credits:
Cover design by Mychal Wynn.
Student Photographs taken by Mychal Wynn.
Stock Photographs by Fotosearch.

Reference sources for style and usage: *The New York Public Library Writer's Guide to Style and Usage* copyright 1994 by The New York Public Library and the Stonesong Press, Inc., and the *APA Stylebook 2004* by the Associated Press.

RISING SUN
PUBLISHING

P.O. Box 70906
Marietta, GA 30007-0906
770.518.0369/800.524.2813
FAX 770.587.0862
E-mail: info@rspublishing.com
Web site: http://www.rspublishing.com

Printed in the United States of America.

Empowering African-American Males

Acknowledgments

I would like to thank those parents, educators, counselors, and mentors who have embraced the strategies outlined in this book and who are working diligently to turn the tide against seemingly insurmountable odds to help Black males experience school success as they discover their role in pursuing the American Dream.

A special thank you to my friends—editor, Dr. Glenn Bascome, a classroom teacher and Director of the Dame Marjorie Bean Education Center in Somerset, Bermuda and an excellent role model; and Karen McCord, a Professor at Solano Community College, for her thoughts and insight. I would also like to convey my sincere appreciation to Ella Tolliver, Vilma France, Ethel Cook-Wilson, Donald Sanders, and Curtis McCord for their support in proofreading the text.

My wife, Nina, who has always been there to protect our sons from the many challenges, obstacles, and pitfalls which claim the spirits of Black males each school day.

I would like to acknowledge and thank all the teachers, coaches, counselors, administrators, friends, family, and mentors who have contributed to the growth, development, nurturing, and maturation of our sons. Nowhere is it more evident, "It takes a village to raise a child," than in raising and nurturing a Black male from boyhood to manhood.

Finally, I would like to acknowledge my mother, father, family, and community, who nurtured, prayed for, guided, and protected me. I recognize too, Mr. Roberts, my fifth- and sixth-grade teacher, at Edmund Burke Elementary School, who inspired learning; Dr. Cheryl Gholar, my high school job placement counselor, at Du Sable High School, who held out hope for my future; and Mrs. Ernestine Whiting, Dean Roland Latham, Harvette Emmett, and the professors at Northeastern University, who helped me defy the odds in becoming the first college graduate in my family. I also thank my former and present pastors, Dr. Frederick K.C. Price, Dr. Creflo A. Dollar, and the Reverend Kenneth Marcus, all of whom have nurtured my spirit and led me into a deeper understanding of God's Word and his expectations of me as a husband, father, and believer.

Dedication

To my wife, for her patience, understanding, and support, and to our sons, Mychal-David and Jalani, who represent the promise and potential of Black males.

Table of Contents

About the Author

Mychal Wynn brings the issues pertaining to Black male achievement to the forefront of educational, community, and household discussions. From his humble beginnings in rural Pike County, Alabama, to the second-grade teacher who told his mother, "I doubt if he will ever make it beyond elementary school;" to becoming an internationally-acclaimed author and educational consultant; his life experiences provide insight into, and an understanding of, the challenges confronting Black student achievement in general, and Black male achievement in particular.

Despite numerous office referrals, suspensions throughout elementary and middle school, and being expelled from Chicago's De La Salle Catholic High School, Mychal Wynn, graduated with honors from Boston's Northeastern University; co-founded, together with his wife, Rising Sun Publishing; and has written over sixteen books which explore issues ranging from school improvement and parental involvement to closing the student achievement gap and paving the way for increasing the number of Black males matriculating into college.

At the original publication of this book under the title, *Empowering African-American Males to Succeed: A Ten-Step Approach for Parents and Teachers (1992)*, his older son was four years old. He is now sixteen, and together with his younger brother (ten years old), their academic success, standardized test scores, and personal achievement represent the promise and potential of Black males. For over two decades, Mr. Wynn has been an advocate for children—provoking discussion, providing training, and publishing books and materials which provide insight, strategies, and solutions to the myriad of problems hindering Black male achievement from primary through postsecondary school.

He, his wife, Nina, and their two sons, Mychal-David and Jalani (both of whom attend public schools), reside in Georgia.

Foreword

When the *Empowering African-American Males Succeed: A Ten-Step Approach for Parents and Teachers* book and workbook were published in 1992, I wholly anticipated they would be adopted by every urban school district in America and regularly referred to by classroom teachers, who, throughout the country, were struggling in their efforts to help Black males become academically and socially successful. In 1992, my wife and I had one son, who was four years old and attending preschool at the First Lutheran Church in Carson, California. At home she and I were doing with him everything outlined in the book. Our older son is now sixteen years old and in the eleventh grade at North Springs High School in Atlanta, Georgia. My wife and I have another son, currently ten years old and in the fifth grade. Their academic achievement and social development are the result of the strategies outlined in the original book, additional strategies contained within this book, and relationships with coaches, teachers, principals, pastors, and mentors who have provided their much-needed web of protection. However, they are the exceptions rather than the rule as Black males in public education continue to be disproportionately placed into special education, disproportionately suspended from school, disproportionately dropping out of school, and virtually at the bottom of the academic achievement gap in every category (i.e., reading, writing, math, and science).

In Nathan and Julia Hare's book, *Bringing the Black Boy to Manhood: The Passage,* they note:

> *The Black race is like an unsteady palace, gigantic and ornate, teetering at its base while people gather around with cranes and complex machinery. The people squeal and squelch and prop the palace up, feverishly, pompously, working to repair it at its cracks and wobbly ceiling, when all the while the problem of the building's unsteadiness is a few missing bricks and broken mortar from its now all but invisible foundation.*

Enabling and empowering Black males requires a few missing bricks (mission, vision, climate & culture, curriculum & content, instruction, and assessment) and renewed mortar (strong relationships, effective collaboration, focus, and direction). In my hope to better assist teachers and serve parents,

I have revised the original book and workbook, providing more strategies, expanding the activities, and providing current census and achievement data. Together, they represent integral components of a larger vision of developing personal empowerment, college aspirations, college planning, and inspiring young men to look beyond their current circumstances to future possibilities. While I have used my family's experiences to illustrate points, I empathize with the added struggles of the many single-parent households raising Black males. However, if single-parents are successful in forming a web of protection and support in response to their unique struggles, I believe that they can replicate our successes.

The most difficult task facing educators, parents, and mentors of Black males in the United States, Bermuda, the Caribbean, Canada, Europe, and Africa is to expand their focus beyond intervention and prevention programs to conceptualizing and implementing empowerment processes. Increasing reading and math scores is not a lofty enough aspiration. Envisioning a young man becoming an entrepreneur; CEO of Merrill Lynch, AOL Time Warner, or American Express; neurosurgeon, research scientist, or head of government provides a framework for learning how to do (i.e., run things) rather than how to get by (i.e., achieve proficiency).

The original version of this book outlined ten building blocks dealing with the critical areas required to build stronger relationships with Black males as part of the transformation of their thinking from excuses to empowerment and from low-performance to high academic achievement. The information contained within those building blocks has been woven into the six components as presented in the book, *Increasing Student Achievement: Volume I, Vision:* Mission, Vision, Climate & Culture, Curriculum & Content, Instruction, and Assessment (see illustration). The components are dealt with from the perspective of overall school improvement through the systemic changes, cultural shift, operational teams, and research needed to pave the way to higher achievement levels for all students. Here, the components are dealt with from the perspective of the unique needs of Black males and their families as part of a holistic set of strategies directed at closing the achievement gap and successfully empowering Black males to move through the K-12 educational system into postsecondary institutions.

Mychal Wynn

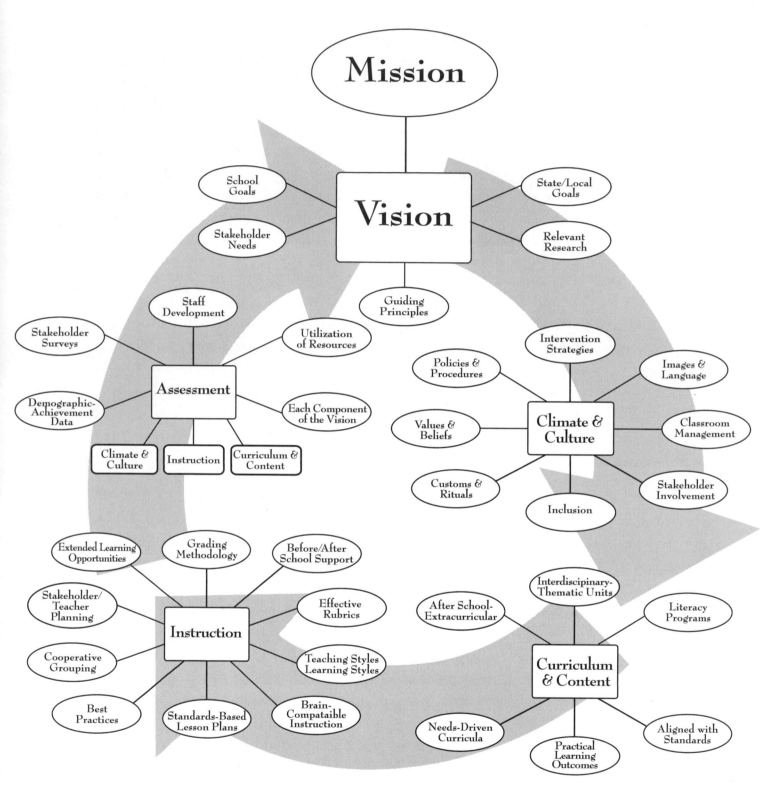

Illustration taken from, *Increasing Student Achievement: Volume I, Vision* (page 5)

How to use this book

This book and the accompanying workbook have been designed to be used as working manuals for parents, teachers, administrators, counselors, coaches, program directors, intervention specialists, mentors, and consultants. As such, they are highly suited to support workshops, staff development sessions, book clubs, and parenting seminars. Depending on your respective role (e.g., parent or teacher), you may be in a position to apply the strategies directly to the teaching and child-rearing of Black males. As a superintendent, principal, or program director, you may be in a position to sensitize parents, teachers, mentors, coaches, and school counselors to the information in hopes of enhancing their relationships with Black males and better understanding the needs of families, thereby paving the way to higher academic achievement and fewer discipline problems. Coaches, counselors, and mentors will expand their knowledge and understanding of the unique issues confronting Black males and their families as they navigate their way through an oftentimes confusing primary-through-postsecondary educational system.

The book raises as many questions as it provides insight—beginning with defining your role, conceptualizing your mission, and clarifying your vision. As an adult stakeholder, you are challenged with answering the questions, "If not me, who? If not now, when?" As much as possible, the author and editor, both Black men (one a Black American, the other, a Black Bermudian), have attempted to depersonalize the issues. However, both are fathers who have worked diligently to overcome the very issues outlined within this book to ensure the academic, social, spiritual, and emotional nurturing of their children. The editor, Dr. Glenn Bascome (a public school teacher), and his wife have seen their two children graduate from college—their daughter is a public school teacher with a Master's degree and their twenty-five-year-old son expects to complete his doctorate in physiotherapy in 2006. The author, Mychal Wynn, and his wife continue to encounter the issues raised in this book as their sons are currently in high school and elementary school.

This book sets forth a process, as outlined in the book *Increasing Student Achievement: Volume I, Vision*, where each Chapter builds upon strategies set forth in each preceding Chapter. To facilitate individual use and stimulate group discussions I have set apart data, research studies, and major points by bullets and numerical lists. Effective teachers and presenters tell you what they're going to tell you; tell you; and then tell you what they told you. As such, readers may find it helpful to review the *Key Points* prior to beginning each Chapter and reviewing them again at the end of each Chapter. Activities designed to further operationalize the ideas and strategies set forth in each Chapter can be found in the *workbook*.

While this book has been written to specifically address the issues relating to Black males, you will find the approach used and strategies provided relate to all children. Whether you are a parent, teacher, coach, counselor, principal, or mentor, you must become a role player in influencing change within your school community. Becoming an advocate for children will require that you no longer wait for new leadership, new programs, or new research. You must become the catalyst to move ideas and strategies beyond discussions to being operationalized.

The "Web of Protection" illustrated in Chapter four, *Curriculum & Content*, will help each role player to understand the importance of communication and collaboration. Strong relationships between role players are paramount to protecting Black males from the many issues threatening their lives and contributing to their lack of academic achievement, unemployment, and high rates of incarceration.

Finally, while this book will explore many of the most plaguing issues, the following books are recommended as additional resources to assist your efforts in developing a comprehensive set of strategies designed to identify a young man's gifts, inspire his dreams, and provide him with a primary-through-postsecondary plan:

- *Ten Steps to Helping Your Child Succeed in School*
- *A Middle School Plan for Students with College-Bound Dreams*
- *A High School Plan for Students with College-Bound Dreams*
- *Follow Your Dreams: Lessons That I Learned in School*
- *The Eagles who Thought They were Chickens*

We can, whenever and wherever we choose, successfully teach all children whose schooling is of interest to us. We already know more than we need in order to do this. Whether we do it must finally depend on how we feel about the fact that we haven't so far.

— Ron Edmonds

Empowering African-American Males

Overview

Why Focus on Black Males?

Every 5 seconds during the school day, a Black public school student is suspended. Every 46 seconds during the school day, a Black high school student drops out. Every minute, a Black child is arrested and a Black baby is born to an unmarried mother. Every 3 minutes, a Black child is born into poverty. Every hour, a Black baby dies. Every 4 hours, a Black child or youth under 20 dies from an accident, and every 5 hours, a Black youth is a homicide victim. Every day, a Black young person under 25 dies from HIV infection and a Black child or youth under 20 commits suicide.[1]

— *Marian Wright Edelman, The Children's Defense Fund*

African-American Males—Black Males

While the title of this book reflects the culturally appropriate term, "African-American" referring to Americans of African descent, I will be using the terminology, 'Black' throughout the text. Whether Black American, Black Caribbean, Black Bermudian, Black Canadian, or Black African, the issues confronting Black males, and their parents, wherever they live, are very similar across cultural and socioeconomic lines. These boys, young men, and men who share a cultural frame of reference, are adversely influenced by peer pressures, frequently struggle in classrooms, are the students most likely to be disciplined, and are likely to matriculate through an educational system which fails to affirm their cultural contributions or connect them to their historical past. My mother, bless her soul, when told of my plans to visit Africa, asked, "Son, why are you going to Africa?" When I told her, "Mama, Nina and I are going on a tour of Egypt and Ghana to trace our roots," she responded, "Boy, you ain't from Africa; you were born in Alabama!" However, when I saw firsthand the statues and artifacts in the Egyptian Museum in Cairo, Egypt; when I went into the pyramids, temples, and tombs in Giza and Luxor; when I journeyed along the Nile to a Nubian village; when I witnessed the monuments and statues in Abu Simbel; and when I flew by airplane across the Sahara, landing in Accra, Ghana and witnessed at the airport the thousands of Black people who looked like the Black people pictured on the walls and chiseled in stone throughout Egypt, I knew, despite thousands of miles and hundreds of years of physical and cultural separation, the Ghanaians, the Nubians, and those portrayed in the temples and tombs of Egypt were "Black like me" and I was in fact home.

I have found African Black males, Bermudian Black males, Canadian Black males, Caribbean Black males, and Black males from Alabama to face similar challenges in education, maturation, college matriculation, and, in gaining full access through the glass ceilings into the ivory towers of business in their respective countries, states, islands, and communities. Subsequently, the strategies set forth in this book, are pertinent to the raising, teaching, nurturing, and empowering of 'Black' males whether they live in the United States, Canada, Bermuda, Africa, or on one of the many islands in the Caribbean.

Addressing the Black male crisis requires first, raising the question, "What's the problem?" If there is in fact a problem, we must raise the question, "What do we want to do about it?" In the original version of this book, *Empowering African-American Males to Succeed: A Ten-Step Approach for Parents and Teachers (1992)*, I cited the 1990 U.S. Census Bureau statistics which showed:

> *African-American males have higher unemployment rates, lower labor force participation rates, lower high school graduation and college enrollment rates, while ranking first in incarceration and homicide as a percentage of the population.*

> *The leading cause of death for African-American men between the ages of 15 and 24 is homicide. And, while representing only 6 percent of the population, African-American men represent 49 percent of prison inmates. Only 4 percent of African-American males attend college, while 23 percent of those of college age are either incarcerated or on probation. While African-American children nationwide comprise approximately 17 percent of all children in public schools, they represent 41 percent of all children in special education. Of the African-American children in special education, 85 percent are African-American males. African-American males, while comprising only 8 percent of public school students, represent the largest percentage, nationally, in suspensions (37 percent).*

The tragic reality concerning the plight of Black males is, in the decade between the 1990 and 2000 census little changed. In many categories, the 2000 census shows a worsening of the Black male condition. Despite the many task forces, state accountability standards, high school exit exams, increased NCAA student-athlete eligibility requirements, and the *No Child Left Behind* legislation, Black males continue to be among the students most likely to be referred to the office, suspended from school, sent to an alternative school, placed into special education, drop out of school, incarcerated in a state or federal prison, or be the victim of a homicide.

Black males suffer from a cultural disconnect in schools and classrooms. Hip-hop clothing, flashy jewelry, earrings, corn rows, brash language, body piercings, and tattoos further the cultural, gender, and generational divide between Black males and teachers.

As evidenced by the data contained in the 2001 report for the National Center for Education Statistics, *Educational Achievement and Black-White Inequality*, there is no doubt there is a problem and something needs to be done about it.

Discipline, Special Education, and Jail

- Black students, while representing only 17 percent of public school students, account for 32 percent of suspensions and 30 percent of expulsions. In 1999, 35 percent of all Black students in grades 7-12 had been suspended or expelled from school. The rate was 20 percent for Hispanics and 15 percent for Whites.

- Black children are labeled "mentally retarded" nearly 300 percent more than White children and only 8.4 percent of Black males are identified and enrolled in gifted and talented classes.

- Black males in their early 30s are twice as likely to have prison records (22 percent) than bachelor's degrees (12 percent).

- A Black male born in 1991 (today's 7th grade student) has a 29 percent chance of spending time in prison at some point in his life. The figure for Hispanic males is 16 percent, and for White males is 4 percent.

- A Black male is 700 percent more likely than a White male to be sentenced to a local, state, or federal prison.

- Black males are imprisoned at a rate of 3,405 per 100,000 (3.4 percent); Hispanics at a rate of 1,231 per 100,000 (1.2 percent); and Whites at a rate of 465 per 100,000 (.465 percent).[2]

Freeman Hrabowski, in *Beating the Odds: Raising Academically Successful African American Males*, notes:

By junior high school, many are working below grade level or barely passing; consequently, they see school as a place where they fail. The environment becomes even more frustrating because of problems between these students, their peers, and teachers and administrators—problems often related to behavior …We see that Black students are more often tracked into lower-ability groups involving general education and vocational education and, in contrast, very few Black students are placed in gifted classes. In fact, White children are twice as likely to be placed in these classes as Black children. We also know that males, in general, are more likely than females to be overrepresented in the educable mentally retarded and learning-disabled children and underrepresented in gifted and talented programs. Ford and Harris report that Blacks, Hispanics, and Native Americans are underrepresented in as many as 70 percent of the gifted programs in the nation, and overrepresented in almost half of all special-education programs.

High School Performance, Course Enrollment, and Graduation

- 17.5 percent of Black students, 13.2 percent of Hispanic students, and 9.3 percent of White students in grades K-12 were retained at least one grade.[3]

- 13 percent of Blacks ages 16-24 have not earned a high school credential. The rate for Whites is 7 percent.

- 30 percent of Black high school students have taken advanced mathematics courses compared to 45 percent of Whites.

- 5 percent of Black high school students take a fourth year of a foreign language with 2 percent taking an AP foreign language course.

- 12 percent of Black high school students take science classes as high as chemistry and physics.

- 27 percent of Black high school students take advanced English.

- Black students take AP exams at a rate of 53 per 1,000 students. The rate for Hispanic students is 115 per 1,000 and for Whites is 185 per 1,000.

- The average SAT scores for Black students is 433V and 426M; for Whites it is over 22 percent higher at 529V and 531M.

- The average ACT score for Black students is 16.9; for Whites it is nearly 30 percent higher at 21.8.

Unemployment

- The unemployment rate for Blacks ages 16-19 is 25 percent.

- The unemployment rate for Blacks without a high school credential is 30 percent, 19 percent with high school but no college, 10 percent with some college but no degree, and 6 percent with a bachelor's degree.

While these statistics may be alarming for the general population, they have left barely any Black family untouched and place all Black males at risk. Societal perceptions, law enforcement interactions, and peer pressures of friends, relatives, and friends of friends who are either undereducated, unemployed, in gangs, involved in criminal activity, or on parole have an immediate and far-reaching impact on the lives of current and future generations of Black males. The issue for the Black community—indeed, for America—is much more than merely closing an achievement gap; it is ensuring that future generations of Black men have jobs, function as fathers, and contribute to the health and economic well-being of their local and national community.

It Takes A Village

Increasing Black male achievement will require a systemic and sustained collaboration between adults throughout the school community—the village. In the case of our sons, their academic and social development, school and personal success, exposure and opportunities, and maturation and spiritual development have been, and continue to be, the result of the village. My wife and I have a role as our sons' parents, but so do our friends and other family members, as do their teachers, preachers, coaches, administrators, school safety officers, and school support personnel, have roles in their protection and development:

1. *Parents* will have to become actively involved in the academic, social, spiritual, and physical development of their sons and provide a household culture built around a set of spiritual core values which encourage and celebrate excellence. Fathers and mothers must accept responsibility for opening communication and building relationships with the influential adults in the lives of their sons, i.e., teachers, principals, coaches, pastors, or mentors. On a regular basis, they must inquire about school, the application of something learned at school, and what their sons are "planning" to do with their lives after high school:

   "Mychal-David, how did physics class go today? What did Ms. A say about your artwork? Have you been working on your Literature Portfolio? We hardly see you doing any work at home. When are you working on it?"

"Jalani, what did you learn in school today?" 'Nothing really, Dad.' "Well, if you're not learning anything in school, then you are going to have to read for an hour and then tell me what you learned from what you read." 'Dad, I really did learn something in school today. In science we are learning the Periodic Table of Elements. The elements we talked about today were ...'

2. *Teachers* will have to be willing to better understand the needs of parents, learning-styles of children, and have a genuine desire to ensure frequent opportunities for Black males to be successful in their classrooms.

   "Mr. and Mrs. Wynn, Mychal-David has been struggling with understanding some of the concepts being covered in pre-calculus. I don't believe he has had the necessary foundation in algebra. I am available to work with him during the mornings and after school, however, I believe he would benefit from working with a tutor. I know several tutors whom I can recommend who are available to work with students on the weekends. Once Mychal-David has a better grasp of the concepts which have been covered, I will allow him an opportunity to retake the earlier tests and quizzes which he failed and he will be able to receive full credit."

3. *Administrative leadership*, whether exhibited by principals, assistant principals, coaches, magnet coordinators, department chairpersons, or program directors must be willing to provide advocacy for Black males within their schools and programs and must encourage and expose students to a wide range of personal, intellectual, and artistic development opportunities.

   "Mr. Wynn, I explained to Mychal-David's honors algebra II teacher that she could not change his schedule from the honors pre-calculus to the algebra III/trigonometry class. We have an open enrollment policy at our school. While teacher recommendations are strongly suggested, any student who wants to enroll in any of the honors or AP classes offered has the freedom to do so. There is a parent waiver I will send home with Mychal-David for you to sign to indicate that you understand his enrollment has not been recommended by his teacher."

"Mr. Wynn, in the classroom today Jalani had some problems which had him pretty upset. I had him spend the rest of the day with me in my office. I don't believe his problem is anything to be alarmed about. After you speak with Jalani this evening, please feel free to contact me in the morning before school if you would like to discuss it further."

4. *School-based support personnel,* i.e., custodians, law enforcement personnel, front office staff, and other non-instructional and administrative personnel must be willing to assume an active role in protecting, encouraging, and nurturing Black males throughout elementary, middle, high school, and college.

   One of the custodians at our older son's high school approached my wife and me one day in the corridor:

   "Mr. and Mrs. Wynn, you know your son thinks he has a little girlfriend. I see them standing together between every class. I'll let you know what her name is tomorrow."

   On another occasion, one of the cafeteria workers approached me at my son's elementary school:

   "Mr. Wynn, did you know Jalani doesn't eat his fruit? He throws his fruit away almost every day. Now, he doesn't throw his cake and cookies away. He's going to get fat and ruin his teeth if he doesn't eat his fruit and stop eating so many sweets. Also, did you know he buys a cupcake almost every day?"

5. *Spiritual support,* through faith-based institutions which understand and serve the needs of families: positive adult role models; youth programs; and initiatives which nurture, develop, and celebrate the many and diverse gifts of Black children; and educational programs and initiatives reinforcing and nurturing the intellectual development of Black children.

Like other school children, Black males begin school interested in learning, experiencing, and engaging in the entire process of school from the classroom to the cafeteria and from the school bus to recess. However, any failure to establish an effective home-school collaboration with shared beliefs, goals, and expectations will most certainly result in classroom disruptions and underachievement. Our older son began experiencing all of the stereotypical, if not predictable, conflicts in school (clashes with classmates,

challenges to the teacher's authority, and frequent off-task classroom behaviors). However, a first-grade collaboration with his classroom teacher, Mrs. Barbara Mabry, helped us to help him discover his passion for drawing and to begin to construct around him a *web of protection* which inspired a dream he has held on to from first grade through today (eleventh grade): he is an honors student in the Math & Science and Visual & Performing Arts Magnet Program at North Springs High School in Atlanta, Georgia.

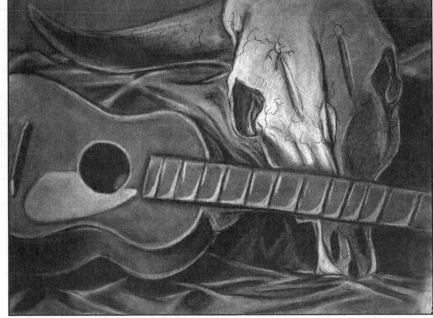

Teacher collaboration is crucial to the success of the village. As such, they must shift their paradigms from viewing the teaching of responsibility as a "sprint"—school opens, they distribute their syllabus, tell parents and

students what their expectations are, and fail those students who don't run THEIR race from the opening bell. Teaching and nurturing Black males through their own self-imposed obstacles and behaviors is a marathon—where parents share what they know about their son's needs, teachers share their expectations, and together they devise strategies to meet student needs. This collaboration recognizes that one young man's pace throughout the race may not be at the same speed as other classmates—

not as organized, doesn't process the information as quickly, is frequently out of step in preparing for tests and quizzes, requires more warm-up time for class participation, isn't always prepared for class, doesn't always have books and required materials, frequently forgets homework, and doesn't always make note of project due dates.

Oftentimes, males simply don't get out of the starting blocks as quickly as teachers or parents would like, or expect them to.

When our younger son, Jalani, was in the fourth grade, my wife and I had a meeting with his classroom teacher, his gifted teacher, and the school's assistant principal. On three occasions during third grade, our son had been referred to the office, twice resulting in in-school suspension. On each occasion, he was in a situation with an adult other than his classroom teacher, with whom my wife and I were collaborating. His conflicts were occurring with substitute teachers, in the cafeteria, and on the school bus.

The year was proceeding reasonably well when he was forced to serve another in-school suspension for "threatening" a little girl. He told the little girl who had demanded he get out of a chair at a computer which she wanted to use, "You'd better leave me alone. I could hurt you if I really wanted to!" At the meeting, everyone was genuinely concerned about Jalani's success. The frustration and exasperation were apparent in everyone's voices as his teacher, gifted teacher, assistant principal, and even my wife shared examples of how they had all been trying to work with Jalani to help him increase his social skills, manage his time, complete his assignments, and perform at a level at which everyone believed him to be capable. Nearing the end of the meeting, the assistant principal turned to me and asked, "Mychal, what do you think we should do?" I responded, "Nothing different; just what we're doing."

This wasn't a sprint! This was a marathon! We were already collaborating and had put strategies into place. My wife and I shared our thoughts about our son and his needs. Some of the issues we identified were:

- Our son was having a difficult time in his gifted class. He was experiencing cultural isolation (there was only one other Black student, a girl in the entire fourth-grade gifted program).

- Our son was struggling with managing his own time. Both in the regular classroom and in his gifted classes—he needed constant reminders to complete his work.

- He was raising his voice, talking over other children in the classroom (a bad habit which was unfortunately being modeled by his older brother who was going through his own issues as a tenth-grader).

- He was generally well-behaved in the classroom, but was having conflicts while under the supervision of adults other than his classroom teacher with whom he had his primary relationship.

Despite these challenges there was nothing else we needed to do. We had already ensured he was in a fourth-grade classroom which was looping.[4] The entire class, together with the teacher, would be staying together for fifth grade. My wife and I recognized one of the challenges our son had was in establishing new relationships. His personal conflicts were occurring largely during the first half of the school year while he was getting to know other students. We also developed, via regular e-mails between us and his teacher, a time-management plan which helped to keep him focused on his responsibilities on a daily basis. All we needed to do was to continue what we were doing to support Jalani and to allow the marathon to continue its course.

As a result of staying with the same teacher and classmates, Jalani was quickly out of the starting blocks in fifth grade. With strong teacher and student relationships, Jalani soared academically and amazed everyone (except me) with his level of personal responsibility, his ability to remain on task, and his ability to avoid conflicts with classmates. He even appeared in his first Shakespearian production, "A Midsummer Night's Dream," where he brought down the house with his performance as 'Nick Bottom.'

Following his performance, we received an e-mail from his teacher.

My, what a journey this has been!!!!!!

Teachers who know of Jalani (but have never taught him) stopped me all day long to comment on how impressed they were with his performance today. What an awesome experience it has been for me to watch the little boy who ran around the front office transform into the confident kid on stage performing one of the lead roles in 'A Midsummer Night's Dream'!!!

Jalani was basking in the stage lights--clearly joyous about being on stage and having full permission to talk--dance, perform, and be a goofball, as well! Have you ever seen more of an advertisement for playing to an individual's learning style? Wow!!!!

I have always loved Jalani--you know I asked to have him in my class for fourth grade. This year has been fascinating for me because I have watched him grow into himself day by day. Mychal, you were right!!!!! I give you full credit--you know your kid, and you could predict the outcome of looping for Jalani--even as he was struggling with relationships last year.

Watching Jalani grow has been interesting because he seems to be developing different facets of who he is: the dedicated student alongside the kind, funny, and caring friend. He is taking responsibility in his academics while goofing off with buddies! What fun!!!!!! These are the qualities we all strive for ... discipline when necessary for career success, and compassion and humor when it comes to family and friends. It is a pleasure to watch him be-bop down the hall with a constant smile on his face now, too. No more sour puss as sometimes found in the past.

What a job you have done--allowing Jalani to be Jalani (and listening to his constant stream of words as he is continuing to grow into himself!!) Thank you for your support, always, and letting me witness and take part in this kid's life. As teachers, we aren't supposed to have favorites, but ... you've got two kids who are completely and totally unforgettable! Favorites who will never be forgotten--for being themselves and helping me to become a better teacher.

Happy Thanksgiving!

These factors in the lives of our children provide clear evidence to support the African proverb, "It takes a village to raise a child." Solutions to closing the achievement gap and increasing Black male achievement are complex processes, comprised of many variables, requiring many strategies, and mandating collaboration between the adult stakeholders within each school community. To create the type of village which nurtures the academic achievement and social development of Black males, we must develop a willingness to objectively assess the effectiveness of how we are serving their needs and the type of relationships we are building with their families, by school setting (i.e., elementary, middle, high school, junior college, and college), and by department, program, grade level, and classroom within the school.

Overview: Key Points

1. Black males, despite socioeconomic, geographical, or cultural differences share cultural commonalities in the areas of academic achievement and social skill development.

2. Black males make up the largest group of low-performing students and represent a disproportionately higher rate of suspensions, expulsions, and special education placements.

3. White students take 200 percent more AP classes; have average SAT scores over 100 points higher (22 percent); and have average ACT scores 5 points higher (22 percent).

4. Home-school relationships must be driven by a common focus.

5. The unemployment rate for Blacks without a high school diploma is 30 percent, while the unemployment rate for Blacks with a college degree is 6 percent.

6. Increasing Black male achievement requires a collaborative effort between adult stakeholders throughout the school community.

7. Systemic, sustainable increases in student achievement are the result of a marathon which must allow frequent opportunities for students who get a slow start to catch up.

8. Thoughtful class placement and teacher assignment are essential to Black male academic success and positive social skill development.

Chapter 1
Mission

*Educators, activists, and assorted sages have given us scores of maxims
that extol the value of education, but the most poignant words I have ever
encountered on the necessity of education for African Americans were those
of a Mississippi slave owner who in 1832 wrote: "Knowledge and slavery are
incompatible." Indeed, they are. And thus, it is not difficult to understand
why at one point in American history it was illegal to teach slaves to read
and write. Just as the denial of education is a proven method of subjugating
a people, there can be little doubt that access to education is potentially a
definitive means to the self-enlightenment and self-realization of a people,
which in turn spells liberation. By that I mean liberation from all the 'isms':
racism, sexism, provincialism, and the individualism that prevents us from
building sturdy Black bridges.*

— Johnnetta B. Cole

Before forging ahead to identify problems, conceptualize solutions, or
develop implementation plans, you must go through the painstaking task
of clarifying your mission, i.e., purpose. Contemplating, conceptualizing,
and clarifying your mission is a time-consuming, self-reflecting, gut-
wrenching task. It requires, amid the chaos and confusion of raising and
teaching children, you stop and reflect on whether you are doing the right
thing, going in the right direction, or have any real understanding of the
challenges, hopes, and dreams of the Black males whom you are raising,
teaching, counseling, coaching, or mentoring. Without devoting the needed
time to clarifying the mission, teachers are hired, the football season begins,
schools open, programs are implemented, and subsequent failure is virtually
guaranteed. This outcome does not necessarily mean people aren't working
hard, the adult stakeholders in the school community don't care, or that
groups of people aren't putting in a lot of time and energy into trying to help
these young men. The problem is, we are so busy doing things, we never
stop long enough to clarify what we want to accomplish, what types of men
we want to develop, and where we ultimately want these young men to go

as a result of all of the energy and effort we are devoting to them.

A clear mission, guides and focuses our efforts. Without one, we are unlikely to identify, conceptualize, or implement the types of self-sustaining systems and programs necessary for substantive, systemic, and long-term increases in the academic achievement levels of Black males. We are more likely to experience a great deal of confusion, high level of personal stress, and seek comfort in resolving that their success, or lack thereof, is really outside our control: "I don't know what to do with these boys today. We've tried everything and nothing seems to be working."

> *Beginning the school year with a purposeful mission, creating a clearly-defined and commonly-shared vision (taking into account state and local learning goals, school goals, stakeholder needs, and driven by relevant research), and cultivating a positive, nurturing, and collaborative school and classroom climate and culture lays the foundation for engaging students within the school's curriculum and content areas ...The school's mission provides the direction with the vision providing the compass that guides the way.*

> *[Increasing Student Achievement, Volume I, Vision]*

A widely-held misconception by parents, teachers, counselors, and coaches is that the exercise of developing a mission statement is something school districts, businesses, and organizations engage in—not something that's important to parenting, teaching, counseling, or coaching. Nothing can be further from the truth. Households without a clear sense of mission have no compass to point the direction toward resolving disputes, directing the family's resources, or identifying the programs and support mechanisms needed to support family and individual goals. Classroom teachers who open the school year without a clear sense of mission cannot conceptualize a holistic set of strategies which integrate classroom management, lesson design, support materials, parent conferences, cooperative grouping, daily procedures, relationships with children and families, or grading practices and methodology. Counselors without a clear sense of mission will fail to fully understand the circumstances and obstacles confronting Black males and what is required to move them into the ranks of exemplifying excellence in character and achievement. Coaches without a clear sense of mission can never fully understand the extraordinary opportunity they have to shape the nature, values, and character of a Black boy's life from boyhood into manhood.

There is no short cut as Stephen R. Covey notes in, *Principle-Centered Leadership*:

Can you go two weeks without milking the cow and then get out there and milk like crazy? Can you 'forget' to plan in the spring or goof off all summer and then hit the ground real hard in the fall to bring in the harvest? We might laugh at such ludicrous approaches in agriculture, but then in an academic environment we might cram to get the grades and degrees we need to get the jobs we want, even if we fail to get a good general education. The only thing that endures over time is the law of the farm: I must prepare the ground, put in the seed, cultivate it, weed, water it, then gradually nurture growth and development to full maturity—there is no quick fix, where you can just move in and make everything right with a positive mental attitude and a bunch of success formulas. The law of the harvest governs.

The *Successful Texas School-wide Programs* research study noted:

These schools did not simply have Mission Statements, their sense of mission was articulated in every aspect of their planning, organization, and use of resources. Almost every decision about the selection of instructional materials; staff development; use of resources; scheduling of the school calendar; assignment of teachers, support personnel, and volunteers; and use of space was guided by a focus on the mission of ensuring the academic success of every student.

A clear and focused mission is also noted as one of the eight correlates identified in *Effective Schools* research:

- *Safe and Orderly Environment*

- *Climate of High Expectations for Success*

- *Instructional Leadership*

- **Clear and Focused Mission**

- *Opportunity to Learn and Student Time on Task*

- *Frequent Monitoring of Student Progress*

- *Home–School Relations*

My mother and father were born in Memphis, Tennessee during the Great Depression. Their parents grew up during the time of Jim Crow laws and the systemic cruelty directed toward Black people and Black families during the post-Civil War U.S. While both my mother and father dropped out of school, the lessons passed on to them were clear: 'The hope and ultimate emancipation of the Black community rest in education.' Lacking formal education themselves, my mother and father were intent on ensuring a college education for their son. Even as I was growing up in Chicago's infamous south side urban ghetto, my father had a clear sense of mission, i.e., I was going to college. At the barber shop, grocery store, when visiting relatives, or simply being introduced to his adult friends,

he told everyone who would listen, 'My boy is going to college.' His mission was clear—an education would represent my emancipation from poverty. He didn't know where I would go to college, what I would study in college, or how our family would even pay for college. However, without question, I was going to college. Subsequently, my K-12 schooling was placed into this context. Although only 50 of the 500 students who entered my high school [Du Sable High School] actually graduated and only 15 of those went on to attend four-year universities, there was never any doubt in my father's mind that I would be one of those students. Due to his emphatic and continual verbal affirmation, 'My boy is going to college,' there was never any doubt in my mind.

The mission, as it relates to student achievement, occurs on four distinct levels within a school community:

1. Mission of the school district.

2. Mission of the school itself.

3. Mission of the department or program within the school.

4. Mission of the individual, i.e., parent, teacher, coach, counselor, administrator, superintendent, or school board member.

Engaging in the process of conceptualizing your mission is unavoidable. If you are unwilling to engage in this part of the process, there is no need to proceed further—the rest of the book will be of little benefit. Without a clear sense of mission, there is no framework to engage in discussions or to assess strategies. This is why many parent-teacher discussions erupt into arguments and why so many parents and teachers have confrontational or adversarial relationships. Parents and teachers must take time to give thought to the questions, "What do I want a child to experience from pre-school through college?" And, "What type of environment is needed to nurture those experiences?" The answers to such questions will determine whether parents and teachers share a similar purpose for the growth, development, and achievement of Black males.

"Mr. C, our son has the academic ability to be successful; however, he is totally unorganized. If we don't monitor him, he is going to forget to write down important test and quiz dates, forget to do his homework, or if he does it, he is likely to misplace it before he turns it in. Despite all our attempts to teach and reinforce honesty, he has become possessed with a 'lying demon!'"

Talk to ten parents and you are likely to hear at least eight similar stories of their sons being possessed by 'lying demons, lazy devils,' and/or 'griping gremlins.' Such parents don't need teachers who believe in allowing children to fail as a character-building experience, or who are unwilling to communicate with parents on an as-needed basis to assist in their efforts to purge their sons of their demonic possession. While our youngest son has been reasonably self-directed toward his academic studies throughout elementary school, our older son has required micro-managing and constant prayer through eleventh grade. As a result of our prayers and teachers' support, my wife and I have witnessed his continuing transformation. He has become more responsible—taking pride in his work, preparing for tests and quizzes (without our constant prodding), and valuing his own grades and test scores.

We are receiving daily text messages between classes:

"Dad, I got a '95' on my physics test."

"Mom, I got a '100' on my Spanish project."

"Mom, I got a '100' on my art homework."

"Dad, I got an '85' on my lit. final."

"Dad, my lit. portfolio was the best in the class!"

"Mom, I scored in the 90th percentile on the Georgia High School Graduation Writing Test!"

Neither my wife, myself, or our son, can take full credit for his current school success. We readily acknowledge, it has been through a shared sense of mission with his teachers, dating back to the 'Traffic Light' book used by his preschool teacher to keep us abreast of his daily behaviors, to the school planner initialed on a daily basis by his middle school teachers to ensure his making note of test dates and homework assignments, to e-mails received from high school teachers, who have willingly kept my wife and me aware of his progress, to advise us of quizzes, and to let us know when assignments have been misplaced and/or turned in late.

This shared sense of mission has extended, more often than not, to coaches and school administrators. As previously stated, my wife and I are doing our part, but the achievement levels of our sons, grade by grade, subject by subject, and standardized test performance can be traced directly to the sense of mission and resulting collaboration which we have had with their teachers, coaches, and administrators.

The two questions which must be answered as you engage in the process of conceptualizing your mission are:

1. What is your role (i.e., parent, teacher, coach, law enforcement personnel, counselor) in conceptualizing and implementing strategies as it relates to Black male achievement?

2. What is the level of achievement you would like Black males to attain as a result of your influence?

The answer to the first question is usually pretty simple:

"As his mother, my role as his parent is to nurture, protect, love, encourage, and raise him."

Okay, mama, what level of achievement do you want your son to reach as a result of your nurturing, protection, love, and encouragement? Get to school on time? Consistently turn his homework in? Learn a set of guiding principles or core values? Develop a strong foundation of faith? Be recognized for athletic prowess, academic scholarship, or both? Learn how to be a husband to his wife, father to his children, and/or leader in his community? Discover his dream, attend college, ascend to political office and/or enter into social or community service?

"As a teacher, my role is to nurture students' social skill development and academic achievement levels."

Okay, Ms. Fourth-grade Teacher. What level of achievement do you want for your *Black male* students as a result of your influence? Do you want them to qualify for the school's honor roll? Do you want them to pursue advanced middle school math and science? Do you want them to develop Standard

English proficiency? Do you want them to begin developing the vocabulary and writing skills to score highly on the SAT/ACT? Do you want them to begin planning to enroll in honors and AP classes in high school and to begin developing a middle-through-high-school plan? Do you want them to begin thinking and talking about college?

"As a pastor, my role is to lead young people into salvation."

Okay, pastor, what level of achievement do you want for the *Black males* in your congregation and within the surrounding community? Do you want them to develop leadership skills? Do you want them to strive for the highest levels of academic achievement? Do you want them to provide positive role models within the community? Do you want them to internalize, model, and demonstrate Biblical principles at school and in their athletic programs?

"As a middle school football coach, my role is to prepare my players for the offensive and defensive system utilized by our high school coaches."

Okay, coach, what level of achievement do you want for your *Black athletes?* Do you want as many A's as yards gained? Do you want their character to be as solid as their blocking? Do you want them to reflect the same confidence and pride in their lives off the field as they display when they rush onto the field? Do want to see each name on your roster listed on the school's honor roll?

Understanding your role and consciously affirming the level of achievement you want to personally influence within the lives of young men are essential to clearly defining your mission.

Role

There are many roles we, as caring adults, can and must play as we influence the cognitive growth, intellectual development, emotional maturation, and spiritual awareness of the young men in our care. The following roles represent some of the most significant adult influences within any school community:

- **Parent:** The role of parents is unquestionably the most important influence in helping a young man along his journey from boyhood to manhood. How young men are prepared to respond to the many challenges, pitfalls, dangers, and disappointments of growing up Black is either consciously strengthened or unconsciously neglected. The way to academic achievement is either paved through parental expectations and involvement or sabotaged through parental neglect, excuses, or low expectations. Since the majority of Black males are being raised in single-parent, female-headed households, the challenges of parenting and teaching them how to become men are magnified.

- **Teacher:** During their primary and secondary school-age years from kindergarten through the twelfth grade, young men will spend more time with a teacher or group of teachers than they will with their own parent(s)—1260 hours per year and 16,380 total hours by the time they graduate from high school. At the high school level, Black males who are involved in extracurricular activities may spend as many as 16 hours a day in school-related activities resulting in 11,520 hours of influence teachers and coaches may have during a young man's four years of high school. At the collegiate level, the lessons, discussions, mentors, and role models will directly impact a young man's journey into manhood. At all levels, teachers, coaches, and administrators, undeniably, have tremendous power to inspire academic achievement and connect the sterile environment of classroom learning to the interests, passions, and aspirations of the young men within their respective schools, classrooms, programs, and athletic teams.

- **Counselor:** At all levels of schooling, i.e., elementary, middle, high school, alternative school, junior college, or college, counselors have tremendous power to influence the academic pursuits, career aspirations, and personal development of young men. However, the unfortunate reality is, if Black males don't belong to one of three groups—high academic achievers, low academic achievers, or discipline problems—they are less likely to develop meaningful contact with, and thereby benefit from the wealth of knowledge and experiences of the school's counselor. The school's counselor has tremendous power in influencing program opportunities for students and parents and providing exposure to a wide variety of support programs, as well as educational, personal development, and career opportunities which expand a child's world beyond the local community on to a global stage.

- **Coach:** Coaches at all levels of schooling have tremendous influence over the lives of young men, and at the professional level, over the lives of men and families. From AAU/USATF[5] athletic teams to high school, coaches are highly influential within the lives of young men and have perhaps the greatest influence in directing college-bound athletes toward colleges and into relationships with college coaches. As such, they oftentimes may have more power than parents and peers to develop the character traits, belief system, and future direction of young men.

- **Administrator:** Principals and assistant principals, as vanguards of the school community, are in a position to exert tremendous influence over the lives of young men. The leadership skills, mission, vision, core values, and guiding principles communicated by administrative leadership can have far-reaching effects beyond the school and throughout the local community.

- **Law Enforcement Personnel:** Law enforcement personnel literally have a life and death influence over the lives of Black males, who have the highest rates of incarceration and are the most likely victims of police shootings. Through the use of firearms, prosecutorial practices, defense preparation, and sentencing, individuals within the criminal justice system have enormous power and influence over the lives of Black boys, Black men, and the strength and success of the Black community, particularly in urban centers and inner-city areas.

- **Clergy:** Although many young men spend precious little time in houses of worship, pastors, bishops, priests, or other spiritual and/or religious leaders have undeniable influence in the lives of young men through the programs, initiatives, and level of community out-reach of their congregations. Historically, the Black church has been at the forefront of creating and cultivating Black leadership, encouraging full participation in the democratic process, and providing a catalyst for civic, legislative, and educational changes; the church has also been a creative outlet for nurturing the oral presentation, musical, dance, and artistic abilities of Black children. White churches are oftentimes highly influential in suburban communities and have undeniable influence with those responsible for ensuring equity and access of Black males to classes, extracurricular activities, and opportunities within suburban school districts.

- **Social Worker:** Social workers, psychologists, and other intervention or prevention personnel are influential in the lives of young men and the overall mental and physical health of their families. Whether they operate from an intervention or an empowerment frame of reference, they exert tremendous influence through the types of resources, programs, and initiatives they create for, and provide to, families.

- **Mentor:** Persons in any of the aforementioned roles may function as mentors; however, the role of mentoring is identified not by blood (i.e., parent) or professional duty (i.e., teacher, counselor, coach) but by choice. More so than any other role, mentors have the power to determine the scope of contact, nature of the relationship, and length of engagement which ultimately determines the breath and depth of influence they will have within the lives of young men and their families. As in the case of coaches, mentors have the capacity to exert tremendous influence over the consciousness, character, dreams, and aspirations of young men, i.e., stay in school and get a good job, or excel in school, go to college, and participate in the running of America.

- **Tutor:** Tutors, not only provide support for academic achievement, social skills development, and/or physical development, i.e., math and science tutors, reading specialists, athletic trainers and nutritionists, but may be a significant factor in determining student achievement levels.

- **Program Director:** Program Directors may run before- or after-school programs, Boys & Girls Clubs, parks and recreation programs, intervention programs, or Upward Bound programs. Program Directors differ from traditional decision-makers in the sense of their having more interaction and closer relationships with program participants.

- **Decision-Maker:** While each of the aforementioned roles certainly qualify as decision-makers, this category represents such individuals as politicians, business leaders, superintendents, school board members, foundation chairpersons, and university presidents. Those individuals, by their power to influence policy and/or direct the expenditure of resources, can profoundly affect the lives of young men and their families.

Define Your Primary Role

As previously stated, there are many more roles which have influence on the lives of young men and in fact, many people will serve in multiple roles, e.g., parent–counselor–coach–mentor or teacher–counselor–mentor. Having a clear sense of your role helps to further clarify your sphere of influence, which in turn provides the focal point from which to develop your mission.

Place a check next to your primary role:

❐ **Parent**	❐ **Teacher**
❐ **Counselor**	❐ **Coach**
❐ **Administrator**	❐ **Central Office**
❐ **Law Enforcement Personnel**	❐ **Clergy**
❐ **Social Worker**	❐ **Program Director**
❐ **Tutor**	❐ **School Staff**
❐ **Decision-Maker (i.e., budgets, resources, personnel, exposure)**	
❐ **Legislator**	❐ **Bus Driver**
❐ **Peer (i.e., sibling, teammate, friend)**	❐ **Mentor**
❐ **Other:** _____	

> What is your role in developing, nurturing, and shaping Black boys in their journey from boyhood to manhood?

Identify Your Level of Influence

While your role may have a general societal definition—parents should raise and nurture children, teachers should provide effective classroom instruction, coaches should teach the skills pertinent to a particular sport—the scope and magnitude of the problems confronting Black males mandate the expanding of traditional roles to meet a far greater set of needs. As a result, the role you play, together with your desired level of influence, provides the framework for further clarifying and defining your mission.

For example, consider the level of influence you would like to have in a young man's life:

- academic achievement (e.g., honor roll, gifted placement, advanced class enrollment, high school graduation, college enrollment);

- academic knowledge (i.e., basic, proficiency, above average, disciplinary expert, master);

- esthetic/cultural development (e.g., creativity, self-expression, appreciation of the arts);

- self-knowledge (i.e., African diaspora, Black history, family lineage);

- moral/spirtual development (i.e., fairness, citizenship, service, independent decision-making, taking responsibility);

- personal development (e.g., social skills, being well-groomed, personal hygiene, strong handshake, well-mannered behavior, strong work ethic);

- leadership skills (e.g., critical-thinking, independent decision-making, team captain, club officer, mentor, tutor, guest speaker); and/or

- athletic achievement (e.g., skill development, knowledge of diet and nutrition, strength conditioning, excellence in a particular sport, college-qualifying times and/or skill level).

Understanding your role and defining the level of influence you want to have within the lives of the young men within your sphere of influence will challenge preexisting, and oftentimes, long-held beliefs, as to your capacity as well as the very potential of the young men themselves. You can't affirm your being influential in their gaining admissions to college if you previously believed in their not having the intellectual capacity or family support to do so. Football coaches are challenged to affirm their ability to influence the social and academic behaviors of players if they have previously believed peer pressure to out weigh the influence of coaches. Teachers are challenged to affirm students' ability to qualify for the honor roll and achieve a level of knowledge qualifying them as disciplinary experts if teachers have previously believed parents' lack of academic support as the root cause of low student achievement. In the case of parents, if a father or mother lacking a high school education, has previously believed only children of educated parents can attend college, he or she is unlikely to demand a college preparatory track of study in high school or communicate an expectation of college enrollment for his or her son after high school. Whether a coach, teacher, or parent, the scope of your influence in the lives of young men will be based, not on what you know, but what you believe.

Ben Carson, a world renown Black pediatric neurosurgeon, in *Gifted Hands*, notes:

Mother had only a third grade education ...Curtis [his older brother], two years my senior, was in junior high school when the school counselor decided to place him into the vocational-type curriculum. His once-low grades had been climbing nicely for more than a year but he was enrolled in a predominantly White school and Mother had no doubt that the counselor was operating with the stereotypical thinking that Blacks were incapable of college work. Of course, I wasn't at their meeting, but I still vividly remember what Mother told us that evening. "I said to that counselor woman, 'My son Curtis is going to college. I don't want him in any vocational courses.'" Then she put her hand on my brother's head. "Curtis, you are now in the college prep course."

Mission

A mission represents the overall guiding purpose of an individual or an organization. This book has been researched and written with the singular mission of, "Empowering African-American Males." The ideas, strategies, activities, exercises, and additional resources have been conceptualized and/or identified as a means of fulfilling this mission.

The book, *Increasing Student Achievement, Volume I*, noted:

As previously stated, the Mission Statement of each school district must be used as a framework for establishing the mission of each school within the district. For a mission statement to be meaningfully relevant to the education of students and to move plans into practice, it must be relied upon as the foundation from which operational strategies evolve. In essence, those who create the mission must be held accountable to make decisions and utilize resources in ways that are consistent with fulfilling the very mission which they have articulated.

The mission of a school is unlikely to be as simple as photocopying the school district's mission. The school district's mission represents the end result of an effective kindergarten-through-twelfth-grade educational system.

As previously stated, the process of clarifying and articulating a mission as it relates to your school, classroom, program, athletic team, social services agency, or household can be a painstakingly time-consuming process. No doubt you will be tempted to avoid it altogether.

"I'm his mother; I don't need a mission statement. He'd better shut up and do what I say."

"I'm the teacher, and I'm tired of placating the needs of these students. They'd better turn their assignments in on time and do the work like everyone else or they'll fail. Pure and simple!"

Prior to taking such extreme positions, consider parents who send their sons to school without a clear sense of mission are unlikely to:

- adequately prepare their sons for testing;
- encourage their placement into honors, AP, or gifted classes;
- identify the appropriate at-home resources and academic support services;
- understand course scheduling or the college admissions process;
- identify or reinforce a clear set of guiding principles, core or moral values, or set of convictions which reinforce high academic achievement and social skill development; or
- fully utilize the available school and community resources to ensure their son's long-term success, including high school graduation, college enrollment, college graduation, and entry into a profession.

Teachers who begin the school year without a clear sense of mission are unlikely to:

- develop a syllabus, study guides, or grading methodology which meet the unique socioeconomic-, cultural-, or gender-based needs of Black males within their classrooms;

- understand how to develop strong relationships with influential adults as a means of reinforcing academic and behavioral expectations;

- understand how to build collaborative relationships and open communication with students and families;

- engage in an open and critical analysis of student achievement and discipline data within their classrooms; or

- take a proactive approach to identifying the areas of personal and professional development needed to increase student achievement and close the achievement gap of Black males within their sphere of influence.

I was recently invited to work with two elementary schools whose student achievement data clearly indicated achievement gaps. I attempted to explain to the two school principals that prior to dealing with the issues of instructional strategies and meeting the unique needs of students and families, teachers needed to engage individually in the process of clarifying their roles and conceptualizing the missions of their grade levels, programs, and classrooms.

"Oh. Mr. Wynn, we have already done that. Each of our schools has a mission statement. We just need for you to tell our teachers how to teach minority children."

When asked if they were willing to invest the time in gathering and analyzing student achievement data, student-family attitudes toward the school, and cultivating stronger relationships between teachers, support staff, parents, and students, they responded, "Mr. Wynn, we don't have time for all of that. Our schools are currently on the low-performing list, and we need for you to tell our teachers how to teach our low-performing students."

The reality of these two schools, as is the case with many schools struggling with conceptualizing and operationalizing strategies to meet the needs of students and families, is an assumption that simply having a Mission Statement posted somewhere in the school means the teachers and support staff have embraced what has been written and have accepted a role in fulfilling it.

These two principals were unwilling to accept that you can't tell teachers what to do (at least not effectively) no more than you can tell children what to do (and expect them to become critical-thinkers). Teachers, as students, must be nurtured through the process of discovering their capacity, defining their purpose, creating a vision of the end result of their efforts, conceptualizing strategies, and establishing the necessary goals to lead them to fulfilling their purpose.

Those who comment, "I don't see color" must see color before they can meet the unique needs of Black males. Many of their needs are inexplicably tied to their 'Blackness'; thus, to increase their achievement and to ensure their school success, their parents, teachers, counselors, and coaches must be driven by a mission which specifically focuses on them as individuals, which includes color.

The sense of mission teachers, counselors, coaches, and administrators have in respect to their own children is clear—they will not allow their own children to fail and they will not abandon them. Almost without question, the teacher's and coach's children are being nurtured, guided, and prepared to go to college. This oftentimes translates to a decision NOT to enroll their children in public schools. I have always found one of the important barometers for measuring a school is, "Do teachers bring their own children here?"

To clarify your mission, move away from focusing on the "big picture," i.e., national mandates, state accountability standards, district-wide increases in student achievement, school-wide projects, and/or achieving grade-level proficiency. Instead, focus on the "little picture," i.e., what you can do to make a difference right here, right now. Don't focus on what you wish you had; focus on what you have. Don't focus on what you could do if it was a perfect world; focus on what you can do right now within the world in which you teach, coach, mentor, or parent. Don't focus on solving the problems of the Black race, entire community, or whole school, but, focus on empowering a single young man. Take all of the information which follows and extract what you can use to effect change and impact the life of one Black male, who today is in need of a miracle and you are going to become his 'Triple-A' warrior—anointed, appointed, and approved!

Write down his name and focus on this one young man as you consider the ideas, strategies, and information to be presented. After you have defined the appropriate strategies, constructed the necessary relationships, and succeeded with one young man, write down the name of another and begin again until you have saved all of the young men whom God enables you to save:

What is Your Role?

Having considered the information presented in this chapter regarding the tremendous influence teachers, parents, coaches, counselors, administrators, mentors, and adults throughout the school community have in the lives of young men describe your primary role and the level of influence you want to have.

Note: The *workbook* contains samples of the roles, missions, and visions, of various adults within the school community.

My primary role and the level of influence I want to have is:

_____

_____

_____

_____

_____

_____

_____

_____

_____

What is Your Mission?

Your mission represents your guiding purpose as it relates to teaching, parenting, coaching, or mentoring the young man whom you are focusing on. Is your overriding mission to build character and leadership skills, close the achievement gap, ensure he enrolls in honors, AP, or gifted classes, ensure he graduates from high school, or ensure he is prepared for, and enrolls in, college?

For example, as a classroom teacher, is it your mission to inspire the young man you are focusing on to discover and pursue his dreams? As a parent, is it your mission to guide him into the schools and classrooms which are most nurturing of his abilities and most reaffirming of his dreams? As a mentor, is it your mission to expose him to the broad range of career opportunities based on his unique talents, gifts, and abilities? Or, as a coach, is it your mission to develop his social, moral, physical, spiritual, and intellectual abilities so he may become a strong husband and father?

State your mission as it reflects your guiding purpose for your involvement within the life of this one young man.

My Mission is:

_____

_____

_____

_____

_____

_____

Chapter 1: Key Points

1. Without a clear mission, substantive, systemic, and long-term increases in student achievement levels for Black males is unlikely.

2. The mission exists on four distinct levels (district, school, department or program, and individual).

3. Each person must answer the questions:
   - "What is my role?"
   - "What levels of Black male achievement do I want to influence?"
   - "How committed will I be to the mission?"

4. All role players must identify their respective roles and work together to ensure student success.

5. The passion of the individual for the mission paves the way to fulfilling the institutional mission.

6. A goal for increasing Black male achievement must be driven by a mission explicitly focused on "Black male achievement" with the emphasis on the work ethic and acceptance of responsibility.

7. The statement, "I don't see color" hinders the development of strategies necessary to meet the unique needs of Black males and families because color is how we are defined and how we define ourselves. It is always a factor, explicit or implicit.

8. Begin with a focus on one child.

Clearly, the mission of schools, teachers, and parents must be to ensure that Black males do not repeat grades. Students who repeat grades are at greater risk of dropping out of school.

According to a May 2004 report issued by the Children's Defense Fund, *The Road to Dropping Out: Minority Students & Academic Factors Correlated with Failure to Complete High School*:

- Only 13 percent of Black fourth graders are reading at grade level compared to 41 percent of Whites.[7]

- Only 7 percent of Black eighth graders are performing at grade level in math compared to 37 percent of Whites.[8]

- 17.5 percent of Black students, 13.2 percent of Hispanic students, and 9.3 percent of White students in grades K-12 were retained at least one grade.[9]

- A longitudinal study of the Baltimore Public School System[10] found that:
  - 71 percent of students who were retained once dropped out;
  - 80 percent of students who were retained more than once dropped out; and,
  - 94 percent of those who were retained both in elementary and in middle school dropped out.

Chapter 2
Vision

What Blacks are now being taught does not bring their minds into harmony with life as they must face it. When a Black student works his way through college by polishing shoes, he does not think of making a special study of the science underlying the production and distribution of leather and its products that he may some day figure in this sphere. The Black boy sent to college by a mechanic seldom dreams of learning mechanical engineering to build upon the foundation his father had laid, that in years to come he may figure as a contractor or consulting engineer.

— *Dr. Carter G. Woodson*

Taking the time to clarify your role, identifying the level of influence you want, and stating your mission must now be translated into a vision, i.e., what must be done to fulfill the mission. Conceptualizing a vision for your classroom, household, school, program, or church will require discussions with and input from the stakeholders who impact and influence the lives of the young men within your school community. To focus more specifically on ensuring the academic achievement and social skill development for the young man whom you have identified, your vision will determine the scope of the goals you set and the goals you encourage this young man to set for himself:

- Do you envision his reaching proficiency or becoming academically advanced?

- Do you envision his graduating from high school or graduating from college?

- Do you envision his escaping poverty or achieving financial prosperity?

- Do you envision his getting a job on the assembly line or being an executive in the ivory tower?

- Do you envision his becoming a talented athlete or a scholar athlete?

- Do you envision his enrolling in the Air Force or Military Academy or signing up at an Armed Forces recruiting office?

- Do you envision him discovering and pursuing his passions or getting a minimum wage job?

No matter how widely the visions vary between teachers and parents, administrators and mentors, counselors and coaches, or the school board and the school community, there must be a willingness to collaborate between the adult stakeholders before there is any real opportunity for anyone's vision to be realized.

- The teacher who envisions a young man reaching proficiency should support the efforts of a parent who envisions his scoring above the 90th percentile on standardized testing.

- The parent who envisions his or her son graduating from high school should support the efforts of a counselor who envisions his attending and graduating from college.

- The coach who envisions a player enrolling in basic classes to remain academically eligible should support the efforts of a parent who envisions her son enrolling in college prep classes.

- The principal who envisions meeting the school improvement goals of a 10 percent increase in reading scores should support the efforts of a teacher who envisions "Stand and Deliver Fridays" to motivate young men to read a book a week.

The vision my wife and I have for our sons has, in many cases, not been totally understood by friends, family, or by all of their teachers. We have been accused of pushing them too hard, having expectations which are unreachable, and holding them to standards which are unattainable. Fortunately, most of those who have not totally understood our passion, our purpose, or our expectations, have generally collaborated with and supported us in our efforts. However, be assured, the greater your vision for the success of Black males, the greater the number of people who will tell you it's unrealistic and who will actively undermine your efforts to achieve it!

Our parental vision, together with the collaboration of our sons' teachers, principals, counselors, and coaches has paved the way to their academic record, standardized test scores, personal achievement, and overall school success. Our sons, as is typical of most young men, have not always enthusiastically studied, prepared themselves, or trained. It has been the combined efforts of parents who have pushed them, teachers who have stretched them, and coaches who have tirelessly worked them—all driven by a vision that they were capable.

The vision you, as a parent, teacher, counselor, coach, principal, or mentor affirm will influence the consciousness, beliefs, and goals the young man whom you are focusing on will eventually set for himself within every aspect of his life. The scope of his dreams will be greatly influenced by the scope of your beliefs, which will be reflected in the affirmation of your vision.

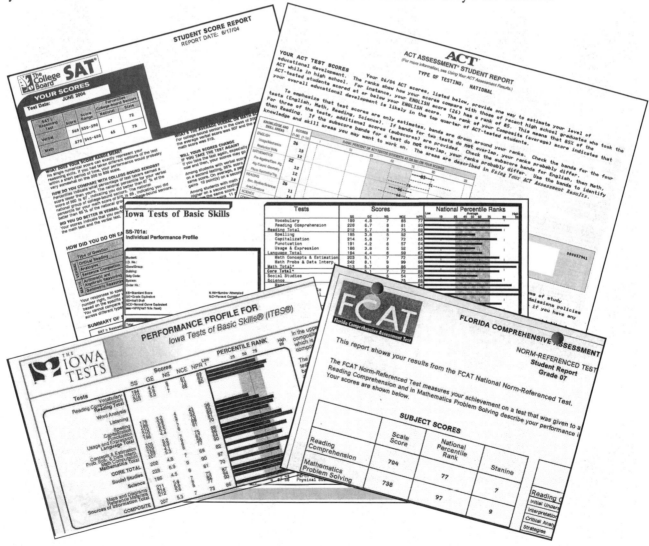

Reality weighs down dreams of college

Wednesday, February 2, 2005

By Lisa Nipp for USA TODAY

In a February 2, 2005 USA Today article, 38-year-old Lisa Turner, who is working on her associates degree at the Community College of Baltimore County, recalls how the failure of role players in her life as a teenager to help her gain focus and develop plans led to her, first goofing off in school, and then to 15 years of working in restaurants and catering firms. Now, a role player within the lives of today's teenagers, she is helping them to develop course schedules and plans that prepare them for postsecondary options and college success. When asked about the lack of advice that she got in high school and the advice given to today's students she stated:

"Nothing has changed. Things have gotten worse, maybe. They thought that they were going to the 13th grade."

Beliefs + Experiences = What You Do

Your beliefs and your experiences have already determined the focus of your mission and now, your beliefs will become more evident through the scope of your vision. Your beliefs and experiences will be reflected in the language you use, lessons you teach, stories you tell, alliances you develop, and the lengths to which you look for information, ideas, strategies, and support.

Jack Addington calls this vision development "Creative Imagination."

Creative imagination forms the mold through which the Creative Process of Life works to produce the manifest Universe. The chair upon which you sit was first an idea in someone's mind. This idea was translated into a visual image in that person's mind. Out of that image came the physical expression of the idea. The great Albert Einstein said, 'Imagination is more important than knowledge.'

Those who have had low academic expectations of Black males will not be able to affirm a vision which inspires a young man's dreams and teaches diligence, determination, perseverance, and integrity as building blocks toward the pursuit of those dreams. Purposefully lifting Black males to the highest achievement levels is a walk of faith many are simply unprepared, unwilling, or unable to take. They are bound by the limitations of their own beliefs. Few would disbelieve a Black male breaking 11 seconds in a 100-meter dash but could those same people believe in his breaking 30 on the ACT or 700 on each component of the SAT? Few would disbelieve a Black male running 100 yards in a football game but could those same people believe in his taking all honors and AP classes during any given school year?

Jonathan Kozol, in *Savage Inequalities*, quotes a Chicago businessman who said:

"It doesn't make sense to offer something that most of these urban kids will never use, no one expects these ghetto kids to go to college. Most of them are lucky if they're even literate. If we can teach some useful skills, get them to stay in school and graduate, and maybe into jobs, we're giving them the most that they can hope for."

In stark contrast, at Marva Collins' Westside Preparatory School on Chicago's west side, they embodied a vision which many (particularly this Chicago businessman) would find impossible to embrace:

All students at Westside Preparatory School must also take an oral pledge before the entire group that they will never bring disgrace to the school and that they will, at all times, uphold the moral and academic standards of Westside Preparatory School and that any student who is guilty of omission in this area does not deserve the right to be called a Westside Prepian. The academic program at Westside Preparatory is nothing less than the basic three R's mixed with a total program that teaches every child that they are unique, special, and that they are too bright to ever be less than all that they can be. The 'I will not let you fail' statement is one that they seldom hear elsewhere. We also hold parent classes, and we teach the very same things to parents that we teach our students.

Revisit your mission from the previous chapter. Was it conceptualized with a focus on his deficits (i.e., below grade level, lack of preexisting knowledge, frequent discipline problems, lack of parental support), or on your capacity (i.e., master motivator, believer in divine intervention, confident in your ability to identify people who can make a connection with him, expert in reading instruction; Multiple Intelligences; learning-styles)? Will you now affirm his potential based on his history or on your capacity; on his inability or your ability; his lack of experiences or your experiences; his foolishness or your wisdom; his lack of support mechanisms or your available support mechanisms; or, his lack of skills or your finely-tuned skills? The most pressing challenge confronting you is not focusing your expectations on what he is incapable of, but on what YOU are capable of. In essence, what do you believe about yourself?

Consider the following:

- Will your conversations with him focus on high school graduation or college matriculation?

- Will your academic support focus on getting A's, B's, or passing?

- Will you talk to him about reaching proficiency or reaching his potential?

- Will you encourage his dreams and aspirations or will you try to assess what is "realistic?"

- Will you encourage him to take the most academically-challenging courses or allow him to choose easy or remedial classes?

- Will you allow him to answer questions in single-word responses, i.e., "fine" or will you encourage him to speak in clearly distinguishable complete sentences, i.e., "I feel very well today, thank you for asking?"

- Will you allow him to submit inferior work or will you encourage him to strive for a higher standard?

- Will you allow him to succumb to the de-intellectualizing of today's youth through hip-hop culture or will you utilize every opportunity to challenge his thinking and develop his critical-thinking skills?

Is it practical to encourage college for a student who is two years below grade level in reading? Is it realistic to encourage a young Black man who dreams of becoming President of the United States? Do we dare demand his

submitting quality work when he can barely write his name? Do we dare take time to talk about his dreams when his school is on the 'low-performing' list and students are failing to meet the state-mandated improvement levels?

Perhaps a more pressing question is, what should we do for the young man who lacks hope?

Answering such questions will determine the scope of your vision, and it is your vision which will determine the goals you set, the discussions you engage in, and the strategies you choose to implement.

Elizabeth Hood, in *Educating Black Students: Some Basic Issues*, notes:

> *Urban schools frequently fail to encourage the urban child to become interested in leadership because the curriculum does not include an adequate number of co-curricular activities. Many teachers and administrators assume that the Black child's primary educational needs are discipline and the three R's. They fail to understand that the heightened sense of power and self-esteem which stem from involvement in meaningful activities will motivate the child to become more self-directed and more anxious to improve his basic skills.*

Winning football games and bringing Black males to proficiency levels doesn't do enough to meet their needs or prepare them for the totality of the challenges and obstacles facing them. The pursuit of your vision will determine how you open the school year and where you focus your energy and efforts in taking the young man whom you identified from where he is to where he needs to be.

Ron Weaver, in *Beyond Identify: Education and the Future Role of Black Americans*, notes:

> *Since Black children are often viewed by their teachers as incapable of success, they tend to perform at low levels and internalize negative feelings. For Black children, as is the case with other minority children usually possessing values differing from those of their teachers, little of what the teachers say or the attitudes <u>instilled</u> are considered related to their life outside the school.*

The experiences of teachers and parents in regards to the lack of motivation demonstrated by Black males in their school work and when doing their chores will undoubtedly influence the scope of their respective visions, as will the statistics cited in Chapter one, i.e., low test scores, high suspensions, low talented and gifted class enrollment, high special education enrollment, low college enrollment, and high incarceration rates. Given our experiences, given these statistics, how do we dare envision, honor roll, advanced class enrollment, college admission, professional employment, and a committed husband and father?

How do we not?

Black males can no longer be absent from academic honor rolls, honors and AP classes, and academically gifted classes, without a community-wide outcry from teachers, parents, counselors, coaches, administrators, and pastors. Consider, if these same young men—the academic underachievers—no longer made their basketball, baseball, or football teams, there would be a public outcry which would shake the foundations of their community. There would be a community-wide call-to-action to get them back onto the basketball courts and football fields because this is where we have come to envision they belong. We have envisioned it, we have affirmed it, we have advertised it, and we have celebrated it with banners, trophies, T-shirts, bumper stickers, pennant flags, assemblies, and newspaper articles. So, too, must we begin to use banners, trophies, T-shirts, bumper stickers, pennant flags, assemblies, and newspaper articles to encourage, recognize, and celebrate their academic achievement.

Coach Ken Carter, former basketball coach at Richmond High School in Richmond, California, was the most recent in a list of educators to have had their vision of the promise and potential of young men portrayed in a movie:

- *The George McKenna Story*

- *The Marva Collins Story*

- *Lean on Me (Joe Clark)*

- *Coach Carter*

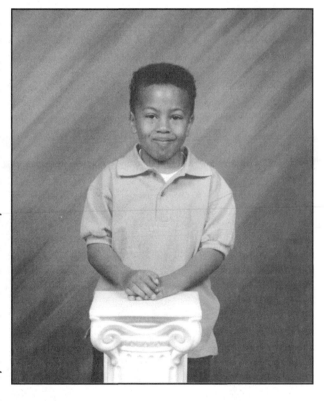

The common thread woven through each story, was a vision, by a coach, principal, or teacher that more was possible for their students and the history of low achievement, seemingly etched in stone, and accepted by adults and students alike, could be changed. Each person envisioned a level of achievement, so far beyond the imaginations of those around them, their principal antagonists were adults, as opposed to the students themselves. Yet, in each situation, their vision inspired hope in their students and players. The most recent visionary, Coach Ken Carter, envisioned a level of achievement in his players off the basketball court few others could understand or appreciate. His energy, strategies, language, stories, lessons, and expectations were all driven by his vision of a level of achievement, determined not by *their* circumstances or even *their* personal commitment, but by *his* experiences and *his* personal commitment. Only by convincing the young men within his circle of

Los Angeles Times, 2001
John M. Glionna

Coach Ken Carter, coach of the 13-0 Richmond High School basketball team, benched his entire 45-player roster on the varsity, junior varsity and freshman squads. He forfeited the next two league games and made the school gym off-limits even for practice. The entire team was benched until players raised their grades.

Coach Carter was quoted as saying, "On the streets and public basketball courts in Richmond and any other city in America, you see the broken dreams of former high school legends who got left behind by life. I was not going to let that happen to these boys."

In 1999, all 15 graduating seniors went on to attend four-year universities or junior colleges.

Coach Carter's tough-school philosophy didn't stop at the lockout. His players—many of whom were from low-income families and whom had never traveled the 10 miles from Richmond to San Francisco—began going on regular field trips to meet with investment bankers and other icons of the business world.

Although his most recent team finished a disappointing 6-13, Coach Carter and his players have their eyes set on a higher prize.

"We're going to college, Coach won't let us fail."

influence, of his commitment, was he able to convince them of their potential. His vision, enabled him to develop the relationships and cultivate the culture needed to lead his players to internalizing this higher level of expectations. Once young men buy in to your vision and embrace your expectations, they are ready to combine their effort with your guidance. Coach Carter's players not only accepted his vision and embraced his expectations, they developed a level of intrinsic motivation which led them to pursue academic achievement with the same passion and commitment as they had previously pursued dunks, cross-over dribbles, and jump shots.

If your vision leads young men to a level of achievement higher than what they have historically experienced or a level beyond what has been customary within your school or program, you must provide the necessary

support and encouragement to sustain them once they begin such a journey. Black males, who become top academic achievers will find themselves separated, and at times isolated, from their peers. Whether they experience cultural isolation in an elementary-through-high school setting or find themselves among only a few Black students on a college campus, you will be challenged to recognize this situation and to provide the needed support and coping mechanisms.

As previously stated, there is a community-wide expectation of young Black men excelling on football fields and basketball courts, while there is no such expectation of their excelling in advanced or gifted classes. My wife and I have successfully convinced our sons of their ability to excel where they want to be (i.e., football, karate, and track & field), and where we want them to be (i.e., academically gifted, honors, and AP classes). However, until more parents, teachers, and coaches share our vision, our sons will continue to experience the cultural isolation of oftentimes being the only Black male in such classes. The camaraderie shared with friends on their football and track & field teams is lost as they enter into their academically-advanced classrooms. Their friends ask, "Man, why do you take all of those hard classes?" Friends and family members ask my wife and me, "Why do you push Mychal-David and Jalani so hard? Isn't it too much for them to play football AND take all of those hard classes?" Such comments did not go unheeded by our younger son, who, throughout fourth grade, persistently asked to be taken out of the gifted program. Undaunted by our refusal to take him out of the program, and unmoved by our attempts to explain why the program needed him to

be an example for other Black children, he came to me at the beginning of fifth grade:

"Dad, I don't want to be in Target [the talented and gifted program] this year. Since I'm going to be playing football, I believe it's just going to be too much work for me. Maybe I'll go back to Target next year."

"Jalani, I can understand how demanding it can be to attempt to balance your school work with the mental and physical demands of playing a sport.
However, you're such an intelligent young man, I know you can balance both of them if you put forth the necessary effort. However, your mother and I don't want to over burden you, so if you're sure that you can't handle it, WE'LL HAVE TO TAKE YOU OUT OF FOOTBALL!"

My son stared at me in disbelief for a moment (this was not exactly the answer he was expecting) and responded:

"That's alright, Dad, I think I can handle it."

Our older son attends one of the most racially-diverse high schools in metro Atlanta where Black and White students, each comprise approximately 45 percent of the student population. However, our older son, like his younger brother, continues to experience a sense of cultural isolation within his classrooms. His experiences through the first semester of the eleventh grade have been:

- *tenth-grade honors literature (4 Black students)*
- *eleventh-grade honors literature (7 Black students)*
- *honors algebra II (2 Black students)*
- *honors pre-calculus (6 Black students)*
- *honors physics (5 Black students)*

- *honors economics (2 Black students)*
- *honors organic chemistry (5 Black students)*
- *AP computer science (3 Black students)*
- *AP US history (7 Black students)*
- *AP studio art (5 Black students)*
- *AP Spanish (4 Black students)*
- *varsity football (55 of 69 players were Black)*

Of the 50 Black students spread across a total of 11 honors and AP classes, there were only 4 other Black males. In a high school ranked in the top 400 nationally, offering more AP and honors classes than any other high school in the county, offering magnet programs in Visual & Performing Arts and in Math & Science, with positive Black male role models on staff and in administration, there is as much opportunity for Black males to excel at this high school as anywhere. However, there is nothing to suggest the tragic underrepresentation of Black students in academically-challenging classes will change until there is a home, school, and community vision that it change. Before we can expect young Black men to succeed in such classes, we must prepare the way with support programs, peer tutors, mentors, and the encouragement needed to overcome their fear into such unknown territory. In essence, teachers must welcome them; parents must encourage them; and the school community must commit to supporting them. The type of strategies needed to pave the way for greater numbers of Black children into the ranks of honors, academically gifted, and AP classes are outlined in great detail in the book, *A High School Plan for Students with College-Bound Dreams*. What's important to note here is, there will be no need to identify the necessary strategies if there is no vision of greater numbers of Black children enrolling into such classes.

Adults within school communities have great power over the lives of children. A power which few deserve, yet, virtually all of them have. From bus drivers to classroom teachers, from custodians to front office staff, from counselors to coaches, from the principal to the safety officer—adults within each school community have enormous power to shape, and oftentimes save, the lives of young people.

Schools like the Harry Daniels Primary Center in Roosevelt, New York and the Flower City School in Rochester, New York, are staffed by administrators and teachers who 'believe' Black males can achieve academically and are marked by customs, rituals, and traditions promoting and celebrating such beliefs. Such a vision is translated into verbal declarations and visual affirmations throughout the school community. A statement of beliefs, core values, and daily affirmations permeate classrooms and ring a resounding chorus throughout the building as adults and children alike feel within their spirits that this is a special place, these are special people, and here, we are developing thinkers and leaders. The corridors, classrooms, cafeteria, media center, gymnasium, front office, and student areas visually reflect the core values and beliefs internalized by administrators and staff. Reaffirming language is heard in student-adult interactions and student-student conversations.

Harry Daniels Primary Center

Dr. Patricia Charthern, principal of the Harry Daniels Primary Center (Roosevelt, NY), has a student population of 300 students (90 percent Black and 10 percent Latino) in Kindergarten through Third Grade. She and her staff have cultivated a school community driven by their clearly-stated primary school mission.

Evolving from their mission is a vision and school philosophy which has shaped staff development efforts, curricular and co-curricular activities, and other school-wide program initiatives leading to a 93 percent attendance rate. She and her staff have led 93 percent of their third grade students to minimum state levels in reading and 99 percent to minimum state levels in math proficiency.

The Harry Daniels Primary Center has chosen for their Mascot the 'Eagle' because they are among the most majestic and powerful of all birds. The Eagle is an intelligent bird and it soars gracefully high in the sky. The students and staff at the Harry Daniels Primary Center model after the characteristics of the Eagle. "We are majestic, powerful and intelligent. We all strive to soar towards high standards."

The Harry Daniels Primary Center, "Home of the Eagles," is a wonderful place where children learn with care, concern, competence and consciousness.

Flower City School

Mrs. Lessie Hamilton-Rose, principal of Flower City School, #54 (Rochester, NY), has a student population which is over 90 percent Black and Latino in grades 3 through 5. She and her staff have a clear sense of their elementary school mission which has led to a clearly-defined vision and statement of beliefs.

This clear sense of mission has led Flower City School in developing the strategies that produced one of the largest gains in reading within the Rochester Public Schools, a 26 percent increase during the 1999/2000 school year. Evolving from that guiding school-wide mission, teachers developed personal missions of becoming recognized as 'Best Practices' instructors within various curriculum and instructional areas (i.e., Math, Social Studies, Standard English, Classroom Management, Multiple Intelligences). Their school-wide mission was the driving force behind such initiatives as the vertical teaming of teachers, establishment of learning communities, kick-off of a 'Backpack Book Club,' with a proclamation from the Major's Office, to improve literacy, and an annual 3rd-through-5th-grade college tour (and the establishment of a college scholarship fund for Flower City alumni who attend college). Local business and mentoring partnerships have also evolved from, and been inspired by, their mission.

Thanks to my mother and, later, Mr. Washington, I grew up with the subconscious conviction that I was going to be somebody, and because of that, there was not going to be room in my life for drugs, alcohol or criminal behavior. Many of those I grew up with foresaw no purpose in their lives. For them, there was no strength of conviction to empower them to resist the allure of drugs and alcohol and crime.

— Les Brown, Live Your Dreams

When school communities envision the level of Black male achievement as envisioned by the *Harry Daniels Primary Center* and the *Flower City School,* customs, rituals, and traditions will follow promoting and celebrating such beliefs. Beyond individual awards and school-wide recognition will be relationships between the school and the community of trust and hope.

Expectations

The struggle with expectations is continual and undeniable. As young men challenge our authority, behave irresponsibly, are rude and ill-mannered, are dishonest, and demonstrate any number of confrontational and/or anti-social behaviors, we are challenged to believe in our capacity and in their potential. Their behaviors are not their burden as much as they are ours. We are the ones challenged with remaining steadfast, keeping our focus, and maintaining our perspective.

Black males, like most people, aspire toward what they know others have done. Their views and ideas of their potential will largely reflect the success achieved by friends, family, and others within their circle of influence and those to whom they have been exposed. Their vision of success will be limited, or enhanced, by those around them. Young Black males aspire to become professional athletes and entertainers because they believe these to be fields accessible to them. They see professional basketball teams starting all Black players and they see entertainment superstars flaunting their material wealth. Shows like "The Cosby Show" which portrayed a Black nuclear family, with a father who was a successful doctor, a wife who was a successful attorney, and children who weren't materialistic and sarcastic, no longer touch the Black consciousness or influence the aspirations of Black children.

The student growing up in a high poverty community is less likely to interact with Black doctors, lawyers, and other professionals and is almost certainly not to see any positively portrayed on television or in feature films. Even on those rare occasions when a Black male in a classroom of 28 students proudly affirms, "I want to become a doctor," he is unlikely to know what is involved, why he must apply himself diligently to his studies, and the number of years he must be willing to sacrifice to achieve such a lofty goal. He is also unlikely to affirm such a career with such modifiers as, "A doctor specializing in AIDS research, in pediatrics, in cardiology, or a clinical psychologist." When a young man boldly affirms, "I want to go to medical school," rather than being exposed to the full range of opportunities associated with such an aspiration from marketing to manufacturing, from research and development to pharmaceutical sales, and from biomedical engineering to opening a medical practice he is more likely to hear adults within his school community question such an aspiration before affirming such possibilities. There are thousands of potential career options for Black males; they need not all aspire to become athletes and entertainers.

Affirming Higher Aspirations

Affirming higher aspirations for Black males will require a change of focus. Instead of focusing on the number of young men on free or reduced lunch, focus on how many opportunities you have to inspire a young man to attend college. Instead of focusing on the number of children who ride the school bus or live in the projects, focus on the number of children whom you can inspire to become teachers. There are 98 HBCUs which should provide enough brochures, T-shirts, and pennant flags to line a corridor from floor to ceiling, helping young men to shift their focus from where they are to where they're going.

Imagine my opening a conversation by saying:

"Hello, my name is Mychal Wynn. I am adopted. I was on the free and reduced lunch program. I would have been held back in the second grade but they had social promotion when I was in school. I wasn't very smart through the fourth grade but somehow by God's grace I graduated from high school. I don't know how I made it into college. Would you like to go out on a date with me?"

Where a child comes from doesn't determine where he or she is going, only his or her beginning. Coaches never complain about the number of players on free and reduced lunch. They devote more of their energy to looking for talent rather than being fixated on a child's deficits (not that being on free lunch should infer an intellectual or social deficit). In fact, players who see athletics as their only way out of poverty are among the most-highly motivated. Such self-motivation doesn't have to end on the football field. With the proper guidance and mentoring these young men may learn to dominate board rooms as they do the gridiron and basketball courts. Magic Johnson and Michael Jordan took their basketball savvy into the Corporate Boardroom, the Barber twins (Tikki and Ronde) have taken their football concentration and applied it to writing children's stories. Former Minnesota defensive lineman and NFL Hall of Fame player, Alan Page, took his passion on the football field into the Minnesota Supreme Court, where he is a presiding Justice.

If we can stop attributing low academic performance to where students come from and instead focus on cultivating an environment driven by their dreams and nurtured by our capacity to assist them, we can begin to engage young men in the frequent and ongoing discussions regarding the totality of their interests and the career options relating to their unique talents and abilities. The aspiring professional basketball player is seeking a job whereas the aspiring team owner is seeking power and influence. The aspiring professional football player is entrusting his life into the hands of coaches, trainers, and team owners, while the aspiring NFL coach is seeking management over front office decisions and control over team personnel. A player's contract is only the beginning of an economics lesson. Total revenues generated by a professional sports franchise, taxes paid to the local municipality, dollars spent on advertising, landscaping, food services, security, and construction amount to billions of dollars and generate thousands of jobs. Revenues from television rights, sales of team paraphernalia, concessions, parking fees, videos, press boxes, and season ticket sales are monumental in comparison to a player's contract, not to mention the fact a team owner can sell a player to another team and pass ownership of the franchise on to his children. Imagine a player with a multi-million dollar contract being forced to uproot his family as the result of a team owner's ten-year-old son's comment, "Daddy, I don't like the way he plays. He caused me to lose my fantasy football game. Trade him to another team. Please!"

From the moment a young man affirms a future, "I would like to become an attorney," we should use his affirmation as a springboard to higher expectations. Assign him a book report or research project on the National Bar Association, historical cases, and significant Black men such as Thurgood Marshall, Johnnie Cochran, or Willie Gary.

"So you want to become an attorney. Let me tell you about Willie Gary:"

Willie Gary was born in 1947, in South Georgia, the sixth of 11 children. The family lived in shacks. No shoes. Nothing.

After graduating from the Historically Black College, Shaw University, and within two years of opening his Stuart law firm, Willie Gary was a millionaire. Over the years, he has donated over ten million dollars to Shaw University, thousands of dollars to local charities, $60,000 to fund a day-care center, and thousands of dollars to Black scholarship programs.

Gary has made his fortune taking big liability settlements from insurance companies in wrongful-death suits. His fee averages 35 percent. That means that if he wins a 100 million dollar lawsuit, he gets 35 million dollars! Unlike a professional football player who has an average career of four and a half years, Willie Gary can practice law for the rest of his life.

He made national news when he reached a settlement of more than 40 million dollars with Florida Power & Light over the 1985 electrocution of seven rural Palm Beach County Florida residents.

He made global news in 1996 when he won a 500 million dollar lawsuit against the Loewen Group, a Canadian funeral home company he had sued for breach of contract. Loewen had been buying U.S. funeral homes and driving the competition out of business. As part of the settlement, he received stock in Loewen and agreed not to sue the company again.

His firm employs 150 people, including 21 lawyers, eight partners, two investigators, dozens of paralegals, a medical director and a public relations specialist. It represents more than 7,000 clients, including two groups of more than 2,000.

Most of the cases are small, less than a million dollars. But a million here, a million there adds up to around 55 million dollars per year in settlements. Most of the clients are small—working men and women, the rural poor, children. Most of the opponents are big—hospitals, chemical companies, insurance companies. Gary's associates call him the giant killer.

The 100 largest U.S. law firms average 400 million dollars in revenues, employ an average of 450 lawyers and generate about 500,000 thousand dollars per year in profits for the partners, according to the American Law Journal. Gary's firm generates almost 3 million dollars per lawyer in gross revenues.

'I'm the rainmaker. Every firm needs a rainmaker, the guy that brings in the business. The stiff-collar, old-school firms might do their marketing at country clubs and on the golf course. I do mine in court.'

Your vision must be greater than their vision. Young men frequently "talk the talk" but more often than naught they are unwilling to "walk the walk." They talk about becoming professional athletes but they are unwilling to develop the necessary work habits, character values, and self-discipline. Oftentimes, coaches and parents, cripple Black males by excusing ill-mannered behavior, overlooking improper language usage, and attributing their standard of dress, lack of grooming, and inarticulate communication to, "That's just the way boys are," or "I don't know what's wrong with kids today," or worst, "I don't know what to do?" The scope of your vision must reflect high expectations in regards to self-discipline and personal responsibility.

Frederick Douglass stated:

It is vain that we talk of being men, if we do not the work of men. We must become valuable to society in other departments of industry than those servile ones from which we are rapidly being excluded. We must show that we can do as well as they. When we can build as well as live in houses; when we can make as well as wear shoes; when we can produce as well as consume wheat, corn and rye—then we shall become valuable to society.

Young men are seldom interested in working at McDonald's or bagging groceries at the local grocery store. Perhaps this is just the rite of passage aspiring football and basketball players need. When our older son played junior varsity football, my wife and I required that he work in the concession stand during the varsity football games and assist in selling spirit wear during lunch at school. We utilize every opportunity to have him and his younger brother answer the telephone, stack books, and fill orders at our publishing company. We look for opportunities for them to perform as ushers at church and we give them a full complement of chores at home. Some of the most positive experiences our older son has had in developing character, learning a sense of responsibility, and expanding his understanding of how to work with and serve others has come from coaching youth basketball and being an assistant instructor at a Martial Arts school. Players from his high school football team learned the values and lessons which will shape them into men by working with, teaching, and mentoring elementary and middle school students at a community football camp—the collaborative vision of coaches, parents, and former alumnus—current NFL Pittsburgh Steelers running back, Verron Haynes. Young men learn best by doing. As such, we must expand their opportunities to practice the values we are teaching them.

Young men are seldom interested in volunteering to feed the homeless or visit senior citizen homes. Perhaps this is an appropriate rite of passage for would-be rappers and recording artists. Each of us must share the responsibility of contributing to a self-centered selfish generation of young people. Their desires to own the latest video games and video game systems; wear the latest hip-hop clothing; adorn the latest hair styles; pierce their ears; tattoo their bodies; and adorn themselves with rings, chains, necklaces and dog tags must be placed into some relevant context. Parents who adorn their sons in the latest clothing and assign little, if any, household chores or responsibilities are crippling them. Parents further cripple their sons by first, purchasing video games and video game systems (oftentimes more than one system), and then, allow their sons to play video games for hours at the expense of homework, school work, and reading.

As parents, my wife and I fully understand how quickly and easily this lack of expectations and connection between what our sons want and what they must learn to do can manifest itself.

One day while in my office, I noticed my young son (Jalani) engrossed in playing a video game (Madden 2005 NFL Football). Throughout the school year, he reads daily and completes his nightly homework without issue or resistance. However, it occurred to me this morning, since his school let out for the holiday break five days ago, I haven't seen him with a book. I have, however, observed him playing this particular video game every day for several hours. Either playing the game, running practice plays, developing a team, or developing strategy, he has been engrossed. My wife and I use to have a rule, 'two to one'—two hours of reading for every hour of video game playing, a strategy which appears to have worked. Both of our sons have excelled in writing and reading proficiency. Yet, here was my son, flying under the radar, quietly playing video games for hours without dad noticing. (He was smart enough to set up his game system outside my office and away from his mother who frequently interrupts his game playing to remind him of chores and other household responsibilities. However, he knew dad was busy writing and wouldn't notice!)

My son, like so many other Black males, is an athlete. In fact, his video game playing is focused almost exclusively on 'Madden 2005 NFL Football.' Since this is the holiday break, I softened our 'two to one' rule. "Jalani, go upstairs in your mother's office and find the book, 'How to Raise an MVP: The David Robinson Story,' and read it. For the rest of the holiday, 'one hour of reading will earn you one hour of video game playing.' However, since you have gone five days without reading anything, today will be your make-up day. The rest of today is devoted exclusively to reading!"

Our older son, as is typical of teenage Black males, is into hip-hop fashions. My wife and I have attempted to reach a point of compromise and establish boundaries. I personally don't like much of what he wants to wear, i.e., baggy pants, brightly-colored shoes, or gaudy jewelry. However, I recognize he is a sixteen-year-old and he and his generation have their fashion statements in the way my generation had ours. I also know some of his fashion statements perpetuate the stereotype of the thuggish Black male who values athletics over intellect, clothing over character, and negative attitudes over positive affirmations. All of this, notwithstanding, my wife and I have attempted to establish boundaries which allow our son to be a teenager without allowing him to fall totally into the abyss of the thuggish image his generation appears to idolize.

Our son has his shopping buddy, my wife. They both know where to shop for the best buys for his generation's hip-hop clothing styles. My wife helps him to select clothing styles and to put together outfits which allow him to express himself—within limits. Also, she has her fingers on the purse strings to avoid the outrageous prices designers and retailers charge for clothing carrying the names of recording artists or designers (i.e., Sean John, FUBU, Phat Farm).

On several occasions we have ceremoniously removed all of our son's clothing from his closet, with the exception of five basic outfits. Throughout the grading period he has been able to earn clothing (since he didn't use his own money to buy anything) with 'A' grades—get an 'A,' buy a shoe; get another 'A,' buy the other shoe—zeros for missed assignments forfeit everything and we start all over!

I took my sons on a research field trip. First we went by the dry cleaners where we saw an entire Korean family working—mom, dad, brother, sister, cousins, and children—all working. Next, we visited a jewelry store where we saw an Indian family—mom, dad, dad's brother, and their son—all working. Next, we went to a Mexican restaurant where we saw the entire family working. Next, we went to an African bookstore where, again, we saw a mom, dad, and children working. By the end of the day we had seen families from a broad range of ethnic backgrounds running businesses, working together, and in virtually every situation, the children were working and learning how to run their family's business.

When we returned home, I asked my sons to call their friends and to do a survey of how their friends had spent their Saturday. Every Black boy whom they called had been either outside playing basketball, inside playing a video game, or just laying around doing nothing. As is the case with thousands of young Black men, what they do on Saturday isn't much different from what they do each school day. When in classrooms I ask for a show of hands of the students who aspire to go to college. Without fail, nearly all the hands of the Black male students go up. Then, when I ask for a show of hands of the 'A' students, those who made honor roll, those who are always prepared for school, and even those who brought paper and pencil on that particular day, nearly all of the hands go down.

Carter G. Woodson, in *The Mis-Education of the Negro*, wrote:

When you hear a man talking then, always inquire as to what he is doing or what he has done for humanity. Old men talk of what they have done, young men of what they are doing, and fools of what they expect to do.

There is a need to engage Black males in such discussions as a means of helping them to understand the quantity and quality of work required for them to be able to do for themselves. Far too many see professional athletics, entertainment, or crime as the only careers or vocations available to them for achieving their dreams. As such, they are putting forth tragically little effort into becoming thinkers, even within the very career pursuits they have affirmed for themselves. Young men interested in pursuing a career in professional sports rarely understand the correlation in developing critical-thinking skills, expertise in muscular development, or an understanding of nutrition and protein synthesis. Young men interested in pursing Rap as a vocation rarely understand the literary foundation, entrepreneurial expertise, or critical-thinking skills utilized in conceptualizing and understanding contractual agreements or investment opportunities as integral to their pursuits. The nature of young men is to do without thinking, and to devote all of their energies to the pursuit of their passions without any thought to developing the foundation to sustain their efforts or to prepare themselves for the inevitable challenges, obstacles, and pitfalls. They are spending more hours attempting to get to the next video game level than they are reading books or developing skills to prepare for the next level of life.

Developing critical thinkers, developing community consciousness, and building community leaders must become a part of our collective school-community vision. Without such a vision we will not teach the lessons needed to help young men understand how what they do, individually, impacts upon the community as a whole, and dispels or perpetuates biases and stereotypes.

Clarity of vision as it relates to the character, moral, intellectual, and spiritual development of young men easily translates into:

- *Lesson Integration:* Black men who provide examples of character, morality, intellectualism, and spiritual enlightenment abound. Biographies of historical figures, newspaper articles of political leaders, businessmen, educators, athletes, and entertainers, and the critical analysis of the nightly newscasts all provide prompts for classroom discussions, topics for research papers, and visual imagery for classroom bulletin boards.

- *Libraries:* There is no shortage of literature written by, and about Black men. My books, *Follow Your Dreams: Lessons That I Learned in School, The Eagles who Thought They were Chickens,* and *Don't Quit* can be used to begin home, classroom, school, church, and community program libraries.

- *Book Stores:* Trips by parents and field trips by schools to local bookstores, together with frequent book fairs at church and school.

- *Expectations:* Standard English usage, situationally-appropriate use of slang, hand shakes, style of dress, style of walk, and the way in which a young man articulates himself are driven by adult expectations.

- *Standards:* Standards of behavior, conduct, grooming, dress, school work, homework, and household chores are reflective of the men whom we envision our sons, students, and players becoming.

- *Academic Achievement:* Any compromise in the area of academic achievement only cripples Black males and perpetuates the racist stereotype of lazy, stupid Black men. Black males do as little as we allow and as much as we demand. What we allow and what we demand is undeniably driven by our vision.

- *Identifying Their Passions:* The passionate pursuits of Black males can be used to lead them into higher levels of learning and a broad-based instructional program. Use their interests in sports, entertainment, entrepreneurship, and video game playing as a framework for literacy, mathematics, science, social studies, internships, field trips, summer programs, mentoring relationships, and developing critical-thinking skills.

The National Center for Education Statistics report, *The Condition of Education, 2001*, notes:

Most high school students formalize their educational plans between 8th and 10th grades, suggesting that interventions to influence students' educational aspirations are more likely to succeed if they take place by 8th or 9th grade (Hossler et al. 1999).

High school graduates whose parents did not go to college tend to report lower educational expectations than their peers as early as 8th grade.

High school mathematics course taking is strongly associated with eventual enrollment in a 4-year institution, and mathematics course taking is related to parents' education.

According to 1999 data, White children who live in two-parent households are nearly twice as likely to have parents who are college graduates:

- 26.4 percent of White mothers and 33.6 percent of White fathers are college graduates.

- 13.9 percent of Black mothers and 16.5 of Black fathers are college graduates.

However these statistics do not account for single-parent households.

Students whose parents did not go to college receive less assistance from their parents in applying to colleges.

Clearly, encouraging and assisting Black males to develop college aspirations must occur at school and through their relationships with teachers, counselors, coaches, and mentors.

College: The Ultimate Educational Goal

Much more can be done to inspire and encourage Black males to aspire toward college. Once having inspired them, teachers, parents, coaches, and counselors must create the support mechanisms to prepare them to succeed once there. The doorway to college may be opened as a result of their athletic, artistic, musical, dramatic, dance, or academic abilities. This is why early identification and nurturing of each young man's unique talents and gifts are critically important. Our older son's way to college began with his first-grade passion for art. Our younger son's fifth-grade talent in acting may become one of the special attributes which paves the way for his college admission.

According to the U.S. Department of Education's data, if young men are encouraged to pursue math and science beyond algebra I and chemistry, they are substantially more likely to attend college. A vision of college-level achievement will directly impact the level of planning by parents and encouragement and intervention by school personnel. The U.S. Department of Education's white paper, *Mathematics Equals Opportunity*, examined the impact of middle school math and science classes on college enrollment through a

National Education Longitudinal Study of 26,000 public and private school 8th-grade students from 1988 through 1996. The report found, low-income students who take algebra I and geometry are almost 300 percent more likely to attend college as those who do not.

A recent analysis by the U.S. Department of Education indicates that high school students who take algebra, geometry, and other rigorous mathematics courses are more likely to go on to college. This is true regardless of their family income. In fact, the benefit of taking rigorous courses is greatest for students from low-income families.

The key to understanding mathematics is taking algebra or courses covering algebraic concepts by the end of the eighth grade. Achievement at that stage gives students an important advantage in taking rigorous high school mathematics and science courses. However, many eighth- and ninth-graders may already be <u>behind</u> in their course selection to get on to the road to college. Some schools do not offer everyone a full selection of challenging courses, or because not all students are prepared for and encouraged to enroll. The results of the recent Third International Mathematics and Science Study (TIMSS) confirm that many students enter high school without a solid grounding in mathematics, closing doors very early for further education and better careers.

The report found:

- 83 percent of all students (71 percent of low-income students) who take algebra I and geometry go on to college within two years of their scheduled high school graduation while only 36 percent of all students (27 percent of low income students) who do not take algebra I and geometry courses go on to college.

- 89 percent of students who take chemistry in high school go on to college while only 43 percent of students who do not take chemistry go to college.

- 60 percent of students who take calculus in high school took algebra in the eighth grade.

The study further determined, enrollment in gatekeeper courses, such as algebra and foreign language, in eighth grade helps students reach higher levels in the mathematics and foreign language pipelines. For example, students who enroll in algebra as eighth-graders were more likely to reach high-level math courses (i.e., algebra III, trigonometry, or calculus) in high school than students who do not enroll in algebra as eighth-graders.

According to the National Center for Education Statistics:

- 31 percent of Blacks ages 18-24 are enrolled in college while the percentage for Whites is 68 percent.

- Only 37 percent of Black college students are male.

- 14 percent of all Blacks enrolled in postsecondary institutions are enrolled in HBCUs (Historical Black Colleges and Universities). 25 percent of bachelor's degrees and 20 percent of first-professional degrees earned by Blacks are received from HBCUs.

The many societal, community, and peer issues distracting and discouraging Black males from academic pursuits necessitate their hearing the college-bound message early and often. Giving young men a college-bound focus

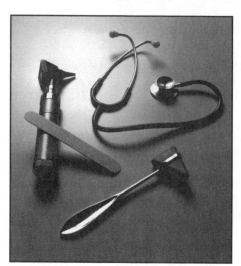

passes the baton of hope and gives them ownership of their own future. Parents can reinforce this message by replacing some of their son's FUBU, Phat Farm, Sean John, and other hip-hop shirts with college T-shirts and their NBA and NFL jerseys with college jerseys. Young men can be encouraged to adorn the T-shirts representing their favorite rapper's alma mater. (Sean "P. Diddy" Combs is an alumnus of Howard University.) Gather brochures and view books from colleges and universities, provide frequent opportunities for young men to be exposed to college graduates and visit college campuses.

Teachers can create a wall within their classroom of paraphernalia from local universities, their alma mater, the alma maters of popular athletes and entertainers and other teachers on staff. Teachers can also look for every opportunity to discuss a student's college-bound dreams, connect a student's interests to college-level study, and continually reinforce class selection and standardized test scores within the context of meeting college admission standards.

Black professionals, particularly graduates of HBCUs, need to get out of the board room and into the classroom. Radio DJ, Tom Joyner, comments:

Intellects like to sit around and discuss whether the need for Black colleges still exists. To that question my response is: 'Don't make me cuss.' We need HBCUs for the same reason we need Black churches, Black radio stations, Black television networks, and Black beauty supply stores. HBCUs meet our needs because they belong to us. They are a part of us. They are us. And we also need HBCUs because Black students who attend them are more likely to graduate. And graduates of HBCUs are more likely to be recruited and hired by major corporations than those who attend White colleges and universities ...Those of us who attended HBCUs ought to be singing their praises wherever we go. We need to be out there talking to youth groups, speaking at high schools and trade schools, and communicating the benefits of attending an HBCU. Dig out that FAMU sweatshirt and wear it whether it still covers that belly or not. Be loud and proud of your alma mater.

What is Your Vision?

Enough said, what is your vision for the young man whom you have identified? How will you utilize the tremendous opportunity you have to influence his emotional, social, and intellectual development in ways which will enable him to overcome the negative influences of peer pressure and media images? How will you inspire the highest academic achievement and affirm the highest educational attainment? Will you develop a vision of a life of hope and promise and be uncompromising in your demand for Standard English usage, social skill development, and developing his intellectual and critical-thinking skills?

If you are a mentor, coach, or pastor, how will you model the highest standards of manhood and communicate your uncompromising expectations of his promise and potential? What lessons will you teach when witnessing ill-mannered behavior, non-Standard English usage, or lack of respect and responsibility?

Your vision will determine your expectations and your expectations will determine your actions.

My Vision is:

_____

_____

_____

_____

_____

_____

_____

Chapter 2: Key Points

1. The scope of your vision will define the scope of your strategies.

2. The school and home vision should be in alignment.

3. Your beliefs and your experiences define what you do.

4. Consider your vision for Black male enrollment in honors, academically gifted, and AP classes.

5. Determine the needed values to be taught and reinforced.

6. Black males should be held to the highest standards and expectations.

7. Lessons should reflect Black men who embody the core values and guiding principles you are teaching and reinforcing.

8. Learn and use a student's passions to lead him into learning.

9. Helping students to discover their dreams can help to place school into a meaningfully relevant context.

10. Consciously affirm and inspire higher aspirations, i.e., college, career, life.

11. Statistics show that students who take algebra I, geometry, and chemistry are more likely to go on to college.

12. Currently, only one out of three Black college students is male.

Chapter 3
Climate & Culture

Walk into any racially mixed high school cafeteria at lunch time and you will instantly notice that in the sea of adolescent faces, there is an identifiable group of Black students sitting together. Conversely, it could be pointed out that there are many groups of White students sitting together as well, though people rarely comment about that. The question on the tip of everyone's tongue is 'Why are the Black kids sitting together?' Principals want to know, teachers want to know, White students want to know, the Black students who aren't sitting at the table want to know ...Why do Black youths, in particular, think about themselves in terms of race? Because that is how the rest of the world thinks of them.

— *Beverly Daniel Tatum*

Understanding the unique issues (i.e., media images, peer pressures, societal perceptions, cultural icons) influencing the attitudes and behaviors of Black males is paramount to developing effective communication, intervention, and empowerment strategies. Perhaps there is no group of students who are more misunderstood than Black students. Teachers and parents are perplexed and exasperated as they openly question:

"Do they value academic achievement?"

"Why do they have such a negative attitude toward school?"

"Do they aspire toward anything other than sports and entertainment?"

"Why do their parents allow them to leave home with their pants hanging down at their knees?"

"Why are they so angry and why are they so confrontational?"

"Why does my son always leave his homework at home? If not for all of the zeros he would be an 'A' student. He just doesn't care."

There are many variables shaping the complex and far-reaching culture of Black males whose attitudes and behaviors will subsequently impact school climate and culture. Negative encounters with law enforcement, store clerks who follow them around, teachers who confront them in front of their peers, mothers who take mole hills and turn them into mountains, fathers who challenge their manhood (i.e., "Don't be such a sissy"), and the multitude of peer-group issues they will experience as a result of being Black—all takes its toll and the miracle is that more Black males aren't losing their minds.

The first step in understanding Black male culture is to take a moment to consider how you would respond to the types of issues confronting them. Read and reflect on the following statements. Use them to stimulate a classroom discussion and listen to student perspectives on each issue. Sit down over lunch or dinner and discuss each statement with the young man you are focusing your strategies on:

- *"Every day is filled with drama: Just going to school, someone is going to challenge your manhood. If you tell an adult, you're a punk. If you fight back you get suspended. If you fight back and really hurt someone you get suspended and go to jail."*

- *"When a girl at school likes you and you don't like her, she is going to talk about you. If you talk about her, she and her friends are going to make life a living hell!"*

- *"When a girl likes you and you like her, it's almost guaranteed someone else is going to like her and he is going to want to fight you. Just because."*

- *"If you go to class to do your work and the teacher doesn't know how to control her classroom, then you are going to have to clown just to fit in ... everyone else is doing it."*

- *"If you are really smart you can't raise your hand too often or else you have to get some questions wrong intentionally or your friends will 'dis' you after class, 'Yo man, you acting like a White boy!'"*

- *"There are certain academic clubs, foreign language clubs, and student associations you can't join or you will be considered a sell-out and you will get dissed."*

- *"You can't come to school with a backpack full of books, and actually have paper and supplies every day or else … you guessed it, you will get dissed."*

- *"If a teacher confronts you in the classroom in front of your friends (or worse, your girlfriend) you have to step, even if it means getting sent to the office or suspended from school. You can't let the teacher 'dis' you in front of your friends."*

- *"If you're walking to school and you hear police sirens you'd better walk slowly, hide, or else you may get shot."*

- *"If you're driving in a car with a group of brothers and the police pull up behind you, your throat gets dry, your heart begins to race, and you see your life flashing before your eyes. This could be your day to die."*

- *"The gun shots, police sirens, and babies crying, keep you up every night. You're lucky to get two hours sleep and when you get to school, the teacher gives you a pop quiz! You don't even care, you just want to get some sleep."*

- *"All over the neighborhood, you see Black men with broken backs and broken spirits, drinking beer at 7:30 a.m., smoking crack in the alley after school, cleaning car windows for a dollar and begging for handouts. You don't want to be like them, but you know some of your friends are going to be exactly like them."*

- *"A lot of your friends just keep you distracted from your school work. They don't study, they don't do homework, and they are barely passing. You want to tell them to wake up, but they're your friends and you figure it's best to just leave them alone."*

- *"After all of the other stuff you have to deal with, just to survive, you have to worry about passing the high school exit exam in algebra I or you won't get your high school diploma and you don't have any other way out of your misery."*

- *"You start school with hopes of going to college, but you wonder if the gangs will let you live to see another day ... so much drama."*

This is just the short list of issues confronting Black males living in urban and inner-city communities. Poverty, homelessness, and foster care brings with it an entirely new set of issues and least we not forget young Black men living in the suburbs. While their parents may have struggled and sacrificed (like my wife and I) to lift themselves out of poverty and provide a safe community to raise their children, they want to go to the ghetto every chance they get and go out of their way to be underachievers and are oftentimes embarrassed to tell their classmates and teammates where they live. They just want to fit it.

One night in the hood ...

One night Freddie and I were walking along Calumet Avenue on Chicago's south side when suddenly two young men leaned out of a first floor tenement window. Less than six feet away, one young man pointed a double-barrel shotgun at us and said, 'Represent.' This shotgun-wielding young man was asking us to proclaim our gang affiliation. This was a rite of passage. The correct response would allow these two thirteen-year-olds to pass unharmed. The incorrect response would send two more nameless and faceless Black males to a premature death.

Freddie immediately pounded his chest with his right fist and proclaimed, 'Disciple thang.' The shotgun-wielding young man responded, 'Disciple thang, walk on.' Freddie and I, at age thirteen, understood the community we were walking through; which gang controlled the neighborhood; how to walk; and how to respond. These survival skills, in that instant, helped us to see fourteen.

What would you have done if confronted with a life-threatening situation such as this? In urban and inner-city communities, young men are growing up on urban battlefields where they must make life-saving decisions daily. Just surviving the day and getting to school is a major accomplishment. Not having paper or pencil is the least of their concerns (and should be the least of ours).

Black Males Need Compassion Not Pity

A sincere desire to understand the issues confronting Black males requires our compassion. However, the sociocultural influences which continually shape Black male culture doesn't necessitate our pity. They need teachers who will teach them, parents who will raise them, and adults throughout the school community who are willing to acknowledge the unique issues confronting them in discussing and developing strategies to empower them.

My wife and I purposefully play the stereotypical good cop–bad cop roles when dealing with the many behavioral issues of our two sons. I issue discipline and she comforts—males need both. They need to know mom and dad have the highest expectations. Dad will establish standards, hold them accountable, and reinforce the consequences. Mom will provide a refuge for comfort, however, under no circumstances will mom undermine dad's authority or join forces with the children to undermine dad's position.

Teachers and parents also have to join forces and agree upon expectations. Parents and teachers can only arrive at this point of agreement if they took the time to clarify their missions and visions. Teachers who associate pity with providing an opportunity for a boy to turn in a late assignment for full credit don't understand his needs, the family's needs, or the mission—teaching and learning. Consider, if a 500-word paper is due on Monday, the teacher could require a 700-word paper on Tuesday, a 900-word paper on Wednesday, and a 2000-word paper if turned in anytime prior to the end of the grading period. Therefore, if a young man puts forth 'A' effort, even when his school work is late, he will have the opportunity to earn an 'A' grade, which *he needs* to stay motivated. The consequence of not submitting the work on time is more work, not a failing grade. Zeros don't inspire young men to do more work. If they don't care about their grades it doesn't even punish them—it punishes their parents! In this day of state and federal school accountability mandates, it ultimately punishes the school. If the assignment was meaningful to begin with, then the important concern is stimulating the intrinsic desire to do the work, and providing every opportunity for the student to put forth the effort to acquire the knowledge.

This is not to suggest teachers excuse late, missing, sloppily done, or incomplete work. Or, that they feel sorry for young men who aren't prepared for tests and quizzes, particularly if they have been announced. Don't feel sorry for them, work them harder. Assign more work. Push them harder. Make them sweat. Learn from coaches, who are oftentimes great motivators of young men. Coaching is all mental preparation, communication, motivation, respect, and most of all, developing a relationship where young people want to work for you. That's the attitude teachers need to have—inspire Black males to want to work for you.

If we want to keep more of our children from failing, we must expand our discussions beyond meeting proficiency levels or minimum standards to:

1. *How do we engage children in an exploratory journey of their talents, abilities, innate interests, creative imaginations, personality types, and learning-styles?*

2. *How do we help children understand the unique ways in which they learn, develop their special gifts, and apply what they know?*

3. *How do we engage children in practical, meaningful, and relevant discussion, debate, and analysis of the real issues, challenges, and decisions that will confront them in their homes, communities, and the world around them?*

4. *How do we help children unlock their creative imaginations, tap their natural geniuses, express their creativity and individuality, and explore their innovativeness, in ways that may ignite a passion, dream, or aspiration?*

5. *How do we help children develop character values, habits, and choices consistent with achieving their dreams and aspirations?*

6. *How do we help children develop or acquire the skills, abilities, behavior, language, attitude, experiences, and knowledge that will allow them to achieve success in school that is consistent with achieving success in life outside of school?*

7. *How do we structure a nurturing, non-threatening and supportive learning environment that allows children to experience success at their varying developmental stages, competencies, and ability levels?*

8. *How do we provide more opportunities for children to receive immediate feedback and intrinsic rewards through the practical application of what they're learning.*

9. *How do we provide children with a passion and purpose for going to school?*

10. *What do children want to learn?*

[Building Dreams: Helping Students Discover Their Potential]

Get a copy of the movie 'Men in Black' and cue the VCR or DVD on the scene where the recruits are being told 'You are the best of the best.' Walk into the classroom dressed in a black suit with dark sunglasses. To be even more dramatic, have some of the football players dress like you and stand around the room with their arms folded. If you are teaching elementary or middle school, borrow some football players from the local high school. Ask for players who have their own black suits and you can provide the sunglasses.

After students take their seats, shout "What's my name?" Have the football players respond, "Mr. Wynn." "What's my name?" "Mr. Wynn."

"I am an 'A' teacher and I only teach 'A' students. They only allow the best of the best to be in my class, so unless there is an error on your schedule, the fact you're here must mean you are the best of the best, and, I don't mean in the school, I mean in the school district. Since you are the best students, in this class you are expected to get an 'A.'

To ensure you get an 'A' I am going to tell you exactly what I am going to do and what is going to be expected from you [begin passing out the course syllabus]. I am not going to trick you. I am going to tell you at least 3 days in advance before I give a test. While I will occasionally give surprise quizzes, they won't count toward your grade, unless you get an 'A.' However, if you don't get an 'A' I will assign more class work and homework to ensure you are learning what you need to know to be an 'A' student. Because I am what? That's right, I'm an 'A' teacher."

Go over the course syllabus and outline in specific detail, exactly what students must do to get an 'A' grade.

"You'll notice on the syllabus, 15 percent of your final grade will be based on homework. The purpose of homework is to reinforce what I am teaching in class and what I will expect you to demonstrate on tests and quizzes. Completing homework is not an option. Late homework is not an option. Sloppily completed homework is not an option. If you turn in homework late, you will be assigned more homework for each day your homework is late. If you turn in incomplete homework, you will be assigned more homework. If you turn in sloppily done homework, you will be assigned more homework. If you turn in any late, incomplete, and/or sloppily done homework after the first week of school I will ask your parent to come to school to speak to me. If he or she can't

make it to school, then I will meet your parent at your home. If I can't meet your parent at your home, then I'll meet him or her at his or her job. You know your mom, dad, grandmother, or grandfather is not going to want to take time  *away for their job to meet YOUR teacher because you are turning in sloppy or late homework. Homework is worth 15 percent of your grade and I intend for you to earn every one of those 15 percent.*

If you have a problem with your homework, see me. If you don't understand something, see me. If you need a place to do your homework, my class is open before school in the morning and after school in the evening."

Engage in a similar conversation in regards to every aspect of the syllabus and explain how you are going to meet students' learning-style needs; why lessons are designed in the way in which they are; any supplemental material which may help students to better understand what is being covered; why some students may benefit from making audio tapes of lectures and why other students may benefit from watching video tapes of lectures; and why other students will learn best from the hands-on opportunities.

"At the end of the grading period, I intend to have a class full of 'A' students because of what?" [Students respond] "Because Mr. Wynn is an 'A' teacher!"

A math teacher who cares about the academic achievement of Black males may have an encounter like the following:

"Mr. Johnson, you got a '65' on the test. See me after school in three days for a retest!"

"Mr. Johnson, you got a '75' on the retest. See me after school in three days for another retest."

"Mr. Johnson, you got an '85' on the second retest. See me after school in three days for another retest."

"Mr. Johnson, you got a '95' on the third retest. I guess we have resolved you are an 'A+' student. Let's try to be an 'A+' student on the first test next time."

Another math teacher stops at the first test and says, "Mr. Johnson you should have studied. You'd better study harder the next time or you're going to fail the class." When is the young man going to learn what wasn't understood during the first test? Who knows what type of personal issues was going on in his life, if there is a teaching-style–learning-style mismatch, if the young man lacks the preexisting knowledge foundation, or if he simply needs more opportunities to 'get it.' Isn't 'getting it' the real goal?

More work increases learning, a failing grade merely punishes a young man for an entirely foreseeable event—young men are going to be late doing their work until they make the transition from irresponsible children to responsible young men. Denying them recess, punishing them with low grades, berating them in front of their peers, referring them to the office, or forcing them to spend long hours in detention doesn't accomplish the primary goal, TEACHING THEM!

To more fully understand this approach, consider Howard Gardner's research in the area of Multiple Intelligences as outlined in his book, *Frames of Mind: The Theory of Multiple Intelligences.*

Gardner identified eight areas through which we demonstrate intelligence (i.e., learn and apply what we know):

- *Verbal/Linguistic*
- *Logical/Mathematical*
- *Interpersonal*
- *Intrapersonal*
- *Visual/Spatial*
- *Musical/Rhythmic*
- *Bodily/Kinesthetic*
- *Naturalist*

Refer to the *workbook* for a complete description of how intelligence is reflected within each of these eight areas. Also, refer to the book, *Ten Steps to Helping Your Child Succeed in School,* for ideas pertaining to how to keep a journal as a means of identify a young man's multiple intelligences, learning-styles, and personality types. The book also outlines, how, as a parent, you can share this information with your son's teachers to get a jump-start on learning. What's important to note here is the dominant intelligences *(Interpersonal* and *Logical/Mathematical)* used by adults in transforming their understanding of Black male culture into the strategies needed to strengthen relationships and open communication. Interpersonal Intelligence deals with the way in which we relate to, understand, and empathize with others. Nowhere is this intelligence more important than in dealing with the many issues of Black males—their attitudes, behaviors, lack of self-motivation, lack of organization skills, lack of critical-thinking skills, and cross-gender communication issues require highly-developed relationship-building skills. Logical/Mathematical Intelligence deals with inductive/deductive reasoning, problem-solving, abstract thinking, and planning. This is the intelligence we rely upon to develop plans and strategies designed to provide solutions to the issues, many of which are entirely foreseeable, which will provide obstacles to learning and thusly, student achievement.

Stephen Peters (pictured with the young men from his *Gentlemen's Club*), a former classroom teacher and Middle School principal, pioneered a program for identifying Black males most likely to contribute towards or

Mychal Wynn · Empowering African-American Males

become involved in conflicts within his middle school. He, together with some of his teachers, developed a program for building relationships with these young men prior to their becoming discipline problems. In his book, *Inspired to Learn*, he notes, how, as a classroom teacher, his ability to develop relationships (i.e., Interpersonal Intelligence) with young men enabled him to empower them and thusly, reduce the conflicts within his school community:

> *'Just send him to Mr. Peters' class,' rang out from my colleagues at C. Alton Lindsay Middle School. They were referring to students who were out of control in their classrooms. These students had already been sent to the office, suspended, conference with, and so on. Nothing seemed to work with them as they continued to repeat the same behavior. Many of the students who were sent to my classroom were children from broken homes with little hope. Lindsay was a large middle school with many children who fit this description. Their chances were greatly reduced when they encountered adults who backed them into corners. Many young people today expect their interactions with adults in schools to be negative experiences.*

The success of Stephen Peters' Gentlemen's Club, the mentoring programs by such organizations as 100 Black Men, Omega Psi Phi fraternity, and the Masons is based on:

- Building relationships with Black males and their families (i.e., Interpersonal Intelligence).

- Developing strategies which take into account their learning-styles, personality types, culture, perspectives, perceptions, influences, peer pressures, and the many issues they are uniquely confronted with, and conceptualize plans allowing and enabling them to be successful (i.e., Logical/Mathematical Intelligence).

> *Our older son is totally unorganized. He knows it and we know. We purposefully sit around the kitchen table prior to the beginning of each semester and organize every binder for every subject. When his teachers distribute their syllabi we three-hole punch the course syllabus for each class and place each one into the appropriate binder. Our son knows exactly what is expected of him each school day (i.e., file his homework, graded work, and notes, and write down the announced test/quiz dates).*

Despite our best efforts, threats of punishment, and depriving of privileges, he will invariably lose control of his binders and papers will wind up everywhere.

My wife used to go through his binders, leap into a fit of rage, scream at him, follow him around the house, and run up her blood pressure (not the highest level of Interpersonal Intelligence). They both would be upset and he would be just as unorganized. Time for a new plan.

Question: What does he love to do?

Answer: Hang out with his friends on Friday evening at the movie theater.

Plan: "Mychal-David, we understand, despite your best efforts, you occasionally allow yourself to get unorganized during the school week. Therefore, your mom and I have decided we will forego a binder check until Friday after school. You'll need to bring home all of your course binders on Friday and have them organized before you go to the movies. If you have any tests, assignments, or quiz grades less than 'A' you will have to spend Saturday and Sunday reviewing your tests, quizzes, and notes for those classes, which means no TV or video games during the entire weekend."

The first Friday we did this, our son, despite his protests, didn't get to go to the movies. His binders were so unorganized, it took him all of Friday evening and much of Saturday to get them organized. Needless to say, every ensuing Friday, he was 'intrinsically-motivated' to do better!

Our younger son requires an entirely different set of strategies because he has a totally different set of needs.

Our younger son loves to talk and to perform. When he was in the fourth grade he auditioned for the Shakespearean play, 'Romeo and Juliet.' Some time after his audition when the parts were announced, we asked if he got a part in the play, to which he responded, 'I didn't get a part.' We could see he was disappointed so my wife and I didn't press the issue.

Nearing the end of the school year during the final parent-teacher conference, I made a comment to his teacher in regards to how the opportunity to have performed in 'Romeo and Juliet' would have really benefitted Jalani who was frequently being reminded about his excessive talking and socializing in class. My son's teacher responded, 'I agree with you totally, that's why I didn't understand why Jalani wasn't in Romeo and Juliet.'

She went on to tell my wife and me how our son had gotten a role which he had turned down because it wasn't the lead role!

A week into rehearsals during fifth grade for the school's performance of Shakespeare's, 'A Midsummer Night's Dream' I received a phone call from a teacher indicating Jalani didn't want to be in the play.

I had the teacher put my son on the telephone and I told him, "Jalani, you tricked your mother and me last year. This year you're going to be in the play. Do you understand?" He responded, 'Yes sir.' Following which I spoke to the teacher and told her, "You won't have any further problems from Jalani." However, the teacher responded, 'Mr. Wynn, if Jalani doesn't want to be in the play, I don't think you should force him to be in the play.' I responded, "Jalani will be fine, thank you for your concern."

The point for teachers and parents to understand is, you must be willing to develop strategies which take into account the unique issues and obstacles impacting Black male culture and Black male achievement. Sometimes the attitudes and behaviors young men have internalized is reflected in an unwillingness to try new things, a reluctance to enter into situations where there is a risk of failure, and a general lack of enthusiasm toward school and school work. Oftentimes, Black males need to be pushed and stretched in unfamiliar ways. The difference between their unwillingness and downright rebellion is in the nature of their relationship with teachers, coaches, parents, and mentors.

Successful relationships:

- inspire trust;

- communicate caring and compassion;

- are based on mutual respect;

- establish a level of comfort that you (as the adult) can be depended upon; and

- establish you as possessing knowledge, wisdom, experience, or some level of disciplinary expertise.

Each school community needs to develop two strategic planning teams:

- one team to be comprised of teachers and parents who are highly-developed in Interpersonal Intelligence,

- the other to be comprised of teachers and parents who are highly-developed in Logical/Mathematical Intelligence.

The interpersonal team focuses on strategies designed to strengthen relationships between students and families. The logical/mathematical team focuses on strategies designed to tap into preexisting knowledge, deepen learning, and tap into students' intrinsic motivation to complete coursework and prepare for tests and quizzes. The teams should be comprised of both teachers and parents because of the different and important perspectives each group brings to the discussions. Student achievement is not a teacher problem or a parent problem, it is a school problem which has far-reaching implications for the school community and the larger society. Strategies must take the unique student and family needs and parent perspectives into account.

Each group will have to take into account such issues as:

- The issues outlined on the 'Circles of Influence' (see illustration).

- The demographic needs of students.

- The existing school climate and culture and the prevailing attitudes of Black males toward learning.

- Data as it relates to student achievement, grade distribution, homework completion, test preparation, and strongest and weakest subject areas.

- Classroom management, time-on-task, and transition times during the class period (i.e., teacher-directed, student-directed, wrap-up).

After gathering and assessing the data reflecting the unique needs of the school community, and after engaging in discussions along the specific lines of building relationships and enhancing classroom and instructional logistics, the two teams should come together to discuss a merging of the strategies. Beginning with one classroom, one subject area, or one grade level the teams should work to develop an action plan with an achievable first goal.

Circles of Influence

Societal Influences

Sexually Explicit Programming

Lack of Positive Black Images

Promotes Violence as a Means of Problem-Solving

Frequent Portrayal of Black Families and Professionals as Dysfunctional

Desensitizes Death and Handgun Violence

Negative Role Models

Home/Community

Lack Academic Reinforcement

Lack Adequate Study Time/Location

Lack of Parental Involvement in Academic Tasks

Lack of Positive Mentoring

Lack of Self-Control/Self-Discipline

Requires Before/After-School Care

Underemployed or Unstable Household

Limited Exposure to Successful Adults

Lack Financial Resources

Glorifies, Profanity, Sarcasm, Sex, and Crime

High Amount of TV Viewing

Lack of Spiritual Foundation

Negative Peer Pressure

Negative Teacher Attitudes Toward Students

School

Low Teacher Expectations

Frequent Referrals/Suspensions

Low Attendance

Frequent Tardies

Verbal/Physical Confrontations

Lack of Respect for School Property

Extended Family/Foster Care

Single-Parent Households or Lack of Male/Female Influence

Glorifies Athletic/Entertainment over Academic Achievement

Holds Teachers in Low Regard

High Percentage of Free/Reduced Lunch

Individual

History of Discipline Problems and Low Academic Achievement

Lack of Respect for Individuals and Authority

Lacks Positive Focus/Direction

Incomplete or Unfinished Homework

Low Household Goals/Lack of Planning

Unorganized Households

Community/Household Void of Inspiration and Positive Images

Violent Outbursts

Negative Verbal/NonVerbal Communication

Low Self-Esteem

Apathy

Exhibits Self-Destructive Behaviors

Few Long-Term Goals

Uses Violence as a Means of Problem Solving

Lack Adequate Supplies and Materials

Limited English or non-English Speaking Households

Illiterate or Marginally Literate Family

Lacks a Middle/Upper Class Mentor

Lacks Nutrition

Poor Grooming & Personal Hygiene

Unrealistic Expectations

Transient Student Population

Lacks Meaningful Relationship with a Caring Adult

Does Not "Connect" Content to Outcomes

Students Frequently Unprepared

Lack of Medical/Dental Care

Low Teacher Morale

Frequent Classroom Disruptions

Students Disruptive in Large Groups

Victim or Perpetrator of Violent Crime

Poor Diet

Negative Peer Values

Many Teenage Pregnancies

Negative View of Women

Verbally/Physically Aggressive

Uses Violence to Resolve Conflicts

Negative Experiences with Law Enforcement

Firsthand Experience with Abuse

Glorifies, Fame, Fortune, and Infidelity

Perpetuates Gender/Race Biases and Stereotypes

The *Hope for Urban Education: A Study of Nine High-Performing, High-Poverty, Urban Elementary Schools* research study noted:

- *School leaders identified and pursued an important, visible, yet attainable, first goal. They focused on the attainment of this first goal, achieved success, and then used their success to move toward more ambitious goals.*

- *School leaders redirected time and energy that was being spent on conflicts between adults in the school toward service to children. Leaders appealed to teachers, support staff, and parents to put aside their own interests and focus on serving children well.*

- *Educators fostered in students a sense of responsibility for appropriate behavior and they created an environment in which students were likely to behave well. Discipline problems became rare as the schools implemented multi-faceted approaches for helping students learn responsibility for their own behavior.*

To more fully understand Black male culture and the influences it has on student achievement within your school community, review the illustration on the adjacent page, *Circles of Influence*, circling those areas of influence which appear to have the most impact on Black male culture within your school community.

While teachers and parents oftentimes agree on the cultural influences, i.e., music, language, style of dress, peer pressures, and lack of positive mentoring, there is general disagreement as to the cultural beliefs and values which the influences reflect. Teachers believe the behaviors exhibited by Black males within their classrooms is reflective of the acceptable norms of their household culture and the devaluing of education, commonplace amongst Black males, is a reflection of 'Black culture.' Parents, on the other hand, vehemently disagree with the behavior of Black males as being reflective of Black culture or family culture. Rather than taking negative attitudes and behaviors *to* school, parents believe their sons bring negative attitudes and behaviors home *from* school.

Having grown up a Black male and, now a parent of two Black males, I have reflected on how I behaved in school through the sixties and seventies, and on the behaviors which my boys have exhibited in school through the nineties and into the new millennium. Neither my behaviors of four decades ago, or my sons' behaviors yesterday, reflect 'Black culture.' Their classroom behaviors, as was the case when I was in school, is reflective of a combination of peer pressures, pop cultural influences, their own personality types, and the expectations communicated by the adult who is present (i.e., what they can get away with). The influence of parental behavioral expectations depends largely on the level of communication between home and school and the strength of the relationship between parent and teacher.

Elizabeth Hood, in *Educating Black Students: Some Basic Issues*, describes the experiences of a Black administrator with three seventh-grade Black males expelled from a classroom:

> *I said to these three small but energetic boys, 'This is the third time in a week that you three have been sent to the office from Miss J's class. What is the problem with you in Miss J's class?'*
>
> *One of the boys responded, 'Miss J just picks on us. The whole class makes noise in that lady's room. She doesn't know how to make us behave. All the kids act up in that room. She doesn't like us three, so she sends us to the office to try to scare the other kids.'*
>
> *'You do get along well in your other classes?' I asked. 'Well, Ma'am, it's like this,' the smaller of the three joined in, 'We do all right when the teachers really get us when we get out our seats and make noise. We don't do nothing wrong in those classes. No Ma'am.'*
>
> *The outcome of the battle was always decided on the first day the students entered the class. If the teacher failed to 'make them' at that initial encounter, the battle was over and the teacher the loser.*

To place the cultural influences reflected in the illustration into their proper context, Black males who walk into classrooms or onto an athletic field must be assessed individually rather than as representative of some larger identifiable 'Black culture.'

To assess Black males individually:

- get to know them individually (i.e., personality type, learning-styles, multiple intelligences);

- get to know their family and family influences (i.e., where they live, who they live with, the type of work their parents do);

- visit their homes and get to know the hopes and dreams of their families;

- get to know the make-up of their family unit (i.e., single-parent, grand parents, only child, siblings, foster care, multiple generations within the household) and do not make assumptions as to their strengths and weaknesses;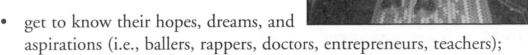

- get to know their peer group, peer culture, and peer values (i.e., wanna be thugs, gang bangers, low academic achievers);

- get to know their hopes, dreams, and aspirations (i.e., ballers, rappers, doctors, entrepreneurs, teachers);

- get to know their role models, heroes, and heroines (i.e., mother, grandmother, father, rappers, athletes, coach);

- understand their reputation without being unduly influenced by it (i.e., frequent office referrals and/or suspensions, loud talking teachers, confrontational attitudes);

- understand their level of pre-existing knowledge (i.e., experiences outside of their community, cultural exposure);

- understand their socioeconomic frame of reference (i.e., living in poverty, homeless, middle class, affluent);

- understand the family exposure to education and careers (i.e., professions, college graduates, incarceration, welfare); and

- understand their experiences with adults within the school setting and whether or not there are any influential adults who can be collaborated with for support (i.e., teachers, administrators, custodians, school bus drivers, coaches).

Getting to know the Black males within a school community requires a willingness to understand what has shaped their attitudes and behaviors and to accept that the influences are oftentimes contrary to the values, beliefs, and cultural frame of reference of their homes.

Beverly Daniel Tatum, in *Why Are All the Black Kids Sitting Together in the Cafeteria?* notes:

> In <u>*The Autobiography of Malcolm X*</u>, *as a junior high school student, Malcolm was a star. Despite the fact that he was separated from his family and living in a foster home, he was an 'A' student and was elected president of his class. One day he had a conversation with his English teacher, whom he liked and respected, about his future career goals. Malcolm said that he wanted to be a lawyer. His teacher responded, 'That's no realistic goal for a nigger,' and advised him to consider carpentry instead. The message was clear: You are a Black male, your racial group membership matters, plan accordingly. Malcolm's emotional response was typical—anger, confusion, and alienation. He withdrew from his White classmates, stopped participating in class, and eventually left his predominately White Michigan home to live with his sister in Roxbury, a Black community in Boston.*

Clearly, Malcolm's attitude toward school, teachers, and White classmates was not shaped by home, family, or community culture but by the school itself through the attitude, language, and behavior of one teacher. A teacher with a clear mission to discourage Black students from pursuing those intellectual and vocational pursuits considered reserved for Whites. While not necessarily rooted in racism, the attitude that Black students should not be encouraged toward certain intellectual and vocational pursuits exists through academic tracking and grouping, vocational or career tracks, recommendations for special education placement, questioning the recommendations and referrals for gifted education placement, denial of Black student enrollment in honors and AP classes, and a failure

by teachers, counselors, and coaches to encourage Black students to aspire toward college. The attitudes and behaviors of adults within school communities are powerful contributing factors to the attitudes and behaviors of Black males.

In regards to the impact of Black household culture on Black youth culture, Tatum notes:

In adolescence, as race becomes personally salient for Black youth, finding the answer to questions such as, 'What does it mean to be a young Black person? How should I act? What should I do?' is particularly important. And although Black fathers, mothers, aunts, and uncles may hold the answers by offering themselves as role models, they hold little appeal for most adolescents. The last thing many fourteen-year-olds want to do is to grow up to be like their parents. It is the peer group, the kids in the cafeteria, who hold the answers to these questions. They know how to be Black. They have absorbed the stereotypical images of Black youth in the popular culture and are reflecting those images in their self-presentation.

Tatum sites other factors influencing the attitudes of Black youth:

- Anger and resentment toward the systematic exclusion of Black people from full participation in U.S. society.

- Rebellion against images associated with 'whiteness' (language patterns, dress, music, dance, hair styles, participation in certain school clubs). In some situations, depending on the overall school and peer culture, academic achievement, and/or enrollment in academically-challenging classes can be associated with 'whiteness.'

- Awareness of attitudes, behaviors, and assumptions directed toward Black people as a whole (e.g., drug use, stealing from retail stores, 'they all want to become athletes or entertainers').

- Noticeable underrepresentation of Black children in academically advanced classes.

- Noticeable overrepresentation of Black children in special education and on athletic teams.

- Assumption of an 'oppositional identity' in which anything associated with 'whiteness' is discarded and all things 'authentically black' are embraced (i.e., music, walk, dress, tattoos, hair styles, language patterns, attitudes toward authority).

Young, Black, Rich, and Influential

Todd Boyd, in *Young, Black, Rich, and Famous*, notes:

When Jack Johnson became heavyweight champion of the world in 1908, a massive panic struck those who were interested in maintaining the mythical sovereignty of the White race. Johnson, the larger-than-life Black champion who was a great fighter and seemingly unbeatable, was far from being deferent or docile, the mode of behavior considered most appropriate for a Black man of his time. Instead he was loud, boisterous, and wanted everyone to know that he had defied convention and become the champion in spite of the overt racism of the day. Johnson once reportedly said, 'I'm Black, and they'll never let me forget it. I'm Black alright, and I'll never let them forget it.'

Today, nearly 100 years removed from when Jack Johnson dominated heavyweight boxing, Black men, dominate the public face of sports and entertainment. Young Black men, some of whom are college educated, others who don't have a high school diploma; some of whom come from middle-class or affluent families, others who  are straight from inner-city ghettos; some of whom have read Malcolm, King, DuBois, Woodson, Dunbar, Bennett, and Baldwin, and others who haven't read beyond the basal readers and chapter books of elementary school. Their faces, cornrows, tattoos, jewelry, gold teeth, earrings, and clothing styles dominate magazine covers, bill board advertisements, transit buses, and music videos.

Adults who are teaching, raising, and mentoring Black males must become in tune to the impact of what may be considered an anti-social, anti-intellectual, pro-sex, pro-alcohol, and materialistic Rap and hip-hop culture. Unlike generations past where the message in the music was anti-establishment—pro-black, anti-discrimination—pro-community empowerment, anti-racist—pro-community consciousness, and anti-police brutality—pro-justice, much of today's rap and hip-hop music glorifies materialism and debases women. Despite the continuing destruction of the nuclear family in the Black community as a result of men who are not fathers to their children and proliferation of AIDS and STDs throughout the Black community, the message from Black entertainers to Black consumers is to have sex, be unfaithful, and buy the biggest house, most expensive car, gaudiest jewelry, and have the most lavish parties as your money will buy.

As Charles Barkley, former NBA player, stated in a Nike commercial, "I'm not a role model," the same must be said of Rappers and hip-hop artists. They are not role models, however, no reasonable or logical argument can be made to discount the power which media, music, advertisements, and the internet has to influence the behavior of millions of Black children.

Tavis Smiley, in *How to Make Black America Better*, notes:

This is not another debate over whether Charles Barkley was right when he said he was not a role model. I'm not suggesting that people have to be role models. The point here is that each of us, as African Americans, has to buy into the notion of being a race model. The term 'role model' implies having met a certain standard of perfection voluntarily. A 'race model' has no choice but to meet that standard. The role model plays to a visible audience of people who choose to admire him. The race model plays to an invisible audience he doesn't even know is admiring him. A role model doesn't bear the burden of having to be all things to all people. A race model does. So let's set out with the goal of being the best Black people we can be. The race is bound to rise as a result.

Cathy Hughes further states:

Black people do not need role models; we need to help ourselves return to our collective standard of decency, honesty, hard work, sharing, caring, and reaching back. When success is based on the motivation of a role model, the entire system of reference is open to destruction based simply upon the possible failure of the role model—that one person. When we aspire, however, to the higher collective standard, no single failure can damage or cause the individual to lose hope. A personal failure is brought back to redemption by aligning the person once again to the collective standard.

The hip-hop and Rap music industry is a multi-billion dollar industry which influences behavior, clothing, hair styles, language, and the purchases of automobiles, jewelry, alcohol, and gold teeth. It is a powerful sociocultural phenomenon influencing the behavior of Black children and Black households to the detriment of education. It is not uncommon to encounter Black children in elementary school who, as non-readers, know the lyrics to popular songs before learning the alphabet. In many high schools, you are more likely to see Black males with headphones listening to rap CDs entering school without paper, pencils, or books. Least we not forget, as early as elementary and middle school you are likely to see Black girls as inappropriately dressed and as sexually provocative as the Black women portrayed in music videos.

Because of these powerful forces influencing the ways Black children speak, walk, dress, style their hair, and pierce and tattoo their bodies we dare not dismiss such influences as "the times in which we live." To the contrary, we must recognize, realize, and conceptualize ways to limit a young person's exposure on the one hand and engage him or her in critical-thinking discussions on the other. Unfortunately, school curricula is not as dynamic as the culture. The lyrics, music video imagery, advertisements, television sitcoms, talk shows, and news reports of the many exploits of the heroes and heroines of today's generation have to make their way into classroom discussions and critical-thinking analysis.

One of the most dangerous things parents can do is to leave their sons at home with a working television with a cable connection and a computer with internet access. Equally as dangerous is allowing a young man, a television, and a computer, alone in a bedroom with the door closed. There is simply too much inappropriate content and too many predators. Far too many young people are below grade level in reading and critical-thinking skills while they have a household full of CDs and 24-7 television access. Parents have to stop blaming everyone for their son's attitude, behavior, and low academic performance and do a check-up from the neck-up! No child should be spending more time watching television than he is reading, engaged in sports, or otherwise being engaged in mentally or physically stimulating activities.

Teachers, coaches, mentors, and parents have to understand the world of today's young men and stop burying their heads in the sand. The only way adults can know the images, language, and messages which young men are being exposed to is to listen to their music, watch their videos, and watch the television programming they are watching and internet web sites they are accessing.

Once you are informed and can make a judgment as to the appropriateness of the content, use what you know to initiate discussions to engage young men in thinking about the messages in the music and the images in the advertisements. As a teacher or mentor who believes certain content is inappropriate and sending the wrong messages, tell parents what you think even if you are told to "mind your own business!" If you are a parent, don't allow your sons to access inappropriate web sites, watch inappropriate programming, or listen to inappropriate music, and tell other parents to do the same. Don't take the position, "Well, Mr. Wynn, if I don't let him watch it at home, he'll just go over to one of his friends and watch it." To use such reasoning is as ridiculous as saying, "Mr. Wynn, I let my son smoke crack cocaine at home because if I didn't he would just go over to one of his friends and do it."

Young men need teachers who will teach and parents who will raise them. My wife and I aren't perfect parents, we aren't even the best parents—as our sons will most certainly attest to. However, as parents, we have a God-given responsibility to do the best we can to counter-balance the values and images our sons are bombarded with through the media and from their peers. As parents, my wife and I:

1. Make education a priority in our household. Rarely a day goes by without my wife and me asking our sons about school. Reading and school work is tied to everything. You can't go to the movies unless your school work is done. You can't play a video game unless you have read for the amount of time you intend to play the video game. Your weekend doesn't begin until your homework has been completed.

2. Take control over the radio station. Personally, I prefer to listen to the Tom Joyner Morning Show in the morning and old school programming throughout the rest of the day. While I give my sons some flexibility in changing the station they know when music is inappropriate and they are quick to change to another station.

3. Our sons are allowed hip-hop fashions, but they have to wear a belt and my wife and I impose limits. Some of the fashions which we feel are too over the top stay at the store.

4. We don't affirm professional sports or entertainment as career aspirations. This is not to suggest our sons couldn't pursue professional sports or entertainment if this reflects their future dreams, however, my wife and I don't affirm them as an alternative to education or intellectual pursuits.

5. We don't allow piercing or tattoos. That's a decision our sons can make when they are grown, on their own, and paying their own bills.

6. We've never taken our sons to a Rap concert or to see a hip-hop artist who promotes sex in his or her music.

7. We eliminate television and video games from Sunday evening through Thursday evening during the school year. Any free time should be spent reading a book or preparing for the next school day.

8. We don't promote athletes and entertainers as role models, heroes, or heroines. However, we acknowledge those athletes and entertainers who espouse similar values, character, and spirituality as we teach in our household.

9. We take advantage of opportunities to discuss the music, fashions, people, and images our sons are interested in.

10. We reinforce Standard English usage and discourage overuse of slang. We consider overuse to represent when you don't know any other way to communicate, but through the use of slang. This is not to imply we do not recognize, value, or validate our own Black cultural frame of reference and culturally unique language and language patterns.

All parents are challenged with counter-balancing the negative language, images, and ideas proliferating the airwaves, television programming, music videos, video games, and movies. Whether spending the day together at a Track and Field Meet or spending Spring Break and summer vacations together, strong families provide the best foundation from which to nurture and develop strong Black men.

The Educational Disconnect

The powerful media influence pertaining to sports and entertainment has an adversely powerful influence on the educational perception of Black males. It is not uncommon to speak to students in an assembly or elementary school classroom and find over 90 percent of the young men affirm professional sports or the music industry as their sole career aspiration. For many of them, they believe physical and/or musical talent to be the single contributing factor to the successful pursuit of their aspirations, and as such, view education as unimportant. Somewhere they have received signals which suggests reading as unimportant to rapping and critical-thinking as unimportant to a professional athlete. Or course, nothing could be further from the truth.

The pursuit of an education for the purpose of becoming educated has been relegated to an education being of value only in so much as it assists in getting jobs and/or pursuing careers. Learning how to write, speak, think, and solve problems is not nearly as important as 'getting paid.' This is the message communicated through the music, the advertisements, and current pop culture. Such messages have had a powerful effect on the mind-set of urban and poor Black children who have internalized speaking Standard English as "talking White" and pursuing an education as "acting White."

Beverly Daniel Tatum, in *Why Are All the Black Kids Sitting Together in the Cafeteria?* notes:

Reflecting on her high school years, one Black woman from a White neighborhood described both the pain of being rejected by her Black classmates and her attempts to conform to her peer's definition of Blackness:

'Oh you sound White, you think you're White,' they said. And the idea of sounding White was just so absurd to me ... So ninth grade was sort of traumatic in that I started listening to rap music, which I really just don't like. [I said] I'm gonna be Black, and it was just that stupid. But it's more than just how one acts, you know. [The other Black women there] were not into me for the longest time. My first year there was hell.

In my book, *Follow Your Dreams: Lessons That I Learned in School*, I share the story of relocating our family from an affluent Atlanta suburb to an impoverished area of St. Petersburg, Florida so we could enroll our sons into a public magnet school for the visual and performing arts. Shortly after getting settled into the house we bought adjacent to the school, we witnessed a conversation between our older son, ten years old at the time, and a neighbor. The neighbor, a Black woman in her late twenties was talking to our son.

"So Mychal-David, your family moved here just so you could attend Perkins Elementary School?"

"Yes ma'am."

"I don't know if I would move a thousand miles from one city to another just so my daughter could attend a certain school."

"Actually, it's not a thousand miles. Atlanta is only 500 miles from St. Pete."

"'Actually.' Mychal-David you talk like a White boy, so proper and everything."

Such a powerful cultural phenomenon reaches into the Black affluent and middle class. In Montgomery County Schools in Maryland, home to some of the highest educated and most affluent Black households in the U.S., and Dekalb County Schools in Georgia, representing one of the highest concentration of middle class Black households in the U.S., Black males from educated and affluent families, who are quite capable, do not perform at a comparable academic achievement level as their White counterparts.

The prevailing Black male peer culture, even in the most affluent schools and communities, devalues academic achievement, Standard English usage, and intellectual pursuits.

My older son made a telling comment when he stated:

"Dad, at my school, all of my White friends are talking about going to college and most of my Black friends are talking about getting a job after high school."

As previously stated, there is a noticeable absence of affluent and middle class Black children enrolled in honors, gifted, and AP classes at the high school level. Despite high expectations, strict home environment, and constant communication with our sons' teachers, my wife and I are engaged in a daily battle with the peer pressures of Black children who do not value education and who refuse to apply themselves to academic pursuits.

Truly understanding Black children requires a willingness to understand the issues and the 'drama' which has shaped their persona prior to their getting off the school bus or walking into the classroom. In their vernacular, we have to 'feel' where they're coming from.

Avoid Stereotypes ...

A young man came into the classroom today angry. Some of the students said, 'Good morning' and the young man snapped, 'Get out of my face.' The young man folded his arms, arched his eyebrows, and walked away. One of the young men came over to repeat his good morning and the young man raised his fist as he shouted, 'Leave me alone.'

The young man was uncooperative, angry, and potentially violent.

Was he from a single-parent home where his mother wasn't properly disciplining him? Or from an inner-city, lower economic, physically-aggressive household? Had he witnessed substance abuse or been exposed to other types of physical or verbal abuse? Which is most nearly true?

Neither!

This was my son one morning at preschool. He was just having a bad day.

Black males represent the complete spectrum of American life. They come from every community, family background, economic status and social strata; from single-parent households to two-parent dual income households. Their parents range from little formal education to Ph.Ds. The clash of cultures between Black males and schools is rooted in the failure of school-based personnel to avoid broad-based stereotypes and generalizations to understanding one child, one family, and one situation at a time. The attitudes and behaviors of Black males will reflect gender-, home-, societal-, socioeconomic-, community-, exposure-, and experiential-influences unique to each community, student, and family. It is not atypical for Black males to maintain a code of conduct at home, and yet, outside the home demonstrate a very different standard of behavior. They share a subculture of different cultural values and behaviors which bonds them to their peers. Their subculture is constantly evolving, yet it remains the same. Although the words have changed, the rituals of "The Dozens," "The Showdown," "Rappin'," and "The Walk" have remained the same for generations.

The Dozens

One of the unfortunate realities of Black male culture is verbal put-downs which has its roots in "The Dozens." Beginning in Black households, carrying into elementary school classrooms, and continuing through athletic programs, Black men are recognized and celebrated for their ability to verbally abuse other Black men. More than any other single obstacle to the success of Black men is what we think of ourselves, what is locked away within our subconsciousness. The language used to describe one's self and one's culture shapes personal and societal perceptions. Call me an idiot and I will behave like an idiot. Call me a "N-----" and I will behave like a "N-----." The current language of Black males has been shaped by the media, particular film and music, accepted amongst themselves, perpetuated by their heroes and heroines (particularly rappers and athletes) and is too infrequently challenged by parents, teachers, and coaches. In essence, the media has told young men how they should talk, which eventually impacts how they behave, and the young men themselves have defined their language and behaviors, while parents, teachers, and coaches sit and watch. In essence, our children are being led by children and parented by an uncaring and disassociated media.

"The Dozens" in its original form was not about putting down as much as it was about lifting up. A ritualistic game believed to have originated in the African country of Nigeria, it was a tribal tradition through which competing boys typically lifted up one's father in this verbal game of one-upmanship to manhood.

"My father is a great warrior who has slain many lions with his bare hands."

"My father is a greater warrior who has slain lions with one hand tied behind his back."

"My father once slew a lion and captured an eagle at the same time."

"My father once stood before a stampeding herd of buffalo and demanded they stop and they all lay down before him."

"The Dozens" has also been called "Cappin', Snappin', Rankin', and Signifyin'." Today's Rap music has its roots in "The Dozens." The purpose of this game, in its U.S. post-slavery version, is to hurl verbal assaults sufficiently clever to be proclaimed the winner by one's peers. This game is generally played by two young men who hurl verbal insults at each other personally and about their lineage while a group of young men cheers them on (or more commonly known as instigate). If neither person gives in, the group eventually proclaims a winner. Occasionally, the game will result in a physical confrontation if one person is unable to withstand the level of insults. This, of course, is tantamount to weakness in the eyes of his peers.

To excel at this game, a young man must be able to communicate verbally through rhythm and rhyme; to think and respond quickly. He must be able to listen, focus, and pay close attention to what is being said so he may counter with something funnier and more clever than what's been said about him or his lineage. (In their vernacular: "Yo Mama.") Richard Prior, Redd Foxx, Chris Rock, J. Anthony Brown, Sinbad, Steve Harvey, Jamie Foxx, and Eddie Murphy reflect the type of extraordinary wit and higher-order thinking skills demonstrated by master comedians, whose craft is rooted in The Dozens.

As a child growing up in Chicago, I played and lost at this game often. Being skinny, fair-skinned, and having a short, stout mother gave my adversaries plenty of ammunition for the ensuing battle. It was common for my schoolmates to listen intently for another adult to say my mother's name, "Ernestine." From then on, "Ernestine" always made a quick entrance into "The Dozens." I lost at "The Dozens" so often I was convinced until I entered college that being fair-skinned clearly indicated I lacked "soul," I just wasn't 'Black' enough.

Many teachers demonstrate their lack of understanding of "The Dozens" by attempting to ban this form of Black male culture. Some will attempt to break up the game with threats of suspension or other forms of punishment, while others are frightened by the young men engaged in the game because of their intensity and boisterous behavior. Teachers who don't recognize or aren't willing to accept this as part of Black male culture may call security or other authority figures to break up the game. However, if the game is banished from classrooms, it simply finds its way into the bathroom, locker room, schoolyard, or onto the street corner.

By recognizing, understanding, and accepting this form of Black male culture and the verbal, thinking, and cognitive skills being developed, we can redirect the negative, degrading language back into its original historical context—affirming the greatness of one's family and community. The young men most likely to destroy others through their verbal tongue-lashing have equal power to uplift, edify, and reaffirm themselves and their peers. By harnessing their talent to write raps, affirmations, and to create a vocabulary of words and phrases affirming the individual and collective greatness of young Black men in their classroom, on their athletic team, and/or within their program, they are provided with a venue to further enhance their skills and reinforce a culture of excellence.

While Black males may put on a tough exterior where they talk bad, walk tough, and talk like they are confident and secure in who they are, many Black males hate themselves and those who look like them. This, despite the fact the entire world wants to be like them. From Japan to the Chicago suburbs, from South Central Los Angeles to the South Bronx in New York, people admire the fashions, music, hair styles, skin, lips, and butts of Black people. Multi-national shoe, clothing, music, and food companies market what Black people eat, wear, sing, and the game Black males bring, throughout the world for billions of dollars each day. Yet, despite being admired and emulated by the world, Black males disrespect, degrade, dehumanize, and dishonor themselves each day on street corners, in classrooms, in music videos, through their music, and particularly in their language.

No matter what you may believe, words have power. In the Biblical book of *Ephesians* [4:29] it states,

Let no corrupt communication proceed out of your mouth, but that which is good to the use of edifying, that it may minister grace unto the hearers.

The negative dehumanizing language the slave masters of 300 years ago directed at the millions of Africans chained and stuffed aboard slave ships and shipped throughout the Caribbean and the Americas is now embraced by the descendents of those Africans and used each day to destroy the image of themselves and of their children. Words have power and Black males must be taught about the power of the language they are choosing to put into their consciousness.

In the *workbook*, is an activity, "The Dozens" which helps young men to continue mastering their thinking, verbal, and communication skills by using "The Dozens" to affirm positive language about themselves and their peers. This can provide a starting point for parents and teachers to help Black males to break the cycle of negative language, jokes, and put-downs and to begin weaving positive comments, language, and affirmations into their vocabulary and language patterns. My wife and I have never allowed our sons to ridicule and put each other down, having instead encouraged them to use language which inspires and uplifts each other. The maxim, "Sticks and stones can break my bones, but words will never hurt me" is simply untrue. Words have tremendous power and the language teachers, parents, siblings, and friends direct at young men can cut deeply and leave lasting scars. While "The Dozens" begins as a playful test of verbal skills, in its current form it oftentimes ends in the destruction of one young man's self-esteem and the perpetuation of self-hate for the winner.

The Showdown

Jawanza Kunjufu, in *Countering the Conspiracy to Destroy Black Boys, Volume III*, notes:

When a Black boy looks at a female teacher with a look of defiance, I call this The SHOWDOWN.

When my older son (now sixteen) was two years old, he was already familiar with "The Showdown." There were times when he didn't get his way, for whatever reason, and would stop whatever he was doing, fold his arms defiantly, arch his eyebrows, and stare directly into your eyes. At two years old, he was more hilarious than intimidating. But what if he did it today, at

sixteen years old? What about the young man, who, by his posture, defiantly ignores the teacher's authority within a classroom; the young man who has issued a personal challenge to his classroom teacher?

"The Showdown" is a culturally-based attitude young men learn, at an early age, to challenge authority and influence others. My son issues it to my wife and young men issue it to their classroom teachers each school day. In urban communities, Black males quickly learn that "The Showdown" is a survival skill. They must either be physically strong, mentally quick, quick-of-foot, or have "wolf tickets to sell!" Without one or more of these attributes, it is difficult to survive. "The Showdown" not only occurs in the classroom, young men issue the challenge on basketball courts and football fields; in schoolyards and barbershops; wherever Black men gather.

I'll never forget transferring to a new school in the seventh grade. Corpus Christi Middle School was a Catholic school located on Chicago's south side. An all Black student body—male students wore white or light blue

shirts with black or dark blue slacks, girls wore white or light blue blouses with plaid skirts. The uniforms caused students to stand out in the community. The Black males would experience the showdown in the classroom as well as on the journey to and from school.

I was prepared for "The Showdown" each day as I left my neighborhood for the journey through other neighborhoods to get to school. Someone would "get in my face" asking for money. Someone else would ask what gang I represented. Someone else would accuse me of seeing someone's girlfriend.

Black males growing up in urban communities, like Chicago's south side, or worse, Chicago's west side, had to know how to respond to "The Showdown." Sometimes you fought; sometimes you ran; sometimes you sold "wolf tickets." "The Showdown" is a rite of survival—an urban rite of passage.

When dealing with Black males, adults have to understand "The Showdown," accept the challenge, and determine the situationally-appropriate magnitude of the response needed.

Clyde sat there, defiantly, his arms folded staring at the teacher. Most of our substitutes were afraid to call on Clyde, so they attempted to ignore him. This only encouraged Clyde to exert more control as he lost respect for the teacher. He became openly disobedient. He raised his desktop, ignored requests to open his book, and taunted the girls seated around him. Eventually, when the teacher could no longer ignore Clyde, she typically would waste a great deal of the class' time: 'Clyde don't do this, Clyde don't do that, Clyde please sit down, Clyde, if I have to ask you again, I am going to send you to the office.'

The teacher had obviously lost the battle and the class was out of control. Even in a private school, the teacher left this assignment with lowered self-esteem and a negative opinion of Black children, particularly, Black males. Any future showdowns will bring similar results. The teacher will convey her opinion of Black males to family, friends, and colleagues. She will mention Clyde to all the teachers in the teachers' lounge, thereby influencing the attitudes and behaviors of other adults throughout Clyde's time in middle school.

I engaged in "The Showdown" as a release from boredom. I generally caught on to my subjects very quickly. As I lost interest in the class, I would begin to doodle, draw, write poetry, or respond with what I thought were witty answers to questions. I was frequently put out of class for one reason or another. Sometimes I was asked to stand in the corridor, other times I was sent to the office, and on a few occasions I was sent home. This was just what I wanted. I had won the battle against the teacher and I had been sent somewhere other than her classroom.

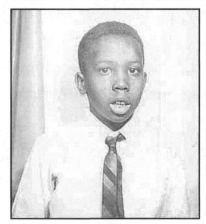

It seemed I was always talking when the teacher was talking or always late for something or always getting into a fight about something stupid. I must have been put out of class or sent to the office at least once a week. Some weeks, I was put out of class every day. I would stand in the corridor and lean against the wall. One of the nuns would always come by and say to me, 'Mr. Mychal, I see you are holding up the walls again today.' I would respond, "Yes, Sister."

'Mr. Mychal, you must stay in class and learn something if you are to become successful in life.' I would respond, "Yes, Sister."

'Mr. Mychal, you must make better choices so you can get an education.' I would respond, "Yes, Sister."

'Mr. Mychal, you are a bright young man with extraordinary potential.' I would respond, "Yes, Sister."

'Mr. Mychal, you must try harder to do the right thing.' I would respond, "Yes, Sister."

'Mr. Mychal, I will see you again tomorrow.' I would respond, "Yes, Sister."

Self-hate

Growing up in Chicago brought with it a set of dangers which few could, or would, understand then, or which teachers and parents understand now. In the neighborhood, we simply referred to the self-destructive and homicidal behaviors of Black men as, "That brother is crazy." Or, "That brother is wound too tight!"

A group of high school kids were playing flag football at Washington Park when a couple of older brothers, in their late twenties, walked up and asked, 'Yo little brothers can me and my boy play?' As the quarterback and one of the captains who chose the teams, I responded, "Yo, bro, can you and your boy wait a few minutes? The game will be over after this next touchdown and we are going to pick new teams." The brother responded, 'Yeah, we'll wait.'

The game resume and the brother and his friend walked about fifty yards from the field and turned around and starting shooting. Pow, pow, pow! 'Won't let me and my boy play, huh? Take that Motherf-----. I'll bust a cap in your football playin' ass!'

The summer before, also at Washington Park, while playing basketball, one young brother was issuing the showdown to another young brother. He was just trash talking and dissing the young brother. Jump shot, 'Take that.' Layup, 'Boy you can't keep up with me.' Dunk, 'What's wrong, you can't jump?' Jump shot, 'And, one. Why you keep hacking me? Why don't you just take your whuppin' like a man? Cause you gon' get whupped!'

The young brother just got served! Over, and over, and over again. We all knew Derek, which is why none of us wanted to guard him. The brother deserved to be on somebody's college basketball team. At barely 5'9" he could out jump everybody and was faster than anybody.

After the game was over, we were all sitting around talking when the young brother who tried to guard Derek walked over to his duffle bag and pulled out a gun. Since this wasn't the first time we had witnessed a "brother gon' crazy" we didn't sit around like they do in the movies and wait to be shot. Me, Derek, Michael Pierce, Dana, and Tuffy took off like road runners. Pow, pow, pow. 'Come on N-----, take me to hole now. What's wrong N-----, where's your game now?'

As a young man growing up in Chicago, I learned how to beware of the brothers who were wound too tight. Jawanza Kunjufu was the first person whom I heard coin the phrase, "Post-Traumatic Slavery Syndrome." Whether their behavior is the result of the aftermath of the 300-year-old systematic and cultural degradation of African people throughout the African Diaspora; the self-hate which results from being turned away from job after job because you're Black; the built-up anger from too many negative encounters with law enforcement where they felt powerless and humiliated by policemen—dealing with their own issues, who satisfy their own twisted sense of power by humiliating other human beings; or the desperation and despair which accompanies 'knowing' that one's circumstances and situation aren't going to change. It doesn't matter whether he is a school-age boy who is going crazy in his elementary school classroom, a high school kid with a gun and an attitude, or a man in his twenties or thirties who flies into a fit of rage because he stopped his car in the middle of the street and someone dared to honk their horn and ask him to move. The psychological and emotional issues Black men internalize continue to consume the lives of countless Black men each year. In 1974, my last year of high school, my constant prayer was to survive and leave Chicago. That year, Chicago had the highest murder rate in the country. As was the case then, and is still the case in 2004, the most-likely victim of a homicide is a Black male. The most-likely perpetrator of his homicide is another Black male.

Being aware of this self-hate and potentially homicidal behavior requires teachers and parents to learn how to calm their own behavior in the wake of this potential storm.

1. Learn how to recognize the showdown.

2. Learn how to diffuse the situation through the use of body language, tone of voice, storytelling, and by removing young men from their audience, i.e., peers.

3. Avoid issuing a challenge which backs a young man into a corner.

4. Learn how to use fewer words, i.e., "Stop talking."

Use your relationship with young men as the primary means of helping them to transition their behaviors from confrontational to collaborative.

You can oftentimes diffuse a situation simply by positioning yourself closer to a young man and placing your hand onto his shoulder, letting him know you understand what's going on and you are not intimidated by his stares.

I don't know if "love conquers all" but I do know demonstrating compassion rather than antagonism will help a young man to overcome his own sense of self-hate and provide an opportunity to open dialogue about his feelings, diffuse his anger, and help him to think through counterproductive and/or self-destructive behaviors. If I pull behind a brother and he has his car blocking the street, I'm not going to honk my horn. I may ask, "Hey bro, do you think I can get around?" as I have in the past. As in the past, I'm more likely to hear, "No problem, dog, my bad" instead of creating a confrontation. I'm just not in that much of a hurry.

The N-Word

When my wife and I were attending Crenshaw Christian Center, in Los Angeles, California, our pastor, Dr. Frederick K.C. Price, preached a sermon, "There is life-giving power in the power of the tongue." Through his message he referred to biblical scriptures which illustrated the spiritual power contained within the words, language, and thoughts conveyed by what we say. Self-help gurus refer to this phenomenon through such axioms as, "Your attitude determines your altitude" or "You are what you say you are." Whether you believe in Religious doctrine or self-help maxims, Black males, through pop culture and Rap music are defining themselves by the lowest possible language, i.e., 'My Nigger,' 'My Dog,' 'Motherf-----' and referring to cars, women, and each other as 'Bitches' and 'Ho's.'

Randall Kennedy, in *Nigger: The Strange Career of a Troublesome Word*, examines such language and comments in regards to the feelings among older Blacks:

Yet it was a word—the word nigger—that lay at the core of a recollection that revealed to me the pain my mother continues to feel on account of wounds inflicted upon her by racists during the era of Jim Crow segregation. Several years ago, I asked her to tell me about her earliest memory of the color line. She began laughingly, telling me about how, in Columbia [South Carolina], she had often accompanied her mother to White folks' homes to pick up and return laundry. Although they typically traveled on public buses, my mother had failed to notice that her mother, Big Mama, always took her to the back of the bus where Negroes were segregated. One day, Big Mama asked my mother to run an errand that required her to catch a bus on which they had often ridden together. This errand marked the first time that my mother rode the bus on her own. She stood at the correct stop, got on the bus, and deposited the appropriate fare. Being a bit scared, however, she sat down immediately behind the bus driver. After about a block, the driver pulled the bus over to the curb, cut the engine, and suddenly wheeled around and began to scream at my mother who was all of about eight or nine years old—'Nigger, you know better than to sit there! Get to the back where you belong!' At this point in the story telling, my mother was no longer laughing. A tear dropped onto her cheek, as she recalled running away from the bus overcome by fright.

Kennedy goes on to comment on the generational differences in perceptions and attitudes toward the word:

There was often a generational difference as evidence in competing uses of the N-word with the younger people experimenting with nonderogatory versions. On the other hand, while some of my younger relatives are adamantly opposed to any use of nigger, believing it to be only and unalterably a debasing slur, some of my older relatives anticipated by many years the transformation of nigger (or 'nigga') that is now widely attributed to the hop-hop culture. Long before the rapper Ice-T insisted upon being called a nigger, my father declared that he was proud to be a 'stone nigger'—by which he meant a Black man without pretensions who was unafraid to enjoy himself openly and loudly despite the objections of condescending Whites or insecure Blacks.

Intellectual discussions notwithstanding, we can't control what children choose to call each other. 'Niggers, Bitches,' and 'Ho's' amongst their peers, around their friends, and outside of the auspices of adult supervision. As they can choose to "Cuss like a sailor," spit, let their breasts hang out and their pants sag in the clubs and while standing on street corners. However, when in school, around adults, they should be held to a higher standard and language which affirms a higher outcome. As parents, my wife and I set standards and adhere to a set of core values which define our household culture. The influence of athletes, entertainers, music, and popular culture is profound on the psyche of young people across socioeconomic, gender, and cultural lines nationally and globally. Yet in the midst of all these influences, teachers must teach, coaches must coach, and parents must parent. As adults, we must recognize the social and societal influences on children. By doing so, we may consciously define the boundaries and affirm our expectations while children are within our sphere of influence. The expectations we affirm, must be done unceasingly. My fifth- and sixth-grade teacher, Mr. Roberts, recognized how the boys in our classroom walked into class and around the school with their backs bent over and their heads looking down at the floor, like so many Black men with broken backs and broken spirits throughout our south side Chicago community. Mr. Roberts, who held us to a higher standard, would walk up to me and grab me by my right hand in a handshake so strong as to force me to lift my head up to make eye contact—with his left hand he would slap me right in the middle of my back, just above my butt, which would straighten me right up. "Good morning Mr. Wynn. How are we today?" Some 40 years later, I can still feel his handshake and my posture is still erect, as I continue my journey in a direction Mr. Roberts, and others like him, affirmed long ago.

Language has power and we, as caring adults, dare not allow pop culture, Rap music, and multi-millionaire high school dropouts to determine the standards we hold our children to. Our expectations should not reflect what is currently 'Phat' or 'Crunk.' School is where children are being prepared to think so they can make their own choices, where they learn the standard so they have the choice of deviating if they choose to. Inside the school is where we must affirm college graduates, politicians, educators, and CEOs. Outside the school, children can choose to be Niggers, Bitches, and Ho's. However, what they choose to call themselves will be greatly influenced by what they learn about themselves, their potential, and their history when in school.

Situational Appropriateness

Many parents provide the love, leadership, and discipline to establish a clear understanding of expected behavior at home. However, school bus, classroom, and school behaviors of their sons may drastically differ from acceptable home behaviors. The Los Angeles Unified School District's Proficiency in English Program (PEP) referred to these attitudes, behaviors, and language usage as "situationally-appropriate."

For example:

- A young man who never uses profanity around his parents or coaches and can be seen standing on a street corner loudly cursing with reckless abandon.

- A young man rarely challenges his father's authority, and yet, challenges virtually everything his mother says.

- Two young men totally disrupt a classroom, and yet, go to football practice with 88 other young men and never challenge the coach's authority.

This phenomenon of young men developing and demonstrating attitudes and behaviors in one environment or with certain persons, and yet, developing very different attitudes and behaviors within other environments or with other persons reflects what young men have internalized as "situationally-appropriate."

Non-Standard English

The use of non-standard or non-conforming language patterns is common among many ethnic- and geographical-cultures. In Black culture, the use of non-Standard English is a bonding mechanism which utilizes culturally-appropriate language patterns and usage, i.e., "I ain't got none, ain't gon' be none, and don't won't none!" Standard English has historically been the 'cash language.' The way White people talk, and, since White people controlled the jobs, it reflected the way Black people had to learn to talk. This is the language used by educators, professionals, and white collar workers. The language educated Blacks learn to use, and most frequently, choose to use.

In *Young, Black, Rich & Famous*, Todd Boyd notes the emergence of a new cash language (at least for the artists and athletes who use it) which is highly influential on the language patterns of Black and White youth:

I see Iverson's [Allen] hip-hop disposition as a most appropriate one. The American Dream for Iverson and all others who subscribe to this hip-hop ethos has to do with making money off of their immense talents, gaining leverage and visibility because of it, and then telling a hostile and often racist America to collectively kiss their 'young, Black, rich and famous' asses in no uncertain terms. This sense of vengeance and retribution, marked by a colossal indifference to mainstream taste and coupled with the money that affords such freedoms, is the new American Dream, or redefined to suit the purposes of those who were excluded from the original version of this otherwise empty concept.

Non-Standard English is the bridge which connects Blacks across socioeconomic, educational, and geographical lines. Split verbs and double negatives, i.e., "ain't gon' be none of that" have an unmistakable and situationally-appropriate place in the oratory of educated and well-spoken Blacks who masterfully use code-switching for emphasis during public oratory.

The "appropriateness" of European-American culture as it relates to survival within a European-dominated American society should not displace the "appropriateness" of African-American culture as it relates to the survival and continuation of the traditions of the Black community. Language patterns are a part of the continuation of African and African-American traditions.

You Know What I'm Sayin'?

An additional influence on non-Standard English usage is the language patterns of pop and hip-hop culture. As opposed to representing a choice between standard and non-standard, young men develop language patterns, vocabulary, and a manner of speaking which becomes their only language. For young men with limited vocabulary and who have limited understanding of Standard English, they are trapped into limited sentence structure, word usage, and experience great difficulty communicating their thoughts verbally.

"You know what I'm saying?"

"That's Crunk!"

"That's Phat!"

"You know what I mean?"

"That's tight!"

"It's aah, aah, aah, you know, it's aah, aah, you know what I'm sayin'?"

As is the case with internet chat room jargon, i.e., LOL, BRB, SYA, TBC, parents and teachers must recognize non-Standard English usage and teach young men what the standard is and how and when it is situationally-appropriate to make the transition to slang and non-Standard English usage. I have found the most effective way to communicate with young people is to simply admit my ignorance.

"What does Crunk mean?"

"What's Phat? Is that good or bad?"

"No, I don't know what you're saying. Could you translate it for me?" In the case of my own children, "No, I don't know what you're saying and I don't think that you do either!"

When having a classroom discussion I will tell students, "You cannot begin a sentence with 'aah.' If you hear anyone begin a sentence with 'aah,' I would like for the entire classroom to give the person a finger snap as a reminder." The first time we do this, thumbs become sore as hardly any students can begin a sentence without saying, 'aah.' The ability to communicate effectively in a professional workplace is a basic skill which, without compromise, we must help young men to develop.

The Cultural Disconnect

There is an undeniable cultural disconnect between Black males and teachers, counselors, and coaches within school communities across the country. Public school teachers, teaching in urban and inner-city communities, are unlikely to live within the communities where they teach. They do not attend church with, see students and families at the local grocery store, or interact with students and families away from the formality of the school setting. This unfamiliarity with students and families is exacerbated in schools as a result of the socioeconomic, gender, and cultural gaps existing between classroom teachers and Black male students. Teachers must recognize the existence of these respective gaps and be proactive in developing a holistic set of strategies reinforcing consistent expectations between home and school.

To develop an effective home–school collaboration you must begin by:

1. Understanding Black male culture and thereby anticipating certain behaviors.

2. Identifying any potential cultural, socioeconomic, and/or gender gaps.

3. Creating a holistic set of strategies which reinforce expectations between school and home.

Before the cultural disconnect can be closed between adults and today's young men, adults must identify as many of the existing gaps as possible:

- *Generational:* While some adults still behave like children, most adults will experience a generational gap between the values, ideas, language, expectations, attitudes, and behaviors between themselves and today's youth. The best way to address this gap, as with all other gaps, is through open and honest communication. Address the differences through critical-thinking, e.g., "That's an interesting style you have wearing your pants around your butt. Did you know that, that style was first popularized by prison inmates? I heard that men did it as a signal they were another man's girlfriend. What statement are you trying to make?" As opposed to an emotional response, e.g., "Boy, you and your friends are just ignorant!"

- *Gender:* If men are from Venus and women are from Mars, Black males are from the twilight zone. Women should anticipate misunderstandings and communication breakdowns.

- *Ethnic:* The best thing for a non-Black teacher to come to grips with is the reality he or she is not Black. The children know it so the teacher may as well admit it. Every ethnic group has a cultural frame of reference which can only be truly understood by those within the culture as is the case with gender differences.

- *Socioeconomic:* If you are not poor, read Ruby Payne's book, *A Framework for Understanding Poverty.* If you are poor, still read the book to better understand the needs of children living in poverty, particularly, the need they have to understand the 'Hidden Rules.' Oftentimes, it is their failure to fully understand the hidden rules as it relates to school behaviors, course enrollment, and college planning which hinders them in developing college-bound plans or even affirming college aspirations.

The Reality of School Culture

More than any other cultural variable, school culture represents the most powerful influence on the academic achievement of Black males. This is not to suggest parents are absolved of their responsibility in nurturing the academic achievement of their sons, however, unless they choose to home school, their children spend more of their waking hours around adults within the school community—school bus drivers, support staff, classroom teachers, and coaches, than they do with parents during the school year. The academic foundation, values, and critical-thinking skills taught at home are either nurtured, expanded upon, or undermined during their son's many hours in school and their involvement in school-related activities.

As a result of the powerful cultural influence of schools, parents must learn how to identify, understand, and intervene when school culture is not nurturing of Black male academic achievement, social development, and college enrollment. Jawanza Kunjufu has coined the phrase, "The Conspiracy to Destroy Black Boys" in his series of books on the topic. Despite state accountability standards, Black male achievement task forces, and school improvement plans, many school communities appear to cultivate the existence of such a conspiracy through their failure to recognize and respond to the negative cultural influences occurring within the school. The reality of school culture is that it is either defined by adults, or by default, is defined by students. Either adults set the standards, define the boundaries, establish the values, create the appropriate customs and rituals, or by default, they are established by students:

In Ms. A's classroom, she cares about and understands the students and families she serves. Based on her understanding of students and families, she is prepared for the first day of school and realizes she only has one opportunity to make a first impression:

She has identified how she is going to greet students and welcome them into her classroom; she has identified the story she is going to tell to introduce her beliefs, expectations, classroom procedures, rewards and consequences.

Based on her knowledge of students and families, she has identified the most influential adults within the lives of her students and has already begun developing relationships with those people.

She recognizes the importance of using the opening days of school to build relationships and establish trust with students and families. Subsequently, she is able to minimize classroom disruptions, office referrals, and cultivate a positive classroom climate and culture. In contrast, in Ms. B's classroom next door, the classroom is constantly out of control, students are openly disrespectful, she repeatedly takes away from instructional time to address student conflicts or to write office referrals, she has no relationships with parents or other influential adults, and there is a clear lack of teaching and learning occurring in her classroom.

This type of contrast can be witnessed in the behaviors of students from one school bus to another, between one athletic team and another, and in programs and activities throughout every school community despite the demographics of the students being served.

Dr. Crystal Kuykendall in her keynote address before the Wholistic Institute tells the story of "Lying Lewis."

"In the seventh grade I had a student called 'Lying Lewis.' Everybody had warned me about Lewis. And when Lewis entered my classroom, I immediately knew that they were right! This boy could lie. And he was good too!

I started telling Lewis that anybody who knows intuitively what to say and make people believe it had a special gift.

I told Lewis that he would make a great politician! I wanted Lewis to know that there was a high road consistent with his special gifts.

Every time that I called on Lewis I would say, 'Assemblyman Hester, or Congressman Hester, or Senator Hester.' I would bring Lewis into the classroom discussions by saying, 'Senator Hester, do you have an opinion on this?'

It got to be so good to Lewis that he corrected me one day and said, 'Call me President Hester!'"

Dr. Kuykendall went on to describe how she continued encouraging Lewis for a couple of years before she lost track of him. She would discover some years later 'Lying Lewis' would become Attorney Lewis Hester, practicing law in Newark, New Jersey. Dr. Kuykendall, through affirming Lewis' greatness, would put this young man on the high road of life!

Adult Attitudes

Adult attitudes toward students and their ability to build relationships with students and families represent the most powerful contributing factors to school culture. Despite the school's demographics—student attitudes, ability levels, intrinsic motivation, attitudes toward learning, home environment, or economic conditions—it is the adults within the school community who have the most powerful influence on school culture. The majority of adults within a school community are teachers, however, oftentimes the MOST influential adults within a school community are administrators—who provide leadership, and coaches—who often have the closest and strongest relationships with students and families. This does not absolve parents of their responsibility in influencing the behaviors of their children, however, once a young man leaves home, the culture he enters into on the school bus, in the corridors, in the gymnasium, in the cafeteria, in the rest rooms, on the playground, and within the classroom itself, has a profound influence on his attitudes, behaviors, beliefs, and values.

There is a clear connection between school-wide culture and Black male achievement as evidenced each school day, in classrooms and athletic programs, where teachers and coaches create a culture of mutual respect, individual responsibility, accountability, and respect for the program and/or classroom.

I have a very close and personal relationship with God. He and I talk on a regular basis and I frequently ask questions regarding the issues which concern and perplex me in education. During one such conversation I asked, "God, what do teachers pray for?" God's response was, "My son, teachers pray that certain children won't return to their schools." 'Oh, God, please don't let Willie come back to our school next year. Oh, God, I know Rashaad was held back a grade, please don't let him be in my classroom next year.'

There was a long silence and then I asked, "How do you answer such prayers?" God responded, "I don't my son!"

School-wide and classroom strategies must be developed to shape a school-wide and classroom culture to displace the disruptive underachieving culture young men bring to school and which is encouraged by peers, with a culture which teaches social skills, conflict resolution, and inspires academic rigor from the opening bell.

On a trip to the Bermuda, my older son, who was in the eighth grade at the time, had an opportunity to spend a week with Bermudian children at Sandys Secondary Middle School. The issues confronting parents and teachers of Black boys (and Black girls) were largely the same as those confronting parents and teachers in the United States: apathy; hip-hop culture; the influence of Rap music on their language; lack of enthusiasm toward academic tasks; a peer culture which valued athletic prowess over academic excellence; the importance of hair and clothing styles; the importance of slang and non-Standard English; and other male cultural icons (i.e., "The Walk, The Showdown," and playing "The Dozens").

Our son, born in California and raised in Georgia, was visiting Bermuda for the first time. Despite the distinct differences in Bermudian British culture and American southern culture, our son was easily able to make the connection with Bermudian Black males. Black male machismo was as common in Bermuda as it was in Atlanta. However, the use of profanity and the term "Nigger" is far less common among Bermudian Black males due to the *influence* of teachers and parents as to its inappropriateness. Bermudian parents and teachers are taking a more proactive role in influencing the attitudes, behaviors, and language patterns of their children.

Teachers

Robert Rothman, in his article, *Closing the Achievement Gap: How Schools Are Making It Happen*, notes:

Educators across the nation are looking to lessons from the Department of Defense schools, where reading and writing performance of Black and Hispanic students is among the highest in the nation.

Teachers at Department of Defense (DOD) schools hold extraordinarily high expectations for Black and Hispanic students, and that is one reason those schools exhibit such narrow achievement gaps, according to Claire Smrekar, an associate professor of educational leadership and policy at Vanderbilt University and an author of a recent study on DOD schools. In a 1998 NAEP survey, 85 percent of Black students and 93 percent of Hispanic students in DOD's domestic schools rated teacher expectations for their performance "very positive," compared with 52 percent of Black students and 53 percent of Hispanic students nationwide.

As a DOD teacher who formerly taught at a predominantly Black school told Smrekar and her colleagues: "In my old district, if a student didn't pass a test, one might say, 'Okay, you tried.' Here they push the kids and don't allow them to settle for less. When they don't succeed, the teacher works harder to get the students to want to excel. The curriculum is not dumbed down."

In the well-publicized study, *A Lesson in Bigotry*, the power of teacher attitudes on classroom learning was demonstrated by Jane Elliott, a teacher in Riceville, Iowa:

On the day after Martin Luther King Jr. was murdered in April 1968, Jane Elliott's third graders from the small, all-White town of Riceville, Iowa, were divided by eye color—those with blue eyes and those with brown. On the first day, the blue-eyed children were told they were smarter, nicer, neater, and better than those with brown eyes. Throughout the day, Elliott praised them and allowed them privileges such as taking a longer recess and being first in the lunch line. In contrast, the brown-eyed children had to wear collars around their necks and their behavior and performance were criticized and ridiculed by Elliott. On the second day, the roles were reversed and the blue-eyed children were made to feel inferior while the brown eyes were designated the dominant group.

What happened over the course of the unique two-day exercise astonished both students and teacher. On both days, children who were designated as inferior took on the look and behavior of genuinely inferior students, performing poorly on tests and other work. In contrast, the "superior" students—students who had been sweet and tolerant before the exercise—became mean-spirited and seemed to like discriminating against the "inferior" group.

"I watched what had been marvelous, cooperative, wonderful, thoughtful children turn into nasty, vicious, discriminating little third-graders in a space of fifteen minutes," says Elliott. She says she realized then that she had "created a microcosm of society in a third-grade classroom."

"After you do this exercise, when the debriefing starts, when the pain is over and they're all back together, you find out how society could be if we really believed all this stuff that we preach, if we really acted that way, you could feel as good about one another as those kids feel about one another after this exercise is over. You create instant cousins," says Elliott. "The kids said over and over, 'We're kind of like a family now.' They found out how to hurt one another and they found out how it feels to be hurt in that way and they refuse to hurt one another in that way again."

Discipline and Classroom Management

As was previously cited:

- A Black male born in 1991 (today's seventh-grade student) has a 29 percent chance of spending time in prison at some point in his life. The figure for Hispanics is 16 percent, and for Whites is 4 percent.

- Black students, while representing only 17 percent of public school students account for 32 percent of suspensions and 30 percent of expulsions. In 1999, 35 percent of all Black students in grades 7-12 had been suspended or expelled from school. The rate was 20 percent for Hispanics and 15 percent for Whites.

Discipline in many schools is out of control. Black males are crippled each school day as they fall further and further behind in literacy, standardized test preparation, proficiency levels for grade-level promotions, and preparation for high school exit exams. Since 1982, I have visited hundreds of elementary, middle, and high schools where I have witnessed firsthand, out of control schools and classrooms. Beginning in the primary grades, Black males, learn the boundaries of school and classroom culture. They are either socialized into a set of core values, guiding principles, and acceptable social behaviors or they continue to exhibit behaviors which may be socially acceptable (if not encouraged) among peers and even productive outside of school.

Establishing the boundaries and communicating social expectations can be achieved through such strategies as:

1. Develop a willingness to openly and honestly gather the data needed to assess your classroom culture (e.g., office referrals, classroom disruptions, detentions, suspensions, parent involvement, student attitudes).

2. Within the context of your data, identify strategies to create the classroom culture needed to optimize student success.

3. Develop a classroom management plan and make a personal commitment to implement the strategies (4Cs: caring, clarity, consistency, and commitment).

4. Gather more data to assess the success of the strategies.

5. Fine-tune or identify new strategies.

Three important areas of concerns classroom teachers must factor into their classroom management strategies are:

1. Stay focused on your mission

Without having a clear mission of the levels of learning you want to achieve as the instructional leader of the classroom and a clear vision of the type of classroom environment necessary for you to fulfill your mission, you cannot conceptualize the strategies appropriate for the unique demographic make-up of your classroom.

2. Build relationships with students and families

Only by observing students and talking to families can you more fully understand the unique socioeconomic-, cultural-, and gender-based needs of Black males within your school community.

In the book, *Perspectives on Teacher Education Reform: Unique Partnership Initiatives*, Vermelle Johnson, in her article, *Developing Leaders: The Greatest Challenge for Education Reform*, notes:

> If teachers demonstrate interest in diverse ideas and culture, it is much more likely that students in diverse settings will flourish during learning. All teachers must be trained on techniques for best reaching the instructional and learning potential of racial, ethnic, cultural, and socioeconomically diverse students and their families, (Garrett, 2002). When the curriculum is relevant of high quality (not just memorizations of skills) coupled with competent teachers, then students are stimulated to learn.

> In the <u>School Achievement Structure Study</u> (1988), administrators carefully selected teachers who possessed the disposition to make a difference in the classroom. Other teachers (focused teachers) with less ability to carry out the subject matter in diverse settings were provided with on-going modeling and regular professional development.

> Student-centered instructional classrooms were emphasized by the principal who aligned the best teachers to work with students in stanines of "4" and below on content skills and concepts. Additionally, small work groups of students, manipulative, and computer-based activities were emphasized throughout the work sessions.

Understanding the importance young men in general, and Black males in particular, place on bonding, mutual respect, and a sense that the teacher or coach is genuinely concerned with them and their lives is critical to effectively building the relationships which provide the foundation of respect, collaboration, and cooperation. All of which are needed to raise academic achievement levels and to achieve effective socialization. When a coach or teacher succeeds in bonding and establishing the foundation of mutual respect, it is easy to discuss the potential problem areas with young men. The goal of discipline is not to 'make them' behave, but to encourage them to think and to develop self-discipline.

African culture of child-rearing is humanistic. With rare exception, Black males need and long for bonding—in relationships between fathers and sons, coaches and players, and teachers and students. Due to the absence of relationships between young men and their fathers in so many households more emphasis is placed on the bonding which occurs in relationships between young men and their coaches, teachers, or other school-based personnel. Coaches and teachers who are effective at bonding with the young men on their teams and within their classrooms discover how relationships drive academic performance and social interactions. They find young men working hard academically and managing their behaviors, not for themselves or as a result of having set personal goals, but because they want to receive the approval of their coach or teacher.

Ron Weaver, in *Beyond Identify: Education and the Future Role of Black Americans,* notes:

> *The social climate developed in the school is associated with the effectiveness of the socialization process. In other words, the way the teacher structures his relations with the children and their relations with each other establishes a behavioral model for them. Accordingly, the organization of the classroom must be examined in relation to the growth and development of the children.*

3. Diffuse confrontational situations

Consider a teacher whose classroom is constantly out of control, has a large number of office referrals, is largely ineffective in communicating with her Black male students, and routinely engages in confrontations with young men within her classroom. In contrast, another teacher, perhaps in a classroom just across the corridor, deals with the same students, yet has no office referrals, few classroom disruptions, and NEVER engages in classroom confrontations with students.

She intuitively knows stepping outside of the classroom with a student removes him from his peer group where he has to save face by 'stepping up.'

She is limited by law from grabbing, cursing, or threatening a student ... in front of witnesses! Away from witnesses she can put her hand onto her hip and allow her nonverbal communication to communicate what needs to be said.

She knows the student has to 'test his manhood' in front of his peers and within the classroom. Outside of the classroom there is no audience and there are no witnesses. Subsequently, she can step up, 'Come on Cletus, there ain't nothing separating us but space and opportunity!' Or, 'What's up, why are you trying to front me off in my classroom?'

In my book, *Ten Steps to Helping Your Child Succeed in School*, I note a situation in which my then four-year-old son, understood what he could get away with as a result of the actions, mannerisms, and language of one preschool teacher, which was in stark contrast to the classroom of another teacher who was able to set certain behavioral expectations through an innate understanding (i.e., Interpersonal Intelligence) of children and by building strong relationships with their families:

When our son, Jalani, was in preschool, we moved him from a classroom where the teacher was unable to effectively manage the 12 children in her classroom. We moved him into Mrs. Lake's classroom despite the fact Mrs. Lake already had 27 children in her classroom. What was most important to us was Mrs. Lake's willingness to work with us to help our son to have a successful school year.

Jalani didn't want to go into her classroom. Every day he would say it was time to go back to his old classroom. He didn't like his new teacher; 'Mrs. Lake is mean!' he'd say. What Jalani didn't like, was that Mrs. Lake wouldn't allow him to get away with the behavior he had been exhibiting in his old classroom. On the rare occasions when Jalani would misbehave, Mrs. Lake wouldn't send him to time-out, she would tell him, "Jalani I'm going to call your mom and dad." To which, he usually responded, "I'm sorry Mrs. Lake, you really don't have to call my mom and dad. I won't do it again, I promise."

Despite Jalani's protests about being in Mrs. Lake's classroom, he went on to have a wonderful year. Through our working in partnership with his teacher, he began to have more good days than bad ones.

Although she had twice as many students, Mrs. Lake had a very well-managed classroom where some of the most difficult students in the school (our son included) learned to work together, play together, and achieve together.

As you review the influences on Black male culture and in fact, the Black male psyche, you are challenged to expand your own levels of interpersonal intelligence to define the language, behaviors, posture, and strategies you will use to avoid confrontations and diffuse potentially volatile situations and create a classroom or household culture which enlightens, enables, and empowers Black males.

Ruby Payne, in her book, *A Framework for Understanding Poverty*, writes:

To better understand students and adults from poverty, a working definition of poverty is "the extent to which an individual does without resources." Such resources would be:

- *Financial: Having the money to purchase goods and services.*

- *Emotional: Being able to choose and control emotional responses, particularly to negative situations, without engaging in self-destructive behavior.*

- *Mental: Having the mental abilities to acquire skills (reading, writing, computing) to deal with daily life.*

- *Spiritual: Believing in divine purpose and guidance.*

- *Physical: Having physical health and mobility.*

- *Support Systems: Having friends, family, and backup resources available to access in times of need.*

- *Relationships & Role Models: Having frequent access to adults who are appropriate, who are nurturing to the child, and who do not engage in self-destructive behavior.*

- *Knowledge or Hidden Rules: Knowing the unspoken cues and habits of a group.*

There are many hidden rules in regards to a young man's journey through public education. Young men from families living in poverty are most in need of advocates, advisors, mentors, counselors, coaches, and teachers who will help them and their family to better understand the hidden rules and develop a primary-through-postsecondary plan. Helping them to develop the respectful, responsible, and self-directed behaviors needed for classroom success will require building relationships with them and their families and better understanding the cultural influences from outside, as well as within the school.

Wade Nobles, in *Infusion of African and African-American Content in the School Curriculum,* notes:

> *Culture is to humans as water is to fish. It is our total environment. As such, education, as well as curriculum development, are cultural phenomena. Culture is as the nature of the water (i.e., salt versus fresh versus polluted) influences the reality (i.e., survivability) of particular types of fish, so too do different cultural systems influence the reality of particular groups of people.*
>
> *When we look at the notion of culture and raise the question of accessing children to a core curriculum, we should be very clear that the core curriculum itself is cultural; and that the <u>teaching methodology</u> that we utilize in teaching the core curriculum is also cultural; and that the <u>site leadership style</u> is cultural, and that the <u>guidance and counsel</u> techniques are cultural, and that the <u>instructional strategies</u> are cultural, and that the <u>school climate</u> is cultural, and that ultimately the <u>aim and purpose of education</u> itself is cultural.*

Gender Issues

In addition to the cross-cultural, socioeconomic, and generational issues influencing school culture, research pertaining to gender issues in schools and classrooms should be closely examined.

Michael Gurian, in *Boys and Girls Learn Differently: A Guide for Teachers and Parents,* notes:

- *Extracurricular Activities:* Girls make up the majority of student government officials, after-school club leaders, and school community liaisons.

- *Academic performance:* Girls receive approximately 60 percent of the A's, and boys receive approximately 70 percent of the D's and F's. Among students performing in the top fifth of high school grade ranges, 63 percent are girls.

- *Specific academic performance:* Girls are approximately one and a half years ahead of boys in reading and writing competency, according to statistics tracked by the Federal Department of Education.

- *Educational aspirations:* Colleges are 60 percent female. The federal Department of Education has found that eighth-grade and twelfth-grade girls have, on average, higher educational aspirations than boys.

- *Learning and behavioral disorders:* Females are less likely to experience a learning, psychiatric, or behavioral disorder. Boys make up two-thirds of the learning disabled and 90 percent of the behaviorally disabled, and nearly 100 percent of the most seriously disabled. Boys account for 80 percent of brain disorders.

- *Discipline problems:* Boys constitute 90 percent of discipline problems in school and 80 percent of dropouts.

- *Culture bias:* The educational system and the individual classroom are not as well designed for male brain development as for female. The system comprises mainly female teachers who have not received training in male brain development and performance; it relies on less kinesthetic, relatively monitored, and less disciplined educational strategies than many males need.

According to a report issued by the National Center for Education Statistics, *America's Teachers: Profile of a Profession*:

- 72.8 percent of public school teachers are female. Of the total number of female teachers, 87.3 percent are White.

- 89 percent of public school teachers are 30 years old or older.

The socioeconomic, cultural, gender, and generational gaps contribute to parent-teacher misunderstandings, student-teacher confrontations, classroom disruptions, office referrals, in-school detentions, out-of-school suspensions, and, by all measures, unsatisfactory academic performance.

Janice Hale-Benson, in *Black Children: Their Roots, Culture, and Learning-styles*, notes the importance of building a bridge between school and home-community culture and consciously seeking to identify the strengths in Black children as integral strategies to lead them into learning, appropriate social behaviors, and full participation in school-wide programs and activities:

> *Black children grow up in a distinct culture. Black children, therefore, need an educational system that recognizes their strengths, their abilities, and their culture and that incorporates these factors into the learning process ...*
>
> *The experiences through which the Black child develops his sense of self, his social orientation, and his world view are provided by institutions (such as family, religion) whose characters, structures and functions are very often unique to the Black community. The school, on the other hand, reflects the culture of the wider society and is often unaccommodating to the culturally different Black youngsters. Indeed, often these differences are defined as deficiencies, which are assumed to be significant impediments to 'proper' learning in school. Therefore, massive attempts at remediation are undertaken (often, to the detriment of the child). In effect, many school practices are inappropriate for treating the educational needs of Black youngsters. An appropriate treatment of the educational needs of Black youngsters must take into account their unique cultural attributes.*

She further comments in regards to how such gaps between students, teachers, and parents impact the school community:

> 1. *The young child learns (probably very quickly because he has older children to help him) that adults in the school do not function in the same way that adults do in his community and that only behavior of gross impropriety (flunking, suspension) will be reported to his parents because school adults are not community agents of social control. He is free to act 'like he wouldn't act at home.'*
>
> 2. *The lore of 'school readiness' suggests that children come to school socialized in such a fashion that the locus of social control has been internalized. Hence, teachers expect Black children to behave as 'good' children should (and good little White*

children do). It seems that the children and the teachers have mutually incompatible expectations of each other. Over a period of time, they tend to work out rather shaky adjustments to each other. The teachers conclude that the children are incorrigible, and the children conclude that the teachers are inconsistent and capricious.

Black children in general, Black males in particular, oftentimes behave at school in ways in which they wouldn't dare behave at home. The language used with teachers, mannerisms in classrooms, and disrespect of adult authority are most often, if not exclusively, directed toward adults within the school community who are unable to bridge the social-cultural-gender divide between teachers and students and between the school and families. Building such a bridge between home and school, where teachers operate as an extension of, rather than in conflict with, family values and expectations is paramount to closing the achievement gap and creating vibrant institutions of learning for Black children.

Mothers

According to the report, issued by the National Center for Education Statistics, *Educational Achievement and Black-White Inequality*:

- 53 percent of Black children under 18 live in single-parent families with 96 percent of those families being headed by a single mother.

- 35 percent of all Black female-headed households are below the poverty level. For Black married couples the rate is 6 percent.

These statistics should not suggest that single mothers, or mothers living in poverty, struggling to survive, can't raise their children. To the contrary, the undeniable history of the Black family is how Black mothers, against seemingly insurmountable obstacles, have successfully raised their children and other people's children as well. However, we can anticipate young men will challenge their mother's authority, attempt to manipulate them, and behave in ways very different from how they would a man.

One day at the market ...

My wife is still working her way through building the foundation for our sons. Generally, you will find my wife meticulously dressed, her nails polished and manicured, her hair neat and very stylish. During her professional career, she has successfully provided counseling and career guidance for hundreds of employees. She has developed good people skills and is the epitome of organization and professionalism.

One day my wife came home frazzled! She came into the house with her hair standing all over her head, several broken fingernails, her clothes soiled, and a run in her stockings, decreeing, "I'm never taking your son to the store with me again. He just acted like an absolute ninny! I've never been so embarrassed in my life. He didn't want to do anything that I told him, he started crying in the store because he wanted me to buy him a beach ball, and then he wanted to open some candy. He wouldn't sit in the shopping cart, then he wanted me to pick him up, and to go from bad to worse he started crying and throwing a fit in the checkout line. When I tried to calm him down, he called me stupid! At that point I was so worn out that I just left the groceries and came home." After all of this, our two-year-old son strolls innocently through the door, oblivious to his mother's distress.

As a father, I rarely experienced this type of behavior with our, then, two-year-old son. The next day I took him to the store (to reclaim our groceries), together with his four-year-old cousin who also had a reputation in the family of being difficult. The three of us spent the entire day together in various situations before returning home. While at home, I did some work on my computer while the two boys played in the yard. On other occasions, my son and I have been in situations ranging from upscale restaurants to museums, and he has never demonstrated such behaviors.

There is a difference in the way in which Black males respond to women and how they respond to men. They will often test women until they demand respect. Even then, males will frequently challenge a woman's authority to the point of screams and threats. Young men are typically unresponsive to a woman's voice when instructed the first time. Often a mother or teacher will make the same request several times before a young man responds.

"Jalani, didn't you hear what I said?"

"Jalani, don't let me have to tell you again."

"Jalani, what's wrong with you, are you deaf?"

"Jalani, I'm tired of telling you the same thing over and over."

"Jalani, you are wearing on my last nerve."

"Jalani, if I've told you once, I've told you a thousand times."

"Jalani, I'm not going to tell you again."

"Jalani, if I have to tell you one more time."

"One ...Two ... Don't let me get to three."

"Jalani, just get out of my face before I hurt you."

"Jalani, just wait until your father gets home." Or, in the case of a single mother, "Jalani, I'm going to tell your coach." Or, in the case of a religious mother, "Lord, have mercy, because I am going to hurt this boy!"

Young men and their mothers go through this scenario from pre-school through high school. In the case of those young men who never leave home, this may continue throughout a mother's lifetime! This behavioral model, which begins at home, is oftentimes unknowingly reinforced by classroom teachers (72.8 percent of whom are female).

Consider the classroom teacher who reminds a young man of a task (i.e., "Didn't you hear me?"); writes his name onto the board (i.e., "I'm not going to tell you again ..."); issues another reminder and places a check next to his name (i.e., "One ..."); issues another reminder and places another check next to his name (i.e., "Two ..."); and finally, issues another reminder, followed by such statements as, "Jalani, why do I have to go through this with you every day? Didn't we talk about this at the beginning of the school year? I just can't keep telling you the same thing over and over everyday." All of this, while writing an office referral (i.e., "I'm going to tell the principal!").

This scenario plays itself out in homes, at airports, in classrooms, at the grocery store, and at the mall. "One ...Two ... Don't let me get to three!" My wife has learned that no matter how tired she is or how busy she may be, when she asks our sons to do something she has to follow with some form of consequence if either or them doesn't respond immediately. She has to constantly and consistently reinforce a previously-defined level of respect, code of conduct, and standard of behavior.

The following rules can help mothers and teachers establish the foundation of discipline, respect, and expected standards of behavior:

1. Establish the rules and consequences early. Enforce them regularly and discuss appending them when appropriate.

2. When you make a request and there's no immediate response, allow the benefit of the doubt and repeat yourself only to ensure you were heard. Since new areas of behavior are always presenting themselves, it is not unreasonable to discuss why certain behavior is expected.

3. If your son is still unresponsive, if the response is slow and lazy, or in any way fails to meet your expectations, enforce the previously-discussed consequences.

With our older son I will simply say, "Mychal-David, did you hear me?" I then announce the consequence. "If I have to tell you again ..." Disciplining young men does not have to take the form of suspension from school or spanking at home. We can develop many forms of discipline based upon our understanding of our sons and students. We can take away privileges and deny opportunities. Young men must be taught the difference between privileges and entitlements. Too many young men receive signals at home and at school that no matter what they do, they are 'entitled' to play on the basketball team, watch television, or buy the latest clothes.

We must establish chores at home which bear a direct relationship to the things they want, establishing the foundation of a "value for value" relationship, value given for value received. Too many young men grow up believing they are entitled to something for nothing.

4. Learn to control your tone of voice. Frequently raising your voice implies you are not serious until you're screaming or threatening.

5. Don't discipline out of anger, discipline out of love. In your mind, you must clearly know why you're enforcing a certain consequence and you must stick to your decision. Don't confuse young men by constantly changing your mind. You have the responsibility to display leadership and enforce your authority.

6. Don't issue idle threats! Young men aren't buying any "wolf tickets." If you are going to discipline, do so. If you aren't, don't threaten.

7. Don't get angry and allow yourself to speak to or threaten young men in a disrespectful way. The foundation of discipline and mutual respect must be established early and reinforced constantly.

In the situation of our sons, I attempt to always issue the consequences when they exhibit behavior I deem unacceptable. I always follow through immediately on any threats I make. I demonstrate respect for their opinions and intellect by explaining within reason, why certain behavior is expected and why other behavior is unacceptable.

I constantly plant the seeds of greatness within my sons' subconscious by telling them they are princes. They must display the highest character, integrity, and intelligence befitting one of royal heritage. I never confront or challenge them on things which I don't feel are important enough for discipline. I never tell them not to do something or to stop doing something unless I'm prepared to enforce a consequence if they don't respond immediately. Finally, I make it a point to acknowledge expected behavior and never to allow unacceptable behavior to go unnoticed, unchallenged, or without consequence!

Every home, school, classroom, and business has an unspoken code of acceptable conduct. Unfortunately, many homes and classrooms are like poorly-run businesses. Most of us have experienced going into a store where the salespeople were poorly trained, rude, lazy, uncooperative, and had a nonchalant attitude. We've also experienced businesses where the salespeople were kind, courteous, eager to help, and made us feel as though our business was really appreciated. People tend to respond in a way consistent with what they've been taught is acceptable behavior.

We, as parents and teachers, must provide the example of acceptable behavior in our homes and classrooms. Failing this, we cannot effectively communicate an acceptable code of conduct to our sons and students and more importantly, get them to buy in to this code of conduct. It is this "buy in" which establishes the foundation for teaching and for learning!

Parents and teachers who have problems with their own self-esteem and self-confidence feel they must demonstrate to young men who's the boss! They unwittingly are drawn into a test of wills. They lose sight of the mission; to teach, discipline, love, and raise young men. Our challenge is to create an environment of acceptable behavior without forcing young men to lose respect and status within their peer group. Our aim is to achieve compromise without controversy, compliance without confrontation.

The history of the Black male in America is one in which we have often been stripped of our dignity, self-respect, honor, and humanity. We were brought into this country as chattel through a Middle Passage which was among, if not the most brutal and inhumane, within the annals of world history. We were not respected as human beings, but treated as property. The slave masters were not concerned with our feelings. They had no respect for our opinions. They had no compassion for our dreams and aspirations. They did everything conceivable to remove the Black man as the head of the household and destroy the Black family structure.

Understanding this history, we cannot establish discipline within young Black men without encouraging and rebuilding self-esteem, integrity, honor, and responsibility. I have usually found young men to respond positively to those who speak to them in a respectful manner; those who care enough to discuss their feelings. I routinely address young men as, "Sir," and "Mr." I model what I expect. It is a very rare occasion when an adult doesn't hear one of our sons respond to them as, "Yes Sir" or "No Ma'am."

Following is a typical situation.

Mother: Gregory, empty the trash and clean up you room.

Gregory: I don't want to!

Mother: Don't give any back talk.

Gregory: Why do I always have to take out the trash? Why do I have to clean up my room? No one goes in there but me anyway!

Mother: Do it because I said do it!

Many confrontations between Black males and their parents and teachers result in the "Do it because I said to it" ultimatum. Parents and teachers find it easier to issue ultimatums than to discuss and explain the reasons why certain responsibilities are given to their sons or students. Displaying this type of dictatorship will not empower young men to make their own decisions. In fact, constantly challenging and threatening them often results in their conscious efforts to disobey!

I'm not suggesting that all of our decisions should be subjected to discussion and debate prior to our sons or students following instructions. I'm suggesting that we can become better parents and teachers by thinking through why we want young men to display a certain standard of behavior and to assume certain types of responsibilities.

For example:

Mother: Gregory, empty the trash and clean up you room.

Gregory: I don't want to!

Mother: Gregory, part of your responsibilities in this household is to empty the trash and to keep your room clean. Why would you want to have trash in the house? You know it attracts bugs and bacteria. You know you're supposed to clean your room every day. One day when you're rich and famous you can hire a maid to clean your room and a butler to empty your trash. However today, these are your responsibilities.

Gregory: Why do I always have to take out the trash? Why do I have to clean up my room? No one goes in there but me anyway!

Mother: Gregory, you know we all have certain responsibilities. I have responsibilities to go to work where people depend on me. I have to prepare dinner daily, plan the family budget, do the laundry, and pay an assortment of monthly bills so the electricity, gas, and telephone aren't disconnected. It doesn't matter if we don't have any guests all week. Whenever someone does come to visit our home, I want to have pride in our home just like I have pride in you. Now, let's not waste any more time complaining. No one has to remind me to pay the bills or prepare dinner. Why should I have to remind you of your responsibilities?

This approach is not as quick and easy as simply saying, "Do it because I said do it!" This does, however, replace dictatorship with teaching. It discusses responsibilities and provides leadership examples. It explains why accepting responsibility is important and why these particular responsibilities have been established. It plants the seed, i.e., Gregory will become successful and he will be capable of hiring maids and butlers. It discusses pride in one's self and one's home and it concludes with the example that complaining is not desirable behavior. It also empowers Gregory for a peer group encounter:

Peer: Why does your mother make you take out the trash? I don't have to do anything at home. I never have to clean up my room.

Gregory: Well, at my house everyone has responsibilities. My mother goes to work, cooks dinner and pays all the bills. So I guess taking out the trash and cleaning up my room is not too much to ask. Besides, it makes her happy to have a clean house, you never know who will drop by.

Never speak to young men in negative terms when censoring their behavior. When CJ doesn't do his homework, it's more encouraging to tell him he is brilliant, he is capable of extraordinary things, and the homework is meant to help him in developing the strong foundation he will need to achieve his goals in life. Rather than "CJ, not again. Why don't you ever do your homework? If you don't do your homework you're going to get an 'F!'" When Alphonso is clowning in class it is more encouraging to bring Alphonso into the discussion by asking him to comment on the topic of discussion or to discuss how the topic is relative to his life, rather than, "Alphonso, shut-up or I'll send you to the Principal's office." We'll often find our most disruptive students possessing extraordinary leadership skills. Our challenge is to properly focus their skills and channel their energies into a positive and productive force within our classrooms, schools, and communities.

If we can help young men to internalize an expected standard of behavior, we can use positive peer pressure to reinforce an accompanying code of conduct. This will make our jobs easier and provide a foundation for reinforcing desirable behavior in our schools and classrooms. A clear code of conduct must be developed at home, in school, and within each classroom. Our two sons, one sixteen years old and the other ten years old, have never had a fight at home. Yet, they each have had multiple fights at school. Parents, teachers, and administrators must share common goals and expectations to ensure that young Black males receive clear, consistent, signals from the entire village.

One cold night in Chicago ...

One cold winter night in Chicago, my friend Jerry and I gathered all of the paper and wood that we could find around the apartment complex that we lived in. We found a nice cozy place under a back porch and dumped all of the paper and wood into a trash can and started a fire. We didn't start the fire to keep warm, we just wanted to see how big a fire we could burn! Fortunately, the janitor of the building came by and put the fire out before we could burn down the building. He grabbed both of us by the collar and took us home. All during the time that my mother was whipping my butt, she kept screaming at me, "Why did you set the fire? Why did you set the fire?" She kept whipping me and asking why I set the fire and I kept crying and saying, "I don't know."

Finally, tired and out of breath, my mother grabbed me and started shaking me saying, "Jerry started the fire, didn't he?" As if on cue, I started nodding my head and saying, "Yes ma'am, Jerry did it, he sure did, I didn't do nothing."

My mother, like so many other mothers, didn't want to believe her son was behaving irresponsibly and had nearly burned down the building. Many of our young men stroll through our homes, schools, and communities refusing to accept responsibility for themselves and their actions. Many parents, after receiving telephone calls from schools or the police about trouble their sons have been involved in, immediately defend their sons and their actions.

They refuse to believe their sons are capable of such behaviors. I've heard mothers excuse the actions of their sons by blaming their peers for influencing their behaviors, their financial circumstances, or on their communities.

Young men don't benefit from our excusing irresponsible, ill-mannered, and disrespectful behavior. It is our responsibility as parents, educators, and concerned citizens to teach young men responsibilities and to hold them accountable for their actions. To prepare young men to become men we must demand they not only do their jobs and perform their chores, but they do them well.

Parents are not helping young men when they feel a sense of accomplishment by simply getting them out of the house to go to school! Or, when teachers feel a sense of accomplishment by simply getting young men to sit still in class! Young men must be given clear responsibilities and held accountable for getting up on time, getting properly dressed, and being properly groomed. They must be held responsible for fulfilling household duties (e.g., making the bed, cleaning up after eating, cleaning up the bathroom) before going to school and after school, homework comes before basketball. The foundation and acceptance of responsibility must begin at home and be reinforced in school and throughout the community.

Na'im Akbar, in *Visions for Black Men*, describes the transition which boys undergo:

A male, a boy, and a man are not the same thing. A male is a biological creature, a boy is a creature in transition, and a man is something that has arrived to a purpose and a destiny. When men become real men and do not confuse their maleness or their boyishness with their manliness, they have come into a true rediscovery of what they are. There are problems with those who confuse their biological functions with their spiritual function as men. There are problems with 'boys' who think they're men—who enjoy playing games, who enjoy riding in fast cars, who enjoy listening to loud music, who enjoy running after women, and who enjoy running real fast rather than being steady and directed as men are.

Encouraging, allowing, and demanding that young men assume personal responsibilities develops character and builds self-esteem. It prepares young Black men for a future of hope and promise.

Ron Weaver, in *Beyond Identify: Education and the Future Role of Black Americans,* states:

Several properties of classroom organization have been identified as important for development of a high degree of self-esteem in children. First, the children, especially minority children, must be afforded a sense of mastery—the degree to which they view themselves as able to manipulate events and achieve desired goals—over what happens to them in school. Through such mastery or decision-making opportunity, children may develop self-responsibility. This, in turn, may provide motivation in the sense that the children feel they, rather than someone else, are responsible for their success and failure. Subsequently, this role of self-direction may provide greater initiative in seeking success in school, since Black children's views of the environment of the school—how <u>open</u> and manipulable the environment seems to be—has been noted as more important to Black children than their competence in determining success.

George Henderson, in the same book, notes:

Studies in the foundations of humanistic education for Black students also indicate that Black students are better served when they have an active voice in the decision-making process which attends learning and accept the responsibility

of the consummation of the decisions made. Indeed, self-concept and
personal esteem are heightened when students share in their own educational
development and emotional growth.

It is important for young Black men, to believe they, rather than someone else, are primarily responsible for their success and failure—whether academic, social, personal, or professional. Black men who learn to approach the challenges and obstacles of life with the same passion and intensity as they display on basketball courts will be prepared to successfully fulfill their roles as husbands, fathers, and contributors.

We must establish and maintain regular dialogue with young men in all areas of responsibility (e.g., sex, drugs, fatherhood, alcohol, cigarettes, jobs, gangs, pregnancy, stealing, and destruction of property). Although religion, prayer, and worship of God are not taught in public schools, parents must assume the responsibility of helping their sons to develop a solid spiritual foundation. Young men must develop a spiritual and moral center combined with critical-thinking skills in order to withstand the tremendous amount of negative ideas, values, and images being constantly directed toward them by the media, popular culture, and peers. The daily, oftentimes life-saving, decisions they must make (i.e.,  drugs, gangs, sex, peer pressure) must be guided by a spiritual and moral set of core values—a compass that points the way.

There are so many issues to be discussed and obstacles Black males have to be prepared to overcome, for us to be at a lost of material, ideas, or issues for book reports, classroom discussions, pep talks, or dinner table discussions. The most dangerous young men within the school and surrounding community are those who aren't being taught how to think, who don't have relationships with caring adults to challenge their ideas, stimulate their critical-thinking, and who don't have a spiritual and moral compass.

Rather than giving advice, leading young men around, or telling them what their daily responsibilities are, parents and teachers must begin to regularly ask the question, "Why?" Or, "What are you suppose to do?" Don't give them the answers, allow them the opportunity to discover the answers.

> Dad: *"Jalani, what are you suppose to be doing?"*
>
> Jalani: *"What?"*
>
> Dad: *"Jalani, what are you suppose to be doing?"*
>
> Jalani: *"I don't know Dad."*
>
> Dad: *"Well, Jalani, just stay in your room until you remember what you're suppose to be doing."*
>
> Jalani: *"I forgot Dad, can't you just tell me this one time?"*
>
> Dad: *"Jalani, I'm sure you'll eventually remember. See you later."*

The stories we tell, lessons we teach, responsibilities we expect, and the level of thinking, planning, and doing we consistently reinforce within young men all emanate from the mission conceptualized in Chapter one and the vision developed in Chapter two. The concepts of diligence, determination, perseverance, fortitude, integrity, and accepting responsibility for one's actions should be a regular part of classroom and household discussions. As a parent, rarely a day goes by without a "teachable moment" where I have the opportunity to engage my son in a discussion or share a story involving a value, personal attribute, principle, or philosophy. The way people behave in traffic, lyrics in a song being played on the radio, report card grade, or school project, all provide such teachable moments. The more you talk to young men, the more knowledgeable you will both become.

Developing a Village

After becoming aware of the issues impacting school culture and subsequently Black male achievement, the question begs to be asked, "Now what?" Perhaps a good starting point is with parents, many of whom have figured out what to do. No matter how large the achievement gap or how dismal the overall achievement levels for the majority of Black students, in every school, there are Black children who are achieving in spite of it all. There are always families with children who have above average, or certainly have the intellectual ability to have above average achievement.

A possible principal or counselor initiated strategy is to reach out to the families of high performing Black students. A collaboration with them can spread to other parents and can provide a much-needed support mechanism for high performing students who, as previously indicated, oftentimes suffer from cultural isolation as the only Black student in their gifted or advanced academic classes. Developing a Black Student or Black Male Achievement Club can bridge the gap between families of high- and low-performing students. You are likely to find that many families have both high- and low-performing students within the same household. They, more than anyone else, have experienced  both pitfalls and successes. Some already have children attending or who have graduated from college and provide a unique perspective on what the problems are and what solutions are needed.

Passing the Baton: A Black Male Achievement Club

1. Analyze your school's data and identify Black students who are successful academically, parents who have been actively involved in the school, and community leaders who would like to support Black male academic achievement.

2. Extend a luncheon invitation to parents of high achieving Black students, parents who have already demonstrated a willingness to be involved, and community representatives who would like to support Black male achievement.

3. Provide several chart pads, easels, broad-tip markers, and tape.

4. Identify a facilitator (a passionate teacher or staff representative).

5. Distribute data pertaining to grade distribution, standardized test scores, EOG pass rates, high school graduation and college enrollment rates, honors, AP, and academically-gifted class enrollment, algebra I enrollment, advanced science enrollment, and discipline data.

6. Distribute copies of the Black male achievement data contained in Chapter one. You may also consider providing copies of the table contained in the *workbook*, "Estimated Probability of Competing in College Athletics."

7. Brainstorm what parents believe to be obstacles to student achievement.

8. Provide attendees with a copy of this book, together with a copy of each of the following books:
   - *Empowering African-American Males workbook*
   - *A Middle School Plan for Students with College-Bound Dreams*
   - *A High School Plan for Students with College-Bound Dreams*
   - *Ten Steps to Helping Your Child Succeed in School*

9. Direct each attendee to complete the 'Web of Protection' *workbook* activity prior to the next meeting.

10. Identify all of the issues and adjourn the meeting. DO NOT TRY TO SOLVE ANY PROBLEMS AT THE FIRST MEETING.

11. Type and categorize the list of obstacles, i.e., student issues, parent issues, staff issues, school climate and culture issues.

12. Create information packages containing the issues discussed, data, and a list of attendees from the first meeting.

13. Reconvene another meeting and divide attendees into teams based on specific areas of focus, based on the categories of challenges identified at the first meeting and begin working toward developing strategies.

14. Identify parents who are interested in forming a college-bound team and support their efforts in following some of the strategies outlined in the books, *A Middle School Plan for Students with College-Bound Dreams* and *A High School Plan for Students with College-Bound Dreams*.

Building strong relationships with Black males will require teachers and mentors to not only convince them that they care about their future achievement but their willingness to assist them in planning how they will get there. The relationship stands on the foundation of compassion and vision.

Tasks for all Role Players:

1. Consciously focus on "What can be" rather than "What you see." Always try to discuss current behaviors within a future context.

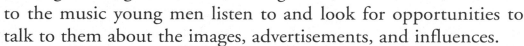 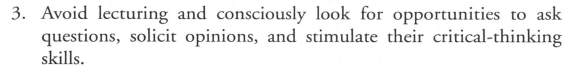

2. Familiarize yourself with the issues and images influencing the language and behaviors of Black males by reading the magazines and listening to the music young men listen to and look for opportunities to talk to them about the images, advertisements, and influences.

3. Avoid lecturing and consciously look for opportunities to ask questions, solicit opinions, and stimulate their critical-thinking skills.

4. Develop a reservoir of stories, examples, and anecdotes which relate to the challenges, issues, and obstacles confronting young men.

5. Develop open communication with parents to share information, communicate consistent messages, and develop consistent strategies.

6. Develop a library of culturally-relevant books and reading material.

7. Connect literacy to your circle of influence. A coach can prepare a reading list for players, a mentor can find books which relate to a young man's areas of interests and use them as a prompt to discuss ideas and interests, a teacher can add book reports to his or her list of extra credit opportunities.

8. Look for opportunities to identify other people to reinforce your message, i.e., athletes, entertainers, coaches, older young men, artists, poets, entrepreneurs, or others involved in work or careers which young men aspire toward.

9. Reinforce Standard English usage while understanding and valuing their culturally-relevant language patterns, polite manners, and strong handshakes.

10. Be patient.

Develop Shared Ownership

Teaching young men how to work together and helping them to develop a sense of shared ownership is another important step toward teaching them; how to overcome their propensity of putting each other down; how to successfully resolve conflicts; and how to appreciate each other's unique talents, interests, gifts, and abilities. The practice of developing teams is consistent with African child-rearing (i.e., humanistic, bonding, shared ownership, assigning roles within the village) and with building bridges between student ability levels.

A teacher, program administrator, or coach may consider organizing young men into teams. It's natural for a football coach to organize defensive linemen, linebackers, running backs, and wide receivers into groups, however, there is usually competition for positions which hinders the sharing of skills, ideas, techniques, or information which will assist each individual player in becoming better, thereby helping the team (i.e., village) to become better. When constructing teams the focus is on team success through the collaborative effort of individual team members. The size of the teams should be an odd number of students (i.e., 3, 5, 7). Each team should have a rotating team leader (i.e., daily or weekly) and a team charter which clearly outlines the process in conducting discussions and resolving conflicts (See Sample Charter in the *workbook*).

"Lets discuss different types of teams and what they do.

Most of us are familiar with athletic teams. What are some of the types of athletic teams?

Did you know that many businesses form various types of teams which are made up of different types of people? For example, in the automobile industry, companies form project teams which are responsible for conceiving, designing, building, and selling automobiles. Such teams could be made up of engineers, business managers, marketing managers, assembly-line workers, and automobile dealers.

Other businesses have quality control teams responsible for inspecting the finished products. Other common business teams are sales teams, management teams, production teams, advertising teams, and customer service teams.

School districts sometimes create task forces which can be made up of business leaders, teachers, parents, and community leaders who review schools and their curriculum to decide if they best serve the students.

Thus, we are going to organize our classroom into 'Success Teams.' We're going to organize our Success Teams so we can benefit from the different skills, backgrounds, and individual goals of each person in our class. Just like a football or basketball team, our Success Teams may have superstars, but our primary goal is for the whole team to win!"

Experiment with different team approaches, i.e., Multiple Intelligences, personality types, ability groups, or learning-styles and structure teams with different objectives in mind. Use one teaming methodology with a student who masters the content area as the group leader to assist you in helping other students to better understand problem-solving approaches. Use Multiple Intelligences teams, grouping like intelligences, i.e., Visual/ Spatial, Logical/Mathematical, Verbal/ Linguistic, or Interpersonal and allow groups the opportunity to work together toward solving problems through their dominant intelligence. Other times, use cross-intelligence groups as a means of  helping students to learn and appreciate diverse intelligences. Similar groups can be developed based on personality types and learning-styles. Experimenting with different types of grouping methodology allows students to appreciate each other's gifts and provides an opportunity to utilize student gifts to assist the teacher by giving high achieving students the opportunity to deepen their own learning—through frequent opportunities to teach others and transfer knowledge.

Parents

1. Develop household rules, expectations, rewards, and consequences with a future focus, i.e., father, husband, college graduate.

2. While you may be your son's friend you MUST be your son's parent.

3. Get involved with your son's school and influence his peer group through the booster club, tutorial program, or other volunteer opportunities.

4. Don't allow your son to go over to anyone's home prior to your having an opportunity to visit their home or know their parents.

5. Encourage your son to use Standard English around you.

6. Don't allow your son to put clothes before learning. What's on his back (or feet) is not as important as what's between his ears!

7. Don't allow your son to disrespect adults, even if he believes he has been wronged. If you feel he has been wronged then you handle it. Adults should deal with adults.

8. Teach your son to keep his manhood to himself and not to make babies until he is married.

9. Don't allow your son to be a thug unless you are trying to raise a thug. If you are trying to raise a thug then you should go to church and allow someone to pray for you!

10. Don't have more DVDs, CDs, TVs, or video games in your home than books and control use of the media that you have!

11. Learn how to listen. Young men who are encouraged to talk will grow into men who have something to say. You will also discover that the longer a young man talks in an attempt to explain or to justify his actions, the more likely he is to "hear" just how ridiculous his actions were!

Providing Culturally-relevant Information

Exposure to the opportunities and discussions of the unique issues confronting Black men provide inroads into shaping the psyche of Black males. Take every opportunity to expose young men to the national, international, and global opportunities their talents, abilities, and intellectual capacity can afford them. Expand their cultural identification beyond the scope of their friends and community onto a world stage. Take advantage of every opportunity to visit other communities, cities, and countries. Restaurants, theaters, musicals, ballets, plays, museums, and events which broaden their horizons and provide opportunities to experience new people, situations, and ideas.

Engage in informal discussions of the African, Black American, Black Caribbean, Black Canadian, or Black British, history and the achievements of Black men and their historical context to the current conflicts confronting Black males amongst their peers and within their respective communities. Weaving historical lessons into the fabric of current discussions is one of the indispensable keys to enhancing the critical-thinking skills needed to confront the daily issues of society and peers. For example, use of the "N-word" cannot be effectively discussed or debated outside of its historical origins. Understanding and appreciating "The Dozens" requires an understanding and appreciation of its historical context, both its African origins (affirmation of tribal greatness, and gender statue) and post-Africa deviation (racial inferiority and gender degradation). The ongoing discussions and historical analysis of the lives, vision, and philosophies of such Black men as Martin Luther King, Jr. Malcolm X, W.E.B. DuBois, Booker T. Washington, Paul Robeson, Jim Brown, Carter G. Woodson, and others provide young men with a framework from which to develop an understanding of the many issues which have led to the crisis within the Black community (albeit the Black community in South Central Los Angeles, East St. Louis, or in the U.S. Virgin Islands).

In July, 2004 Columbia University graduate and the first Black editor of the Harvard Law Review, Barack Obama, a State Senator of Illinois on track to become only the fifth Black U.S. Senator in America's history delivered a speech at the Democratic National Convention reminiscence of the days of Martin Luther King, Jr., Jesse Jackson, and Andrew Young. However, his speech, on a national platform was not carried by any of the major news networks. Yet, the same night, news stations across America carried stories of Black athletes and entertainers together with countless images of Black men being paraded through the criminal justice system.

There are many influences on culture, of which the media is a very powerful one. However, there are many variables which shape the complex and far-reaching culture of Black males: economic status; education; gender; family structure; community structure; media influence; role models; peer values; higher-order thinking skills; and access to mentors and mentoring programs are some of the many influences on Black male culture. Black male culture reflects the totality of the experiences of Black men in the society. Black male experiences within their households, churches, schools, athletic programs, and community organizations all shape Black male culture.

Dr. Molefi Kete Asante, Dr. Asa Hilliard, and others have published a wealth of scholarly literature outlining how to infuse African and African-American literature, historical, and cultural achievements into the school curriculum and into community and religious programs. Parents and teachers must consciously adorn their homes and classrooms with visual imagery (i.e., pictures, posters, calendars, statues, kente cloth, fabric, book covers, and artifacts) positively portraying Black people. They must also develop libraries of biographies, short stories, novels, chapter books, encyclopedias, coloring books, poetry, magazines, video tapes, DVDs, and reference materials relating to Black people in general, and Black men in particular.

> *We realize that our future lies chiefly in our own hands. We know that neither institution nor friends can make a race stand unless it has strength in its own foundation; that races like individuals must stand or fall by their own merit; that to fully succeed they must practice the virtues of self-reliance, self-respect, industry, perseverance, and economy.*
>
> *— Paul Robeson*

Chapter 3: Key Points

1. Black males need compassion to understand the unique issues confronting them, followed by strategies in response to those issues.

2. Zeros and F's aren't a proven intrinsic motivator and should be reconsidered in lieu of strategies which inspire the necessary effort and levels of learning.

3. Frequent opportunities for young men to increase their grade by demonstrating gradual, systemic increased levels of learning better prepares them for standardized testing and end-of-course exams.

4. An understanding of Multiple Intelligences helps to develop holistic strategies which builds relationships and conceptualizes effective processes.

5. Building relationships with parents helps to ensure consistent expectations and a focus on meeting student needs.

6. Visiting a student's home can help you learn the hopes and dreams of his family.

7. Seek to understand the attitudes and perceptions of Black males toward the school community.

8. Understand the rap and hip-hop influences which impact the beliefs and aspirations of Black students.

9. 'The Dozens,' 'The Showdown,' and inappropriate language have histories in Black culture and are predictable behaviors requiring proactive strategies.

10. Do not compromise in teaching 'Standard English.'

11. Gather data and honestly assess school and classroom culture regularly.

12. Teach young men how to work together through frequent use of teaming.

There's A New Day Coming

When the Sun announces the dawning day
Just flex your muscles and start on your way
Go over, or under, around, or through
Any obstacles or hurdles that challenge you
There's a new day coming

Cast aside the failures of yesterday
Forget the peaks and valleys that have paved your way
Wipe the sweat from your brow and the dust from your shoe
Take a breath and relax so that you may begin anew
There's a new day coming

Forget the burdens and obstacles that have held you back
Focus on your dreams and prepare a plan of attack
There are battles awaiting to challenge your success
Daring you to stand tall and to give it your best
There's a new day coming

No matter how great the journey, or how heavy the load
How steep the mountain, or how rough the road
When your arms grow weary and legs give way
Stop and rest for a moment, it will be okay
There's a new day coming

As shadows spring forth from the setting Sun
Take a moment and savor the battles you've won
Sleep peacefully tonight and enjoy your rest
Awaken tomorrow and continue your quest
There's always, a new day coming

— Mychal Wynn

Chapter 4
Curriculum & Content

Kunta Kente was the product of a society that held its young in high esteem and developed a network of role models and functional institutions to assist him in his social development. Until the day he was attacked and kidnaped by slavers, Kunta Kente had been raised in a fashion that clearly defined who he was, his responsibility to his parents, relatives, and community, and his sense of manhood.

— Useni Eugene Perkins

The area of curriculum and content encompasses such hotly debated issues as:

- Whether or not to formally recognize 'Ebonics' as a curriculum component.

- The infusion of Afrocentric thought into an otherwise Eurocentric curriculum.

- Ensuring that diverse cultures and viewpoints rise to the level of critical-thinking and classroom discussion.

- Addressing the gender, racial, religious, and cultural stereotypes in literature and social sciences.

- Whether or not students are introduced to the needed levels of scientific and mathematical thinking to compete globally.

- Whether or not there is too little, too much, or just enough content being covered during the school year.

- Whether or not there is sufficient alignment between what is taught in the classroom and what is tested on standardized, grade-level proficiency, end-of-grade, or high school exit tests.

- Whether or not subject-area teachers effectively design and pace their lesson plans to cover the necessary curriculum components.

The intellectual and far-reaching nature of the debate on what, when, and how to teach is far too complex to be addressed within the scope of this book. Additionally, it is outside the mission of this book, "Empowering African-American Males." As such, what will be addressed here is:

1. How to create a web of support to assist in teaching the necessary lessons and values.

2. The type of lessons and values needed to examine a hip-hop culture which frequently fails to affirm the very values the artists and athletes themselves have internalized as the primary means of their success, i.e., diligence, determination, persistence, and perseverance.

3. How to ensure full access to whatever curricula is being utilized within the school district. Particularly, in the areas of advanced science, math, and reading literacy.

Creating a Web of Protection

In the Biblical book of *Job* [Job 1:10], Job is a man of great wealth and prosperity as long as he is protected by God's 'web of protection':

Hast not thou [God] made a hedge about him, and about his house, and about all that he hath on every side? Thou hast blessed the work of his hands, and his substance is increased in the land.

When God temporarily removes his web of protection, Job is stricken with illness, his friends leave him, and he suffers greatly. However, once God restores his web of protection, Job and his children are blessed with even greater wealth and prosperity.

As previously stated, 53 percent of Black children under 18 live in single-parent families and 96 percent of those families are headed by a single mother. Since the days of the Atlantic Slave Trade, when Black men were forcibly removed as the head of their households and families were torn apart, Black single mothers have a legacy dealing with the many roles forced upon them—mother, father, teacher, counselor, doctor, nurse, dentist, psychiatrist, protector, cook, bread winner, head of household, and spiritual leader. In addition to all of this, today's single mothers must raise their children while balancing school schedules, work schedules, extracurricular activities, and careers (oftentimes more than one), and dealing with the many complex issues unique to raising Black males who oftentimes lack positive social interactions with their fathers. Added to their nearly unbearable stress is dealing with what is oftentimes confrontational, rather than collaborative attitudes from teachers and school staff who rarely understand, or care to understand, the challenges facing mothers in ensuring the safety, social development, and academic achievement of their sons. Subsequently, there is an undeniable need to ensure that their children have interactions with positive male figures and their families have advocates at school. Girls need to be exposed to the type of men whom they may one day choose as spouses and husbands, young men need to be exposed to the type of men who will help them along their journey from boyhood to manhood, and single moms need to meet some good men themselves.

We must consciously construct a web of protection around Black males to protect them against the many negative influences and increase their opportunities for academic and personal success. The illustrations on the following pages represent the web of protection that my wife and I have constructed for each of our sons. Each ring of the illustration represents various levels of influence. The rings closest to our sons represent the most significant influences, however, the people or influences represented have the power to reinforce or undermine the values, expectations, and standards my wife and I have established. For many young men, the outer ring (Societal Influences) of television programming, music, hip-hop culture, video games, and peers displaces their inner circle, thereby providing the primary influence through which they are having their values defined and reinforced. For other children, "School" represents their most significant influence, displacing their inner circle. Clearly, such children are at risk and are in need of caring adults who will be proactive in developing the necessary web of protection. Doing so, requires:

1. Identifying the role you will play, values you will convey and reinforce, and the relationships you will develop with others within his web of protection.

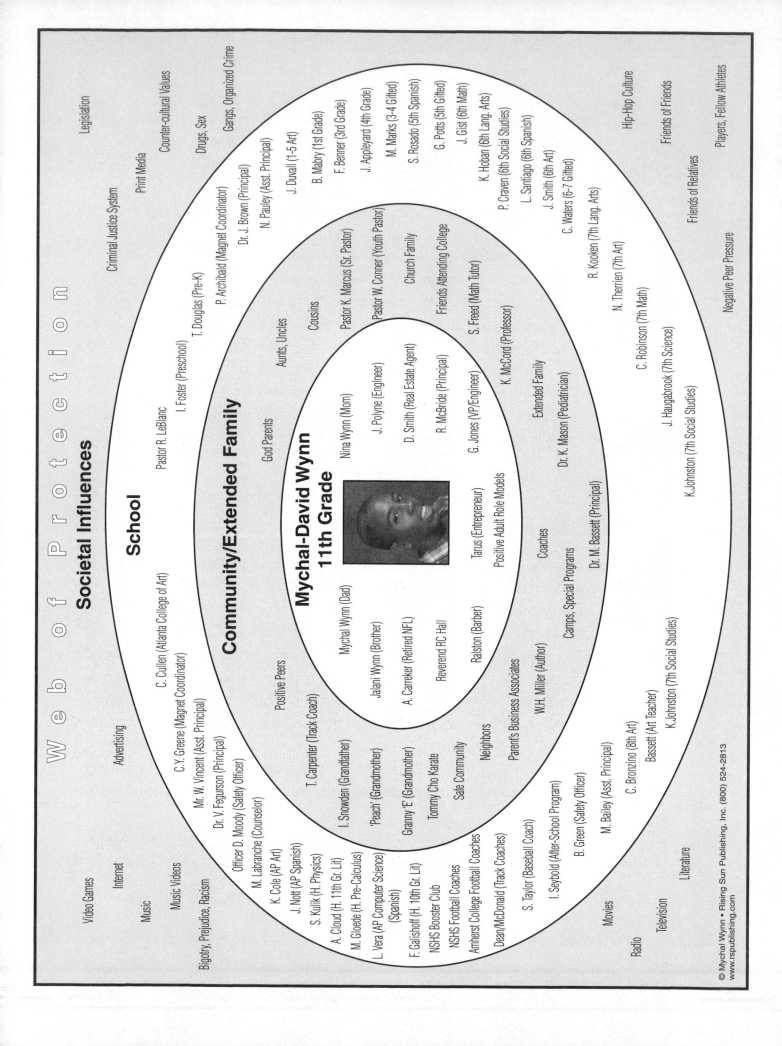

Web of Protection

Societal Influences

School

Community/Extended Family

Mychal-David Wynn
11th Grade

Societal Influences (outer ring):
- Legislation
- Counter-cultural Values
- Print Media
- Criminal Justice System
- Drugs, Sex
- Gangs, Organized Crime
- Advertising
- Hip-Hop Culture
- Friends of Friends
- Players, Fellow Athletes
- Friends of Relatives
- Negative Peer Pressure
- Video Games
- Internet
- Music
- Music Videos
- Bigotry, Prejudice, Racism
- Movies
- Radio
- Television
- Literature

School (ring):
- C. Cullen (Atlanta College of Art)
- Pastor R. LeBlanc
- I. Foster (Preschool)
- T. Douglas (Pre-K)
- P. Archibald (Magnet Coordinator)
- Dr. J. Brown (Principal)
- N. Pauley (Asst. Principal)
- J. Duvall (1-5 Art)
- B. Mabry (1st Grade)
- F. Benner (3rd Grade)
- J. Appleyard (4th Grade)
- M. Marks (3-4 Gifted)
- S. Rosado (5th Spanish)
- G. Potts (5th Gifted)
- J. Gist (6th Math)
- K. Hoban (6th Lang. Arts)
- P. Craven (6th Social Studies)
- L. Santiago (6th Spanish)
- J. Smith (6th Art)
- C. Waters (6-7 Gifted)
- R. Kooken (7th Lang. Arts)
- N. Therrien (7th Art)
- C. Robinson (7th Math)
- J. Haugabrook (7th Science)
- K. Johnston (7th Social Studies)
- K. Johnston (7th Social Studies)
- Bassett (Art Teacher)
- C. Bronzino (8th Art)
- M. Bailey (Asst. Principal)
- B. Green (Safety Officer)
- S. Taylor (Baseball Coach)
- I. Seybold (After-School Program)
- Dean/McDonald (Track Coaches)
- Amherst College Football Coaches
- NSHS Football Coaches
- NSHS Booster Club
- F. Galishoff (H. 10th Gr. Lit)
- L. Vera (AP Computer Science) (Spanish)
- M. Gloede (H. Pre-Calculus)
- A. Cloud (H. 11th Gr. Lit)
- S. Kulik (H. Physics)
- J. Nott (AP Spanish)
- K. Cole (AP Art)
- M. Labranche (Counselor)
- Officer D. Moody (Safety Officer)
- Dr. V. Fegurson (Principal)
- Mr. W. Vincent (Asst. Principal)
- C. Y. Greene (Magnet Coordinator)

Community/Extended Family (ring):
- God Parents
- Aunts, Uncles
- Cousins
- Pastor K. Marcus (Sr. Pastor)
- Pastor W. Conner (Youth Pastor)
- Church Family
- Friends Attending College
- S. Freed (Math Tutor)
- K. McCord (Professor)
- Extended Family
- Dr. K. Mason (Pediatrician)
- Dr. M. Bassett (Principal)
- Positive Peers
- T. Carpenter (Track Coach)
- I. Snowden (Grandfather)
- 'Peach' (Grandmother)
- Granny 'E' (Grandmother)
- Tommy Cho Karate
- Safe Community
- Neighbors
- Parent's Business Associates
- W.H. Miller (Author)
- Camps, Special Programs
- Coaches
- Dr. K. Mason (Pediatrician)
- Positive Adult Role Models
- Tarus (Entrepreneur)
- Ralston (Barber)
- Reverend RC Hall
- A. Carreker (Retired NFL)
- Jalani Wynn (Brother)
- Mychal Wynn (Dad)

Inner circle (family):
- Nina Wynn (Mom)
- J. Polyne (Engineer)
- D. Smith (Real Estate Agent)
- R. McBride (Principal)
- G. Jones (VP/Engineer)

© Mychal Wynn • Rising Sun Publishing, Inc. (800) 524-2813
www.rspublishing.com

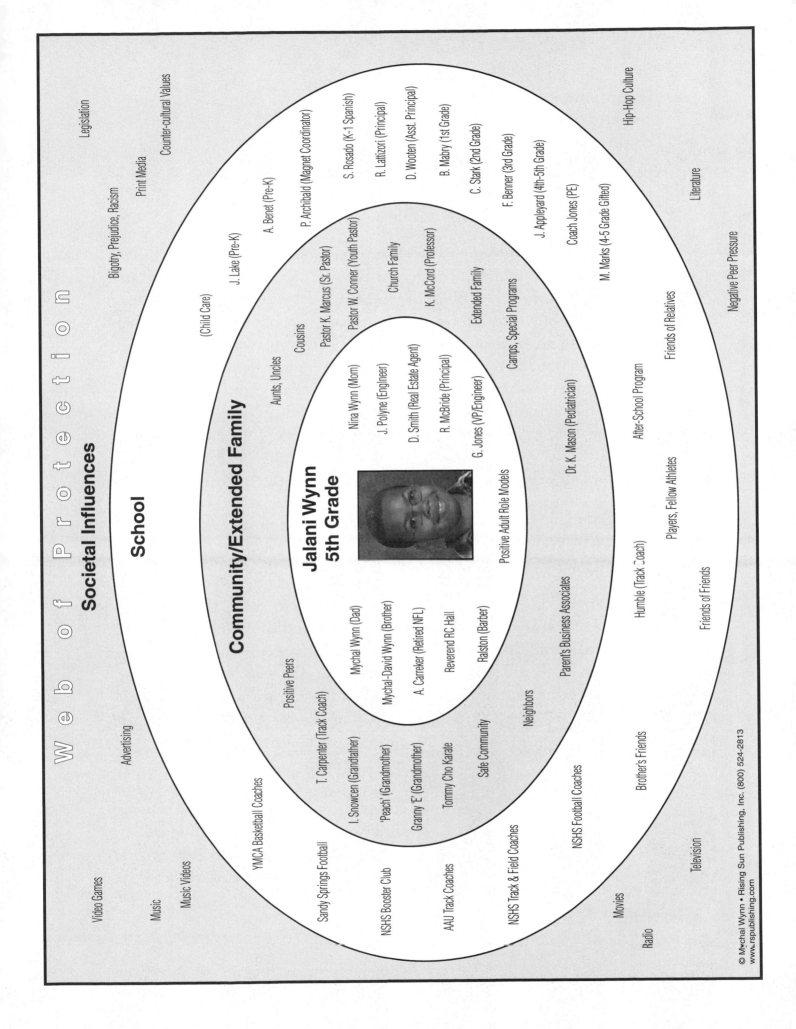

Web of Protection

Societal Influences

School

Community/Extended Family

Jalani Wynn
5th Grade

Inner circle (Community/Extended Family center):

Nina Wynn (Mom)
J. Polyne (Engineer)
D. Smith (Real Estate Agent)
R. McBride (Principal)
G. Jones (VP/Engineer)
Positive Adult Role Models

Mychal Wynn (Dad)
Mychal-David Wynn (Brother)
A. Carreker (Retired NFL)
Reverend RC Hall
Ralston (Barber)

Community/Extended Family circle:

(Child Care)
J. Lake (Pre-K)
Aunts, Uncles
Cousins
Pastor K. Marcus (Sr. Pastor)
Pastor W. Conner (Youth Pastor)
Church Family
K. McCord (Professor)
Extended Family
Camps, Special Programs
Dr. K. Mason (Pediatrician)
After-School Program
Players, Fellow Athletes
Friends of Friends
Humble (Track Coach)
Parent's Business Associates
Neighbors
Safe Community
Tommy Cho Karate
Granny 'E' (Grandmother)
'Peach' (Grandmother)
I. Snowcen (Grandfather)
T. Carpenter (Track Coach)
Positive Peers

School circle:

A. Benet (Pre-K)
P. Archibald (Magnet Coordinator)
S. Rosado (K-1 Spanish)
R. Lattizori (Principal)
D. Wooten (Asst. Principal)
B. Mabry (1st Grade)
C. Stark (2nd Grade)
F. Benner (3rd Grade)
J. Appleyard (4th-5th Grade)
Coach Jones (PE)
M. Marks (4-5 Grade Gifted)
NSHS Football Coaches
Brother's Friends
NSHS Track & Field Coaches
AAU Track Coaches
NSHS Booster Club
Sandy Springs Football
YMCA Basketball Coaches
Friends of Relatives

Societal Influences (outer):

Legislation
Counter-cultural Values
Print Media
Bigotry, Prejudice, Racism
Advertising
Music
Music Videos
Video Games
Radio
Movies
Television
Negative Peer Pressure
Literature
Hip-Hop Culture

2. Identifying individuals and programs needed in other circles and constructing relationships with them to ensure reinforcement of common values and consistent expectations.

3. Identifying the negative influences or counter-cultural values and working to reduce their influence, e.g., turning off the television, limiting involvement with certain peers.

You will notice that our sons share many influences, i.e., church, family friends, relatives, and athletic coaches. My wife and I have consciously identified the need for such influences which has led to the choices we have made as to which church to attend, which athletic coaches we allow to coach our sons, which friends and/or relatives we allow our sons to spend time with, and which after-school or recreational programs we allow them to participate in. These influences have provided positive male role models, reinforced our values, communicated consistent expectations, and provided people to intercede when our values and expectations are challenged by peers. Academically, our sons share a powerful set of influences—teachers. Our sons have had the same first-, third-, fourth-, fifth-grade, and gifted teachers. Subsequently, classroom instruction, classroom management, academic expectations, and home-school communication have provided a strong academic web of protection. Although our sons are six years apart, the relationships which my wife and I have had with their teachers has invariably and immeasurably contributed to their academic success.

To facilitate the growth, development, and maturation of boys, we must consciously understand and identify the web of influence which surrounds, protects, nurtures, and reinforces the needed values and lessons. In the *workbook,* is a 'Web of Protection' activity which I believe all teachers and parents should

complete. Better understanding the support mechanisms which may be missing from a young man's life will help parents, teachers, and coaches to structure a web of protection to provide support and positive influence to counteract the negative media images and peer pressures being directed at young men.

Negative Media Influences

The power of the media to influence both the images which Black males have of themselves and the images which the society at-large has of Black males is undeniable. The powerfully negative influence of the media on the attitude, behaviors, and consciousness of Black males is only countered by the nature and amount of positive influences within the inner rings of the web of protection. You'll notice from the illustrations how the media influences within the lives of our sons are preempted by family, friends, relatives, teachers, coaches, programs, and positive adult influences. The absence of Black men as fathers, mentors, coaches, and teachers, to provide positive male influences, and the fact that mothers, many of whom are single-parents, are overloaded with jobs, managing a household, managing a budget which is frequently short of money, and raising other siblings; television programs, commercials, movies, music, and music videos have far greater influences within the lives of many Black males and are defining their values and influencing their behaviors (most of which are negative, counterproductive, and antagonistic). Typical of media imagery is:

- Aggressiveness in walk, talk, and demeanor.

- Use of profanity and combative behavior when confronting authority figures.

- Sexual promiscuity, sexually explicit language, degradation of and violence toward women.

- Idolization of intimidating clothing styles, use of tattoos, hand gestures, a confrontational mentality, and certain body images (e.g., hair, weight, piercings).

- Desensitizing of violent acts.

- Association of alcohol and drug use with being cool.

- The ultimate goal of financial success is to purchase cars, motorcycles, jewelry, houses, and to have sex.

- The use of violence as the primary means of resolving conflicts.

- Fame and financial success is associated with manhood and such success insulates a person from having to face the consequences of his actions.

- The primary opportunities for personal and financial success for Black males is in entertainment and professional athletics. Neither of which require education as a prerequisite.

Negative Peer Pressure

Each of the media influences is exacerbated through the continual reinforcement among peers who have, themselves, been influenced by media images and popular cultural norms and values. Peer pressure is exerted within the school community, on athletic teams, and through the daily formal and informal interactions between males. These pressures to a great extent influence attitudes and behaviors as males seek to conform and belong to peer groups.

As Black males struggle with a sense of self-identity the magnitude of media influences and peer pressures bear a correlation to any accompanying lack of long-term focus and a young man's higher-order decision-making abilities. As a result of many Black males growing up in poverty, lacking access to positive male role models and influences, and lacking exposure to successful Black professionals and college graduates within their family units and/or surrounding community they frequently lack a future focus. It is not uncommon to hear urban males talk about being lucky to live to '21.' Minor disagreements escalate into fatal encounters. The lack of long-term focus is compounded by males who have not developed higher-order and critical-thinking skills. When males in the primary grades fall behind in literacy and fail to develop the regions of the brain responsible for complex thinking and problem-solving, their actions are highly impulsive. Males who are not taught how to think, reason, and problem-solve continue to demonstrate emotionally-driven responses to conflicts well beyond normal adolescent development. The added media influence of desensitizing children to violent acts results in frequent and tragic consequences.

Peer group pressures reinforces and/or influences:

- Negative attitudes and language toward women.

- Irresponsible sexual behavior (i.e., "I ain't your baby's daddy!").

- Inappropriate sexual behavior and use of inappropriate sexually explicit language.

- Use and dissemination of sexually-explicit and pornographic materials.

- Perpetration of violence through street gang, athletic team, or fraternity initiation rites and peer influences.

- Random acts of gun violence, robbery, burglary, and assaults.

- Random and unexplainable escalation of seemingly simple disagreements into violent and uncontrollable responses.

- Confrontational attitudes toward adult authority.

- Encouragement of disruptive classroom and/or school-wide behaviors.

- Disrespect and destruction of other people's property.

- Lying to parents, teachers, and coaches.

- Devaluing of academic pursuits.

- Devaluing of Standard English usage.

Transition Through Adolescence

It is incumbent upon adults to pay closer attention to the values, attitudes, language, and behaviors which are being directed toward young people through the media and internalized by their peer group. Given the magnitude of the negative images being directed toward and portraying Black males, parents and teachers must understand that teaching reading, writing, and arithmetic must be supplemented by a systemic and consistent focus on values, personal responsibility, standards of excellence, language, attitudes, behaviors, and mannerisms.

Young men are too frequently receiving their information pertaining to manhood, personal responsibility, treatment of others, and relationships with women from peers and the media. Few formal rites of passage programs exist within churches, schools, and communities, and those most influential within the lives of young men (i.e., coaches, teachers, parents, pastors, and administrators) frequently fail to recognize the lessons which must be taught.

Such personal attributes as diligence, determination, dedication to purpose, fortitude, perseverance, compassion, respect for self, and respect for the property and rights of others must be taught and continually reinforced through the thoughtful committed efforts of the adults who are influential within the lives of young men. In workshops I have frequently raised the question, "What is the least effective method of instruction?" Without hesitation, audiences respond, "Lecture." Then, when I ask, "What is the most frequently utilized method of instruction when dealing with the negative behavior of Black males?" Parents and teachers alike, begrudgingly admit, "Lecture."

We must recognize that young people, as they make their transition through early adolescence, puberty, young adulthood, college students, and even into the ranks of newly-weds, will be in need of the continuing guidance and wisdom, which only those older, more experienced, and who genuinely care about them can offer. While they need our guidance they are unlikely to listen to our lectures.

To effectively convey the messages and reinforce the needed values we must identify and use:

- lessons
- stories,
- proverbs,
- parables,
- programs, and
- other adults

Developing leadership skills and implementing the strategies needed to encourage and nurture these values will only occur when we incorporate such lessons into our vision of the type of men whom we are helping Black males to become.

Limiting Access to Negative Media Images

Television Programming: My wife and I limit the amount of time and access to television programming. We simply believe that if our sons aren't 'A' students there isn't any time for television during the school year between Sunday evening and Thursday evening. In the case of our younger son, who is an 'A' student, between the amount of time devoted to after-school activities, e.g., martial arts, football, rehearsals for school plays, track and field, completion of school work, and preparation for tests and quizzes there is no time for television.

We do not see the cultural, intellectual, artistic, or intrinsic value in the vast majority of talk shows, sitcoms, music videos, or reality shows for elementary, middle, or high school students. The value to adults is debatable, however, adults can decide their own programming. Our sons don't have the luxury.

Music: My wife and I try as much as possible to listen to the lyrics within the music our sons listen to. Clearly, censorship is required to varying degrees for both of them. We don't allow either of them to listen to music through head phones when we are gathered together at home or in the car. Whatever, music is being played, everyone listens to, subsequently, the music has to be appropriate for everyone to hear. The same applies to movies, both at the theater and on DVD.

Internet: My wife and I have eased the restrictions on our sixteen-year-old son in regards to internet access and participation in internet chat-rooms. As a high school junior, he is a year away from college and subsequently our ability to monitor his internet access. While we continue to limit access to internet web sites and the time in internet chat-rooms, we are constantly reaffirming how a person's core values and beliefs should not be discarded behind the cloak of screen names and the anonymity of internet users. Our older son doesn't have internet access in his bedroom or behind a closed door in any room. Our ten-year-old son doesn't have any unsupervised internet access and isn't allowed to participate in chat-room discussions.

Engage young men in critical-thinking discussions of the language, values, and images being communicated:

1. Develop bulletin boards at school and post onto the refrigerator at home, news stories, magazine articles, magazine and newspaper ads, music lyrics, and interviews. Use them to stimulate critical-thinking discussions of the images, values, and behaviors being promoted.

    "Is this the type of woman you would want to marry or to be the mother of your children?"

    "Does this represent your definition of manhood?"

    "If there is so much money available to be spent on cars, motorcycles, jewelry, gold teeth, tattoos, drugs, and alcohol why is there so little money available for schools, teachers, community programs, recreation centers, college scholarships, or for young people to start businesses?"

    "Would you want your mama or your daughter shaking her butt in a music video?"

    "If Michael Vick [Atlanta Falcons (NFL) quarterback] could get a 137 million dollar contract, how much money do you think Arthur Blank [Atlanta Falcons team owner] makes?"

    "If Lebron James [Cleveland Cavaliers (NBA) basketball player] received a 90 million dollar endorsement from Nike, how much money does Nike make by selling shoes and sportswear?"

    "How many high school basketball players are there in the United States [549,500]? How many high school football players are there

[983,600]? Only 3 out of every 100 basketball players will have an opportunity to play on a college basketball team. Only 8 out of every 100,000 will be drafted into the NBA. Only 6 out of every 100 high school football players will have an opportunity to play college football and only 25 out of every 100,000 will be drafted into the NFL."

2. Develop a bulletin board of the major problems confronting your community:

    - AIDS and STDs
    - Teen pregnancies
    - Crime and violence
    - Gangs
    - Drugs
    - Suicides
    - Abuse
    - Unemployment
    - Lack of recreational facilities
    - Lack of positive role models
    - Police brutality
    - High school dropouts
    - Incarceration

3. Use whatever problems you identify as captions across the top of the bulletin board.

4. Begin gathering articles, lyrics, advertisements, and interviews representing positive and/or negative influences by recording artists, athletes, politicians, the media, or other influential people. Post onto a bulletin board or have students maintain scrap books.

5. After a period of time of gathering and discussing articles have students write a paper on what they would do to positively influence their community if they achieved their career dreams.

6. Discuss how the self-image of people is tied to the clothing labels, shoes, team jerseys, tattoos, hair styles, and other images promoted by athletes and entertainers and why some people are willing to kill others and risk life in prison over a pair of sneakers or a team jacket.

Consciously Influence Peer Culture

Counteracting the negative influences exerted through peer pressure requires a direct and active involvement by adult stakeholders throughout the school community. Whether it is parents taking the time to visit classrooms or have lunch with children in elementary school, supporting clubs and student events in middle school, supporting the wide range of athletic programs and student activities in high school, or providing mentorship to college students, adults must be involved in the lives of young people. Strategies should include both direct and indirect adult influence (i.e., through peers).

Adults exert direct influence by:

- having relationships with young people which provide frequent opportunities to share experiences, provide insight, and share stories which inspire hope and provide suggestions for dealing with issues and conflicts;

- establishing the parameters established in classrooms, households, and in school-related programs and activities which define an expected standard of behavior, acceptable methods of resolving conflicts, and the level of compassion expected to be directed toward others;

- being physically involved in activities and at events which may result in conflicts and/or inappropriate behaviors;

- consciously recognizing, rewarding, and validating a code of conduct and standard of behavior;

- being aware of the issues unique to your school community, e.g., sexual promiscuity, suicides, depression, anxiety disorders, gangs, drugs, bullying;

- spending quality time involved in the activities which are important to young men, e.g., sports events, movies, concerts, parties, shopping, outdoor activities;

- taking advantage of long rides, vacations, or evenings together as opportunities to talk about issues of concern to young men or sharing hobbies and areas of interests;

- taking advantage of opportunities to exert direct influence by coordinating activities, planning events, and/or exposing young men to a wide range of opportunities;

- taking advantage of the opportunity to discuss music, fashion choices, hair styles, and the other cultural images; and/or

- taking advantage of opportunities to discuss current issues, topics being discussed at school, and issues emanating from popular culture.

I consciously work at spending quality time with my sons. The time spent together takes many forms—coaching their respective athletic teams (basketball, track, baseball, football, and soccer); attending public events (sports, theater, plays, musicals, Olympics); attending school events (plays, sports, awards, school-wide programs); fishing; amusement parks; travel; vacations; college visits; church; track and field meets; movies; playing video games; assisting with homework and school projects; taking photographs of school-related activities; and commuting to and from school. I have taken advantage of the opportunity to sit and talk with them and their friends as an opportunity to better understand what they think, to challenge their ideas, and to share my ideas, wisdom, and experiences.

On a typical school day I drive my older son to and from his high school and rarely a day goes by without our discussing school, friends, issues, and current events.

Whenever I am with my younger son I look for opportunities to challenge his thinking, further expand and explore his ideas, and to help him to think through his thoughts and behaviors.

These scenarios are repeated between my wife and our sons. She too, is always probing their thoughts and consciously trying to stay in touch with the issues they are challenged with each school year and as they journey through each new level of physical, emotional, social, and intellectual growth and development.

We also utilize the opportunity to have family dinners on Sundays. This is the time when we pause in our busy lives to eat together as a family. Sometimes we light candles and enjoy a formal dinner at the dining room table. Other times we sit informally in the kitchen. Wherever we are sitting we take the time to go around the table and to allow each person to share some of their issues of concern or to simply share some of the things which happened in their lives during the previous week.

Oftentimes young men are most in need of adult influence when they least want adults to be involved. Particularly, during puberty and their teen years. While our ten-year-old son is fine riding the school bus, it's a blessing to have the opportunity to drive our sixteen-year-old son to and from school. In the twenty-minute drive we have an opportunity to discuss a lot of issues. There are times when my wife and I can tell there are things on his mind which he isn't going to share with us. This is why we consciously constructed his web of protection. We try to be sensitive to when young people need other adults of other young people to talk to. As was outlined during the discussion on constructing a web of protection, there are steps which adults can take to positively influence the Black male peer group.

Adults exert influence through peers indirectly when they:

- identify those young men who are respected by their peers and who model the type of values and level of achievement which you would like others to aspire toward and use them to inspire their friends;

- take seriously the responsibility of identifying young men as captains of athletic teams, officers in organizations, or project leaders in classrooms as an opportunity to identify and recognize those young people who embody the types of values and provide the types of examples you want to reinforce;

- provide opportunities for interaction with young men who have gone through some of the difficult choices confronting their respective age group, i.e., professional–college, college–high school, high school–middle, and middle–elementary;

- coordinate town-hall style meetings or discussion groups where young men have an opportunity to share and challenge each other's ideas and opinions;

- coordinate opportunities for cross-socioeconomic, cross-ethnic, and cross-gender discussion groups to stimulate discussions pertaining to academic goals, attitudes, dreams, aspirations, and current issues;

- identify clubs and organizations to involve young men in, e.g., 100 Black Men, fraternities, Upward Bound, Jack and Jill, Masons, Boy Scouts, Boys & Girls Clubs, Big Brothers Big Sisters, after-school programs, summer programs and camps, mentoring, and leadership organizations;

- take advantage of opportunities for long rides to museums, plays, college campuses, concerts, and athletic events to listen to the thoughts, ideas, beliefs, values, and opinions of peers; and/or

- take a young man out of organizations or activities that do not reinforce your values and expectations and be aware of the time spent with peers in unsupervised activities.

Using and Accessing the Curriculum

To combat the negative influences received from the media and reinforced by peers requires:

1. Use of the existing curriculum to teach and reinforce the needed lessons.

2. Identifying supplemental materials and programs (i.e., literature, stories, proverbs, guest speakers, field trips, writing, art, and oratorical competitions).

Having previously identified the cultural issues, peer pressures, and circles of influence impacting upon the attitudes and behaviors of young men, we need simply to use what we now know to identify the stories contained within the literature, history, social studies, mathematics, and science lessons to expand their thinking and subsequently influence their actions. There are frequent opportunities to build self-esteem, expand the consciousness, and combat the negative influences of media imagery and peer pressures by:

- identifying and recognizing facts as they relate to Black influence across subject areas, i.e., writers, poets, actors, actresses, scientists, inventors, explorers, mathematicians, educators, architects, political figures, entrepreneurs, and world leaders;

- identifying opportunities to demonstrate learning through multiple intelligences-related activities, i.e., constructing models, oral presentations, musical, dance, and theatrical performances, artistic renderings, plays, skits, role playing, raps, poetry, and videos;

- utilizing multiple intelligences-related activities to structure cooperative groups where students accept research and presentation responsibilities within their dominant areas of intelligence contributing to multi-media and multi-faceted group presentations;

- creating visual imagery through bulletin boards, walls, display cases, T-shirts, and posters, recognizing and reinforcing Black achievement to be displayed throughout the school and throughout the school year;

- creating visual displays of career themes relating specifically to areas of the curriculum which in essence answer the question, "Why do I need to know this?";

- utilizing opportunities to introduce young men to Black writers and literary figures in a conscious effort to wean them away from television and video games into reading and literary analysis;

- encouraging research in regards to Black historical figures for required book reports and research papers;

- encouraging research in regards to Black historical figures within student interest areas, i.e., professional sports, entertainment, clothing manufacturers, hair stylists, artists, actors, and musicians; and/or

- encouraging students to tailor assignments to areas of interests or to areas of need (i.e., learning more about who they are, where they came from, and the historical achievements of Black people).

Schools created a whole new lexicon for today's miseducated students. They are called At Risk Students, Learning Disabled, Mentally Educable Handicapped—the list is infinite. I call them the students of Teacher Inabilities, rather than learning disabilities.

Think for a moment—Abraham Lincoln was fourteen years of age before he learned to read. By today's standards, he probably would have been placed in a learning disabled class and never had the opportunity to become President of the United States.

Einstein was often accused of daydreaming in the classroom. The teacher never bothered to discover that he was trying to determine the radius of the shadows that came through his classroom window.

It is said that Edison tried over two hundred times to develop the light bulb and finally declared, 'At least I now know how not to do it.' Each of these people used stumbling blocks as stepping stones. Each of these individuals turned lemons into lemonade. Can't we, too, do that with our students?

— Marva Collins, Ordinary Students: Extraordinary Teachers

When our younger son, Jalani, was in the fourth grade, his class did an interdisciplinary unit of study involving the Medieval historical period in Europe. His teacher supported his desire to focus his research on the historical development of the Moorish civilization in North Africa and their influence on European culture during their incursion into Europe and conquest of Spain.

The culminating activity for the unit was student presentations of their research through book reports, research papers, art renderings, skits, models, poetry, songs, musical performances, and displays. What, for many students could have easily been a boring unit of study, was able to tap the intrinsic motivation of students by allowing opportunities to express their understanding of the unit of study through their unique gifts and abilities. In the case of our son, he was not only able to focus his research efforts on an area of study which was of interest and provided cultural relevance, his studies helped to reinforce lessons and values my wife and I teach at home, i.e., personal pride, the significant pre-slavery achievements of Africans and African descendents, and the importance of reading, research, and education.

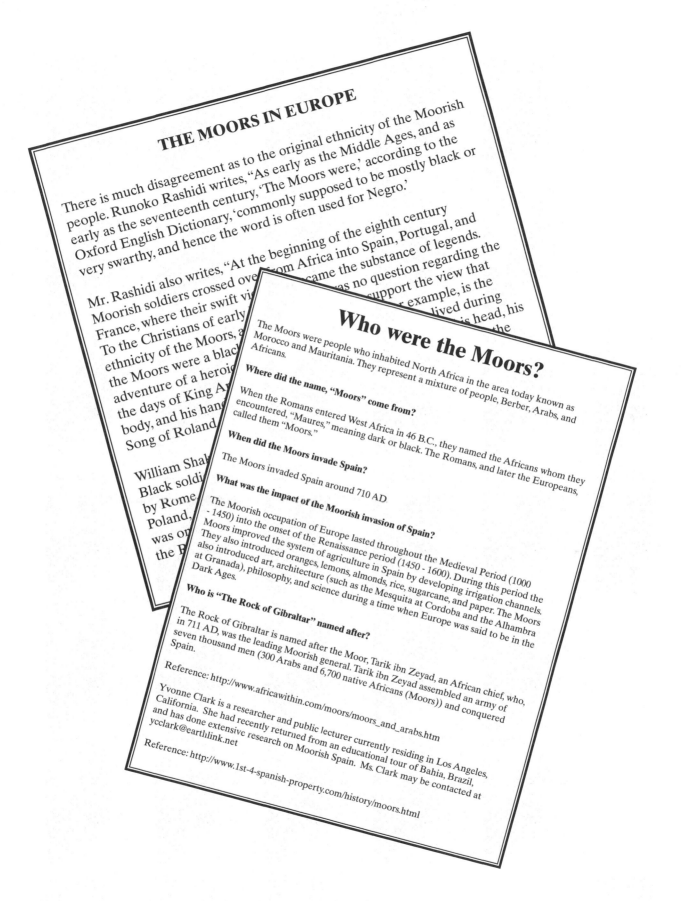

THE MOORS IN EUROPE

There is much disagreement as to the original ethnicity of the Moorish people. Runoko Rashidi writes, "As early as the Middle Ages, and as early as the seventeenth century, 'The Moors were,' according to the Oxford English Dictionary, 'commonly supposed to be mostly black or very swarthy, and hence the word is often used for Negro.'

Mr. Rashidi also writes, "At the beginning of the eighth century Moorish soldiers crossed over from Africa into Spain, Portugal, and France, where their swift vi[...] came the substance of legends. To the Christians of early [...] as no question regarding the ethnicity of the Moors, a[...] support the view that the Moors were a blac[...] lived during adventure of a heroi[...] [...]s head, his the days of King A[...] [...] the body, and his han[...] Song of Roland[...]

William Shak[...] Black soldi[...] by Rome[...] Poland,[...] was o[...] the P[...]

Who were the Moors?

The Moors were people who inhabited North Africa in the area today known as Morocco and Mauritania. They represent a mixture of people, Berber, Arabs, and Africans.

Where did the name, "Moors" come from?

When the Romans entered West Africa in 46 B.C., they named the Africans whom they encountered, "Maures," meaning dark or black. The Romans, and later the Europeans, called them "Moors."

When did the Moors invade Spain?

The Moors invaded Spain around 710 AD.

What was the impact of the Moorish invasion of Spain?

The Moorish occupation of Europe lasted throughout the Medieval Period (1000 - 1450) into the onset of the Renaissance period (1450 - 1600). During this period the Moors improved the system of agriculture in Spain by developing irrigation channels. They also introduced oranges, lemons, almonds, rice, sugarcane, and paper. The Moors also introduced art, architecture (such as the Mesquita at Cordoba and the Alhambra at Granada), philosophy, and science during a time when Europe was said to be in the Dark Ages.

Who is "The Rock of Gibraltar" named after?

The Rock of Gibraltar is named after the Moor, Tarik ibn Zeyad, an African chief, who, in 711 AD, was the leading Moorish general. Tarik ibn Zeyad assembled an army of seven thousand men (300 Arabs and 6,700 native Africans (Moors)) and conquered Spain.

Reference: http://www.africawithin.com/moors/moors_and_arabs.htm

Yvonne Clark is a researcher and public lecturer currently residing in Los Angeles, California. She had recently returned from an educational tour of Bahia, Brazil, and has done extensive research on Moorish Spain. Ms. Clark may be contacted at ycclark@earthlink.net

Reference: http://www.1st-4-spanish-property.com/history/moors.html

Not only is it important to use the existing curriculum to teach and reinforce the necessary values, young men must be encouraged to fully access the curriculum in terms of the variety of classes and academic levels of available classes. Walk through the classrooms of both urban and rural high schools and the numbers of Black males in honors, AG (academically talented), or AP (Advanced Placement) classes is so small they are barely noticeable to anyone but themselves. They know they sit alone, separated from friends and isolated from their social-cultural support system. They are further isolated in the locker room, at parties, or at weekend gatherings where they cannot share classroom experiences with peers.

Perhaps Carter G. Woodson best summarized this phenomenon in *The Mis-Education of the Negro*, where he notes:

> *When you control a man's thinking you do not have to worry about his actions. You do not have to tell him not to stand here or go yonder. He will find his 'proper place' and will stay in it. You do not need to send him to the back door. He will go without being told. In fact, if there is no back door, he will cut one for his special benefit.*

The unspoken signals Black males are receiving in regards to their 'proper place' is that they belong in lower level academic classes. The experiences of my wife and I with this issue is a highly personal one, as witnessed through the experiences of our sons, conversations with other Black students and parents, and our discussions with teachers. While the reasons for the tragic lack of Black males in higher-level math and science classes is not explained by definitive research, the anecdotal evidence and experiences of Black students and families identifies several areas which can, and should be addressed.

As previously cited:

- 30 percent of Black high school students take advanced mathematics courses compared to 45 percent of Whites.

- 5 percent of Black high school students take a fourth year of a foreign language with 2 percent taking an AP foreign language course.

- 12 percent of Black high school students take science classes as high as chemistry and physics.

- 27 percent of Black high school students take advanced English.

- Black students take AP exams at a rate of 53 per 1,000 students. The rate for Hispanic students is 115 per 1,000 and for Whites it is 185 per 1,000.

- The average Black SAT scores are 433V and 426M, for Whites they are 529V and 531M.

- The average Black ACT score is 16.9, for Whites it is 21.8.

Ensure Full Access

Black males are unlikely to fully access the complete range of programs, opportunities, clubs, and extracurricular activities within any public school district. Despite a wide-spread belief that they are unmotivated, the fact is, neither the young men or their families are likely to fully-understand the complete scope of the opportunities within the school district and the potential impact such programs can have on a young man's long-term dreams and aspirations. For example, our older son has had an art focus since his passion for drawing stick people revealed itself in the first grade. His passion for drawing was woven through his educational class schedule, summer camps, and after-school programs, as part of a long-term college admission plan. Many Black boys reveal their passion for art through the graffiti on subway trains, freight trains, buildings, freeway overpasses, sidewalks, desks, and rest room walls. Research has shown Black children are actively engaged in the creative intelligences, i.e., music, art, acting, and dance as early as three years old. Helping parents to understand how to enroll their sons into such programs and helping them to develop kindergarten-through-college course schedules which provide frequent opportunities for their sons to be actively engaged in passionate areas of interests can hook young men on learning early and connect them to school in a way which insulates them from the many negative influences of peers and pop culture messages which devalue education. The books, *A Middle School Plan for Students with College-Bound Dreams,* and *A High School Plan for Students with College-Bound Dreams* can assist parents in developing a complete seven-year plan for their sons from the sixth grade through the twelfth grade. It is important for teachers, counselors, and coaches to understand the obstacles of many young men and their families who simply do not know how to plan a kindergarten-through-twelfth-grade journey through the typical public school system. Course schedules, extracurricular opportunities, special programs, student clubs, and even the complete range of athletic programs often go unnoticed by Black males and their families.

AP Classes

There is a commonly-held misperception by Black males that honors and AP classes are beyond their capacity. While the classes can certainly be more challenging, many young men are surprised to discover they are able to do extremely well in such classes. Particularly, in those classes where teachers recruit, support, and encourage them. When I refer to the illustration in workshops where I help parents to understand the potential tuition savings they can receive as a result of their children receiving college credit for AP classes taken in high school I have seen parents turn to their sons and say, "You're smart enough to take some of those AP classes. You like to draw don't you? Don't tell me you can't take AP Art!"

5 AP classes and a score of '5' on each AP exam can save $39,620.00 in freshman tuition, fees, room, and board at Yale by enabling a student to achieve advanced standing and enter as a sophomore:

2003-2004 Yale COA = $39,620.00

If each AP class is worth an additional 7 quality points[6] being added to a student's GPA, the student would receive a higher class ranking as the result of receiving an additional 35 quality points.

5 x 7 = 35

This illustration was taken from page 71 in the book, *A High School Plan for Students with College-Bound Dreams*

It is important for parents and students to develop strong relationships with their high school counselor. The typical high school has so many course offerings and so many teachers there will be many opportunities to both succeed and/or fail. One class which appears difficult is made easier through an effective teacher. Another class, seemingly less difficult can result in a failing grade due to an ineffective teacher. Our older son took a regular chemistry class when he could have, and should have, taken the honors class. Both the regular and honors class were taught by the same teacher who was an excellent teacher and made both the regular and honors classes interesting for students. His counselor didn't advise us and he didn't suggest it. It was only in conversation with another Black parent who asked, "I thought for sure Mychal-David would have been in the honors chemistry class, Nick loves it." As a result of that conversation, our son began his journey into honors physics, honors tenth-grade literature, honors eleventh-grade literature, honors algebra II, honors pre-calculus ...We have also consciously sought to build relationships with the parents of other young men to encourage their sons to take honors and AP classes.

Corrective Actions for Teachers:

- Ensure that each young man has a kindergarten-through-twelfth-grade course schedule based on his areas of interest, i.e., art, music, dance, science, math, athletics, computers, acting, or talking.

- Help each young man to set up a subject-area binder for each class, each school year to contain the course syllabus, assignment log, monthly calendar, study sheets, and tabs (i.e., homework, notes, tests and quizzes, extra credit).

- Discuss and/or create a visual of how each class relates to his kindergarten-through-twelfth-grade plans.

- Create a parent information sheet which outlines what parents can do to assist students in achieving the highest grade in your class and establish a preferred home-school communication method.

- Tell students/families at the beginning of the grading period what they will be expected to know at the end of the grading period.

- Clarify the standards in parent-friendly language.

- Create at-home tips (refrigerator sheets) to reinforce content areas.

- Ensure that unit tests, quizzes, and exams are aligned with the standards, reinforce problem-solving approaches, and reinforce testing language (i.e., contrast, compare, and most likely).

- Identify student incentives (i.e., grading methodology, make-up policy, extra credit opportunities) to tap students' intrinsic motivation.

- Establish a goal of 100 percent time-on-task, for example:

55 minute period:
5 minute student-directed transition activity
5 minute teacher-directed transition activity
20 minute instructional activity (major concept)
15 minute student-directed study, discussion, or application
5 minute teacher-directed wrap-up
5 minute student-directed transition

Thus, a 55 minute class period is fully-planned and accounted for

- Provide students and parents with clear grading rubrics for major projects and assignments which are written in parent-friendly language. Grading rubrics should provide examples of quality work and clear step-by-step instructions of how to successfully meet your expectations.

Book Report Grading Rubric:
  5 points: Cover Page
20 points: 2 pages, double-spaced, correct grammar
50 points: Answer who, what, when, where, and how (10 pts. ea.)
10 points: 5 questions that the reader should be able to answer (2 pts. ea.)
10 points: Answer key for each question (2 pts. ea.)
  5 points: Attach grading rubric to back page

100 points total

15 points possible extra credit for typed, illustrated, or submitted early (5 pts. ea.)

Fostering Reading Literacy

The importance of reading literacy, fluency, and an appreciation of books and published literature cannot be underestimated or compromised. The current school, community, church, and household influences of Black male literacy simply does not do enough to encourage reading and reading literacy. Young men are receiving their information from radio and television talk shows, music, and music videos. Black males are more likely to have a trophy case full of athletic awards, medals, and trophies than they are to have a single book in their bedroom. They are more likely to have a collection of video games rather than a  collection of books, and they are more likely to receive a video game from an adult for Christmas or their birthday than they are to receive a book!

Lack of reading fluency and proficiency is a clear predictor of future incarceration. A popular, yet unproven, internet story suggests that third grade reading scores are used to predict the number of prison beds which will be needed in the future. Whether or not there is any validity to this story research does show the majority of the state and federal prison inmates lack high levels of literacy, many of whom are functionally illiterate.

In *Reading for Change: Performance and Engagement Across Countries*, published by the Organization for Economic Co-Operation and Development (OECD), it's noted:

> *Lewis (2002) claims that some states in the United States use third-grade reading statistics to determine how many prison beds they will need in 10 years' time. Though this might seem far-fetched, it has been reported that half of all adults in U.S. federal prisons cannot read or write at all. The typical 25-year-old male inmate functions two or three grade levels below the grade actually completed. (Bellarado, 1986).*

The Ohio Rehabilitation and Corrective Services noted:

In Fiscal Year 2004, 23,866 offenders were committed to the state prison system (20,987 males; 2,879 females).

The average reading level of inmates received by the Department is a grade level of 7.6. Further 85.5 percent of the offenders do not have a verified high school diploma or a high school equivalency diploma (GED). Approximately 30 percent of the males and 20 percent of the females are tested with reading levels of less than sixth-grade level and are considered functionally illiterate.

A 1984 Lehigh University study for the National Institute of Justice noted:

Of more than 1000 male and female prison inmates in three states, the study found that 42 percent had some kind of learning deficiency, defined as functioning academically below the level of fifth grade.

Corrective Actions to Increase Literacy:

*   Young men should see adults read.

*   Read to children early, often, and regularly.

*   Build reading time into your area of influence, i.e., classroom, athletic team, home, church, or community program.

*   Establish the connection between literature and a young man's dreams, aspirations, and interests, i.e., video game playing, sports participation, and extracurricular activities. The easiest and obvious connection for parents is to have their sons read the books that movies and cartoon programs are based on.

*   Start a 'Back Pack' book club on your team, and in your church, community program, and school. Require young men to be actively engaged in reading a book for 365 days a year (with the noted exception of leap year). Have them live with their current book by keeping it in

their back pocket or in their backpack. Randomly stop them and inquire as to the book they are currently reading, to explain what the book is about, and what they're learning from reading it.

- Ensure that every young man has an in-home library reflecting a broad range of literature.

- Provide frequent opportunities for students to read aloud, whether through classroom presentations, reading to younger children, or reading at home to parents.

- When traveling together, turn off the radio and have young men read to you and encourage them to read for meaning.

  When my older son was nine years old, he and I took a drive from Atlanta to Florida. I turned off the radio during the entire seven-hour drive and I had him read aloud from the book, Aesop's Fables. I encouraged him to change his voice when reading quoted dialogue, pausing at periods, and demonstrating the appropriate expressions of the characters.

- Don't assume young men can read because of their physical size or grade level. Many young men have become experts at masking their lack of reading proficiency.

- Integrate reading, writing, and book reports into your strategies of character, moral, intellectual, and spiritual development. Rather than referring a child to the office or in-school detention where he is able to sit idly, assign reading, writing, language, and vocabulary-building activities.

- Closely monitor reading proficiency and standardized reading, writing, and language scores.

- Ensure early intervention.

- Create a literacy rich environment by keeping books wherever there are young men, i.e., in your car, on tables, in kitchens, in locker rooms, in classrooms, in churches, and in recreational centers.

- Create a reading list for young men within your sphere of influence, i.e., parent, coach, counselor, teacher, or mentor. Encourage young men to develop their own list of favorite books and authors.

- Create reading corners (e.g., home, school, or church).

- If you coach an athletic team, require players to have books for each road trip, track meet, and overnight stay.

- Parents should assign children weekly book reports.

Changes in the Teaching of Math & Science

Algebra is considered the gateway class to higher-level mathematics. The typical high school math track for students being prepared for college enrollment is algebra I, geometry, algebra II, and either algebra III/ trigonometry or pre-calculus. Many school districts provide students with the opportunity to not only successfully complete algebra I and geometry during middle school, but award students high school credit toward their high school graduation requirements. Subsequently, students are able to enter onto an even more aggressive math track in high school (e.g., pre-calculus, calculus, AP calculus AB/BC, AP statistics, and AP computer science) which may provide college credit (in the case of AP classes) and provide excellent preparation for technical or pre-medical areas of study in college, i.e., medicine, science, and engineering.

Black males are among the least likely students to enroll into advanced math and science classes and are among the most likely students to be directed toward trade and vocational studies rather than college preparatory studies. They are still being directed toward becoming employees rather than employers, toward become voters rather than policy makers, not to mention they are the most likely students to be relegated to remedial and lower level classes. Changing this dynamic requires a radical change in thinking and raising of expectations. An example of such a revolutionary change in thinking is the *Algebra Project* in Cambridge, Massachusetts which is inspiring and preparing Black students for entrance into higher-level high school mathematics classes:

The Algebra Project was born out of one parent's concern with the mathematics education of his children in the public schools of Cambridge, Massachusetts. In 1982, Bob Moses was invited by Mary Lou Mehrling, his daughter's eighth-grade teacher, to help several students with the study of algebra. Moses, who had taught secondary school mathematics in New York City and Tanzania, decided that an appropriate goal [vision] for those students was to have enough skills in algebra to qualify for honors math and science courses in high school. His success in producing the first students from the Open Program of the Martin Luther King School to pass the city-wide algebra examination and qualify for ninth-grade honors geometry was a testament to his skill as a teacher. It also highlighted a serious problem: most students in the Open Program were not expected to do well in mathematics.

The answers to the questions, 'What is algebra for?' and 'Why do we want children to study it?', play an important role in the Algebra Project. The project assumes that there is a new standard in assessing mathematics education, a standard of mathematical literacy. In this not-so-far future, a broad range of mathematical skills will join traditional skills in reading and writing in the definition of literacy. These mathematical skills will not only be important in gaining access to college and math- and science-related careers, but will also be necessary for full participation in the economic life of this society. In this context, the Algebra Project has as a goal that schools embrace a standard of mathematics education that requires that children be mathematically literate. Such a goal will necessitate a community of educators including parents, teachers and school administrators who understand the paramount importance of mathematics education in providing access to the economic life of this society. An answer to the question 'What do we need to include in the mathematics education of every middle school student?' also frames the Algebra Project.

Bob Moses, is not only a positive male role model, but has a clear vision of the level of math and science literacy necessary for Black students to fully participate in government, business, and society at-large. He believes math literacy is a civil rights issue and failure to prepare and encourage Black students to pursue higher-level mathematics denies them opportunities and full access to educational and career pursuits.

Science

Dr. Freeman Hrabowski, a graduate of Hampton Institute and President of the University of Maryland Baltimore County, developed the highly successful Meyerhoff Program for aspiring Black scientists. The program, which began in 1989, was developed with a clear mission/vision to provide mentoring of targeted Black men initially, then Black women, to prepare them for careers in science, engineering and medical research. The first group of Meyerhoff Scholars were 19 young Black men who enrolled in the fall of 1989. A year later the program was expanded to include Black women and students from across

the country. The program has graduated more than 200 students to date, 98 percent of whom are Black. The vast majority have gone on to graduate school. Hrabowski attributes the success of the program to committed professors who foster a culture of collaboration, responsibility, and high expectations among students:

The sophomores help the freshmen and so on. Not only are they expected to excel academically, but they are encouraged to work with inner-city kids and pursue artistic interests as well.

Hrabowski further sites:

Today, UMBC has become the leading producer of African Americans going on to earn Ph.Ds in science and engineering.

The average combined SAT score for incoming freshmen in the program for fall 1997 was 1285, considerably higher than the national average for Black freshmen (859) or White freshmen (1060). A student's success is further assured by the individualized attention Meyerhoff Scholars receive. All Scholars attend regular meetings with UMBC President Freeman Hrabowski, and the Meyerhoff Program staff work with students on a day-to-day basis regarding academic advisement, counseling, scheduling, and completing the necessary documents for graduate school and summer internships.

The success of the program provides a clear example of how strategies conceptualized within each of the components covered thus far, i.e., Mission, Vision, and Climate & Culture are needed to inspire, encourage, and achieve high levels of academic achievement for Black males. To increase the number of Black males pursuing such highly rigorous academic programs, more strategies must be developed throughout elementary, middle, and high school education designed to ensure enrollment and success in higher-level math and science classes.

Corrective Actions for all Role Players:

- Create a collaboration between elementary, middle, and high schools to identify young men who are gifted or interested in math and science in the primary grades and create a program to encourage and support their enrollment in academically-challenging classes.

- Develop programs which recognize and celebrate math and science achievement as pompously as Pop Warner football, AAU/USATF track and field, and youth basketball.

- Match young men with professionals, students taking higher-level math and science in high school and college, and teachers who serve as faculty advisors to math and science clubs in middle and high school with primary-age boys to inspire and encourage long-term scholarly achievement.

- Have AP and honors high school teachers collaborate with middle and elementary school teachers to identify and nurture the qualities and traits to prepare students to become successful high school students.

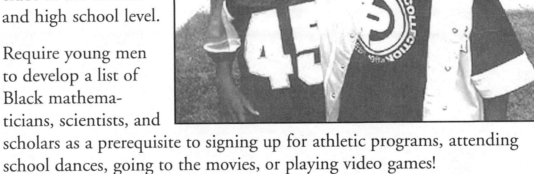

- Create math and science clubs in the primary grades which feed into companion clubs at the middle and high school level.

- Require young men to develop a list of Black mathematicians, scientists, and scholars as a prerequisite to signing up for athletic programs, attending school dances, going to the movies, or playing video games!

- Require athletes to compute, maintain, and explain the statistics pertinent to their sport, i.e., batting averages, on-base percentages, free throw percentages, scoring proficiency inside the red zone, or average yards per carry.

- Require athletes to be able to explain those components unique to their sport, i.e., speed, agility, lactic acid, metabolic rates, resting heart rates, protein synthesis, carbohydrates as a source of energy, or carbohydrate-versus protein-rich food sources.

- Identify young men who have high interest levels and/or highly-developed math and science abilities and push them into challenging classes, enroll them in challenging programs, and identify after-school and summer programs to nurture and further develop their math and science skills and abilities.

Identify The Values and Principles That You Need to Teach

Teaching the lessons and cultivating the core values and guiding principles needed to counteract the powerful media influences and peer pressures is going to require some work from the adult stakeholders within the school community through a fourfold approach:

1. Identify the values and principles you want to teach.

2. Identify the resources needed to teach them.

3. Confront the negative values, images, attitudes, and behaviors.

4. Sift through the values and images to identify the real dreams and aspirations of young men.

The Overview outlined the sense of urgency needed to address the Black male condition. Any parent, teacher, coach, or mentor has the capacity to immediately address each of these four areas. This is not to deny that more can be accomplished and the level of influence can be substantially increased through school-wide, community, or programmatic efforts. However, the sense of urgency demands that parents, teachers, coaches, and mentors work with young men within each of the four areas immediately.

In Chapter two, the question was raised, "What is your vision for the Black males within your sphere of influence?" Review the following list of qualities and attributes and circle those qualities, values, or attributes which you would like to influence:

Passion	Purpose	Perseverance	Integrity
Determination	Diligence	Persistence	Dedication
Commitment	Devotion	Enthusiasm	Energy
Fortitude	Kindness	Humanity	Generosity
Selflessness	Tolerance	Awareness	Service
Leadership	Teamwork	Cooperation	Humor
Thoughtfulness	Originality	Innovation	Imagination
Independence	Judgment	Honor	Morality
Experimentation	Resilience	Idealism	Vision
Compassion	Responsibility	Mission	Respect
Sense of duty	Entrepreneurship	Creativity	Initiative

This is a short list of those values which should become a part of any household, classroom, athletic team, or mentoring program attempting to teach, inspire, and empower Black males. Having considered the impact of media images and peer pressure on Black males, is this list comprehensive enough?

Following is a list of some of the important values and attributes my wife and I have undertaken to teach our sons, their cousins, and any of their friends whom we have the opportunity to interact with and influence:

- Respect for self and others through your language and behaviors (regardless of race, sex, sexual orientation, religion, or social status)

- Responsibility to yourself and others as evidenced by your account-ability for your actions

- Diligence, determination, persistence, and resiliency as evidenced through chores, school work, and participation in athletics and activities

- Humanity, integrity, honor, and humility as evidenced through your faith, treatment of, and service to others

- Originality, leadership, innovation, and creativity in your approach to solving problems

- Initiative in your willingness to do what needs to be done and the quality with which you fulfill your work and responsibilities

- Developing a quest for excellence in all personal pursuits

- Being a race model by understanding the far-reaching impact of what you do and/or don't do has on all Black people

- Holding the family name in high regards and being a vanguard of the family legacy

- Having a purpose-driven life with identifiable goals and aspirations

- Being driven by intellect and emotion by interweaving both to accomplish goals and to avoid conflict

- Developing the temple of the body through prayer, meditation, diet, nutrition, rest, and exercise

- Appreciating and developing God-given talents and abilities

- Truthfulness in your actions reflective of your faith

- The manner in which your carry yourself and communicate your ideas to others

- Developing the language skills, vocabulary, and ability to speak Standard English

As a parent, teacher, coach, or mentor you must revisit Chapter two, *Vision,* and clearly identify the complete range of personal qualities and attributes you wish to influence. Identify in as specific detail as possible (e.g., hand shake, personal instruction, language skills, vocabulary, clearly audible voice, dress, walk, mannerisms, standard of behavior, or eye contact). The principle question is, "What type of man am I trying to help this young man to become?"

Identify Who Will Teach Them

As previously stated, everyone acknowledges lecture as largely ineffective. So why do we do it? It's easy. How often have you, or an adult whom you know, been guilty of placing your hand onto your hip, or pointing your finger in the face of a young man decreeing:

"What's wrong with you?"

"If I've told you once, I've told you a thousand times."

"You are wearing on my last nerve."

"You know better."

"You make me so mad I could spit!"

"Why would you do something so stupid? You know better."

Moving away from lecture to teaching the lessons and conveying the values young men need to learn requires:

1. Preparing for the all-to-familiar behaviors and/or situations that you can reasonably expect to encounter with young men.

2. Identifying the lessons, stories, proverbs, and parables you will rely upon, rather than lecture, when confronted with those behaviors and/or situations.

I frequently tell the story outlined in my book, *The Eagles who Thought They were Chickens*, as a means of exploring the attitudes and behaviors commonplace in school communities. The story provides many parallels to the attitudes, behaviors, and language used by young men in reference to themselves and in relating to peers.

John Alston in, *Story Power: Talking with Teens in Turbulent Times*, beautifully outlines the method of using storytelling as a means of bonding and communicating with young people.

Story Power conveys a new approach to communicating with teens. It is about listening to stories that they bring to us, as they attempt to thrive and survive.

Story Power is a way to understand what they are telling us and tell them what we want, so they can truly comprehend.

The core of a story well expressed can mold thinking and serve as a guide for behavior, so this communication tool I call "story power" can develop strong character, integrity, and decency in the young adults we are nurturing. Children will become older no matter what we, as parents and concerned adults, do to influence them. The influence we provide is crucial to the kind of adults they become.

I have discovered how a well-timed and well-told story or parable can be literally a life-saver when dealing with young men. It quickly grabs their attention in situations where all else seems to fail. It provides a means for a parent, teacher, coach, or mentor to share a lot of personal information and experiences within a relatively short time span and provides a bridge of communication to crossover and effectively open dialogue. Examples of stories are included in the *workbook*.

'You boys are going to go to the library and check out books. You're going to read at least two books every week. At the end of each week you'll give me a report on what you've read.'

By reading so much, my vocabulary automatically improved along with my comprehension. Soon I became the best student in math when we did story problems. After I started pulling ahead in school, the desire to be smart grew stronger and stronger.

— Ben Carson, *Gifted Hands: The Ben Carson Story*

Identify Programs and Activities

Martial Arts and organized sports provide further opportunities to teach respect, develop character, and increase self-discipline within young men. When parents assess involvement in youth sports they must look beyond won-lost records to the example provided, and beliefs articulated, by the coach or instructor.

Areas to be considered are:

1. What is the coach's philosophy as it relates to teaching self-discipline, personal responsibility, respect for authority, camaraderie among teammates, and sportsmanship?

2. What is the personal model of character, language, and behavior exhibited by the coach or instructor?

3. Is there genuine concern by the coach or instructor with the personal development of players and communication with parents?

4. Does the coach or instructor have clarity of purpose, "Why are they there?"

5. What is the coach's or instructor's perception of players, e.g., do they feel sorry for poor kids, do they have a low opinion of a player's intellectual capacity, do they have low expectations of player behavior off the field, in classrooms, and at home?

Athletic coaches and martial arts instructors have tremendous power to shape a young man's consciousness, influence his behavior, and contribute to his overall perspective as it relates to sports participation and sportsmanship. Parents should assess AAU, USATF, youth programs, and high school coaches before entrusting their sons into their care. Special attention should be given to high school coaches and the statistics they generate. Not the number of wins and losses but the number of players who graduate from high school and go on to attend and graduate from college; the number of players who enroll in honors and AP classes; the number of players who are encouraged to assume leadership positions in student clubs and organizations; the number of players who are recruited by colleges and who actually graduate from the colleges they are recruited

by; and the players who the coaches recognize and celebrate. For example, do the coaches formerly recognize players who are academic achievers, players who score highly on the SAT/ ACT, players who consistently qualify for the school's honor roll, and players who model the character, values, beliefs, and principles which the coach espouses?

Is the coach willing to bench a player who behaves disrespectfully or performs poorly in his class work? Or, are there special exceptions made for star athletes? The same question can be asked of parents. What are the important values you would like for your son's coach to reinforce? Do you want to see your son play at any cost or is it more important for him to learn to become a man, even at the expense of being a star athlete?

Both of our sons struggled with behavior throughout elementary school. While they were both considered bright and intelligent children, both were suspended from school on more than one occasion and referred to the office multiple times. Both, notably had some of the best teachers in the school. The problem was simply, both of our sons are opinionated, refuse to back down, and are males. Nationwide statistics clearly indicate that Black males are disproportionately referred to the office and suspended from school. As

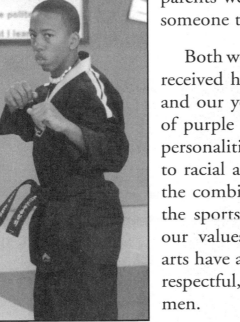

parents we clearly understood that our sons needed someone to reinforce our lessons in self-discipline.

Both were enrolled into martial arts. Our older son received his black belt when he was eight years old and our younger son has currently earned the rank of purple belt. While they both have very different personalities, they have both struggled in responding to racial and gender conflicts in school. We believe the combination of our lessons, careful selection of the sports teams and coaches who have reinforced our values, and their involvement in the martial arts have all helped them to become well-mannered, respectful, and reasonably well-disciplined young men.

Church

We must recognize that Black males are involved in a spiritual warfare for their very souls. Media images and peer pressures have tremendous influence over their attitudes and behaviors and rarely affirm positive behaviors and aspirations. The values, principles, and influences are in direct conflict with the Biblical principles needed to provide the compass to guide their actions and behaviors. As coaches and instructors must be carefully selected, so too, must parents select the churches which will best meet the needs of their sons. I remember as a child how I sat in the back of the church, typically falling asleep in the pew. While I didn't pay much attention to the sermon, didn't sing in the choir, didn't study the Bible, and don't recall any meaningful experiences in Sunday School, the fact that I was in church, surrounded by people who loved and cared about me had a positive influence.

As is the case of identifying the coaches and athletic teams which will best meet the needs of your sons, so too, must you choose a church which will best meet their needs:

1. Does the church have an active youth ministry and a youth minister who can genuinely make a connection with young men in your son's age group?

2. Does the church offer programs which will meet the unique needs of your son, e.g., SAT prep classes, college tours, tutorial classes, athletic programs, youth Bible Study, or youth church?

3. Does the church have opportunities for active and engaging involvement between your son and other males, e.g., band, choir, mime groups, theater, ushers, youth deacon board, leadership groups, youth organizations, or boy scouts?

4. Does the church provide the type of atmosphere for young men which encourages and excites them about attending and being involved in church?

5. Does the church have Black men who serve as positive role models for young Black men?

In many communities not only is the church no longer the focal point of the community, but there is clearly an absence of a direly needed church-school partnership. I was fortunate to be a part of the reemergence of such a partnership through the Texas Educational Agency Region X offices and local churches surrounding the issue of "Parenting and Teaching African-American Males." The three-prong effort of presenting educational workshops for administrators and teachers, a parenting workshop at a local school, and a community workshop hosted by a local church is the model needed nationally. There is clearly a role which teachers, counselors, and administrators must play within our schools to make use of the types of ideas presented and to implement the types of strategies needed. There is clearly a role which parents must play in teaching values, respect, and responsibility, while encouraging academic excellence. However, Black males must be taken back into the church where they can continue the journey toward understanding, realizing, and fulfilling their purpose. There must be a merging of education and spiritual empowerment if Black males are to overcome the many media forces, societal, and peer pressures which are moving them away from their moral and spiritual center.

Some of the strategies which may be employed are:

1. Identify a local church, synagogue, temple, or mosque to partner with a school.

2. Use the facility to host workshops, teacher meetings, and student performances.

3. Use volunteers to assist with school functions as a means of bringing a service and calming spirit into the school community.

4. Use the talents and abilities of volunteers to build cabinets, paint, lay carpet, hang pictures, troubleshoot computers, and decorate the school as a show of fellowship and support.

5. Remember, when concerned adults are in the school (classrooms, cafeteria, corridors, playground) they usually provide a positive influence on school climate and culture.

6. Perform an interest and talent survey to identify mentoring opportunities for connecting volunteers with students based on student dreams and aspirations.

7. Host special days at the church, synagogue, temple, or mosque for career, college, community, or dream day.

8. Collect books, musical instruments, clothing, athletic wear, and supplies for donation to the school.

9. Provide tutorial assistance.

10. Create a celebration of academic achievement.

Our church, Turner Chapel AME, in Marietta, Georgia provides SAT prep classes, HBCU tours, tutorial services, sports, mentoring, and a youth ministry which reaches out to youth and families within the local schools. We also offer scholarships, recognition, and celebration during the worship service for academic achievement. In most communities, one church—one school is not an unreasonable goal.

Spiritual empowerment and educational enlightenment go hand in hand. The power of the Holy Scriptures can only be unlocked through literacy. On this issue there can be no compromise.

Strategies mentors can employ are:

1. Invite a student and his or her family to worship service and/or to church-sponsored events.

2. Keep the family informed of special programs, workshops, tutorial services, college trips, SAT/ACT prep classes, and other programs which would benefit the family.

3. Provide an example of service, character, and moral turpitude for the student and his family.

4. Maintain a college-bound focus.

5. Look for opportunities for social activities among other spiritually-centered adults and children.

6. Pass on books relating to spiritual empowerment, discovering one's purpose, values, beliefs and guiding principles.

7. Take advantage of opportunities to attend movies or host movie nights and provide opportunities for post-movie discussions of the issues confronting young people.

8. Take advantage of every opportunity to shake the hand of a young man and to reassure him of your willingness to listen to his hopes, dreams, and issues.

9. Provide opportunities for the young men whom you are mentoring to interact with your sons, nephews, brothers, other relatives, or friends who are close in age and provide positive examples.

10. Take advantage of opportunities to take your mentee to local lectures to hear speakers with positive, spiritually-centered messages.

The fourth group of Teachers. They understand the significance of subject matter, but they also believe that you shouldn't teach the most comfortable way, but the way children learn. Therefore, if you have a greater percentage of right-brained thinkers, you should increase the percentage of right-brained lesson plans. These students are holistic learners and look for a larger meaning. They prefer cooperative learning, and can learn with a higher noise level and greater movement. Their strengths lie in music, art, and physical activities.

My last group is Coaches, who understand subject matter and pedagogy, but also, understand the need to bond with students first. Coaches care, respect, and appreciate the culture of their students. They fully understand that there can be no significant learning until there is a significant relationship. Author and professor Peter Murrell, Jr., calls these people 'community teachers.' Scholar and policy-maker, Martin Haberman penned the book Star Teachers of Children in Poverty. *Coaches understand the child and their neighborhood and provide complementary curriculum and pedagogy. They are less concerned about discipline and order and more concerned about creating lesson plans that excite and engage students. Star Teachers, in Haberman's terminology, convince students that effort is more important than ability.*

— *Jawanza Kunjufu, [Black Students: Middle Class Teachers]*

The Professional Sports Dream

When surveying young men in schools as to what their dreams and aspirations are, upwards of 90 percent of them aspire toward careers in professional sports. I have come to refer to this almost singular aspiration that has millions of young Black boys focused on a sports, oftentimes NBA, career as "The Michael Jordan" phenomenon. Michael Jordan, one of the most gifted, competitive, and charismatic basketball players in the history of the National Basketball Association was idolized by millions of young men. World-wide, he was one of the most recognizable and popular athletes ever. You could walk into any school and ask young men what their dreams and aspirations were and countless numbers of them would immediately respond, "I want to become a basketball player like Michael Jordan." Well-intentioned adults would say things, like, "That's nice, Willie, but what if you don't make it?" Unfortunately, Willie was entirely sure that he would make it and he wasn't devoting any attention to a "What if" scenario. Willie could be seen playing basketball on snow-covered playgrounds. He, and countless others like him, knew the NBA statistics of their favorite players. They could be found cutting classes to spend the entire day in gymnasiums. Such young men have developed a passion, have tunnel vision, and absolutely believe basketball is their "ticket" to a better life. Such young men aren't listening to any "What if?" scenarios.

Today, "The Michael Jordan" phenomenon could easily be labeled, "The Allan Iverson, Tracy McGrady, Shaquille O'Neal, or Lebron James" phenomenon. Our challenge, as adults, is to expand the knowledge of such would-be NBA stars in regards to the dreams that they are intent on committing a good portion of their lives to pursuing. Personally, I would rather more young men dream of empowering their communities, becoming CEOs, teachers, of entering into any of the thousands of other careers to make a difference in their lives and in the world around them. However, I also know they, like anyone else, are entitled to be encouraged and supported in whatever their dreams are (as long as they are socially and morally acceptable). As such, I believe we should harness their passions and use their dreams to teach them how to think critically and to expand upon a broad range of skills and intelligences.

Willie, who wants to pursue a career in professional basketball, wears the sneakers of his current NBA idol. He also has a matching jersey and warm-ups. Obviously, Willie has identified a hero and role model. Resist the urge to ask Willie, "What if you don't?" Instead respond, "Great!" Then, encourage "Air Willie" or "King Willie" to visualize himself as the greatest basketball player, ever, and to visualize himself becoming a confident and eloquent public speaker. Encourage Willie to develop his public speaking potential as he may become a spokesperson for the young men who may never have his opportunity to succeed (familiarize him with the tables on the following pages).

Willie has some work to do. To expand his basketball skills he needs to become a good learner, listener, and team player. When Willie begins to receive national recognition, he will have to be prepared to handle interviews, read contracts, and prepare letters of acceptance or decline to the colleges which recruit him.

Depending on Willie's grade and ability level, there are many other aspects of his dream which can be tied directly to the curriculum through math, social studies, language arts, science, oral presentations, research, and book reports. Role playing and skits between Willie and other

students can explore nutrition, muscular development, cardiovascular training, interest rates and return on investments, and automobile, real estate, and contract negotiations.

In basketball, they call this a "back door play." This is a play where you lull the defender into watching the ball while a player sneaks around the defender and receives the pass for an easy layup or dunk. By allowing Willie to focus his attention on his dream, we are able to sneak research, reading, language skills, science, social studies, math, and critical-thinking skills in through the back door!

By encouraging Willie's dreams you can further encourage his setting goals aligned with his dream by:

- reviewing the tables on the following pages so he clearly understands the odds of his making it onto a college team, and the additional odds of making it onto an NBA team;

- meeting NCAA guidelines for college-bound student-athletes;

- registering with the NCAA clearinghouse;

- developing a kindergarten-through-twelfth-grade plan of the needed courses, GPA, and SAT/ACT qualifying scores; and

- developing the attitude and personal attributes consistent with becoming a professional athlete.

By allowing Willie to retain his goal, we simply work with him to understand and develop himself for achievement in the areas leading up to and following a career in professional basketball. This activity can be utilized for any professional sports dream, i.e., Baseball, Football, Soccer, or Golf. If Willie somehow beats the odds and makes it into the ranks of a highly-paid professional athlete, he will be better prepared to handle the fame and fortune. If, as is more likely, he doesn't fulfill his dream of becoming a professional athlete, he will have developed a broad range of other skills, knowledge, and insight into his dream that he will be better empowered to pursue other careers.

Refer to the exercise in the *workbook* to direct Willie through a research, writing, and presentation activity involving his dream of pursuing a professional sports career.

> *To me, competitive doesn't mean 'hating to lose,' it doesn't mean doing a bunch of talking. Being competitive means working your Butt off. If you're saying you're competitive, and you don't work, you're just talking.*
>
> — *Jim Brown*

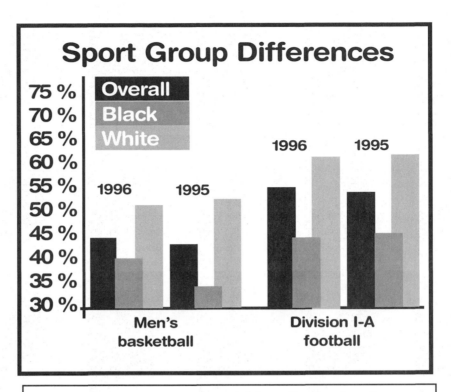

NCAA Division I-A Student-Athlete Graduation Rates

Division I-A football student-athletes in the 1996 cohort graduated at a 54 percent rate, one percentage point higher than the 1995 class but seven percentage points below the 1996 student body. Men's basketball players overall were at 44 percent for the 1996 class compared to 43 percent for 1995. Neither group has graduated at a higher rate than the student body in any year since graduation rates began being tracked with the 1984 class, but both have experienced increases in each of the last two classes. It is also important to note that these groups of student-athletes do tend to graduate at higher rates than their gender and ethnic group counterparts in the student body.

Rates continue to be high in women's basketball, as the 1996 class posted a rate of 66 percent, one percentage point higher than the 1995 group.

[Increasing Student Achievement: Volume I, Vision]

NCAA Student and Student-Athlete Graduation Rates

Source: http://www.ncaa.org/grad_rates/2003/d1/index.html

School	1996-97 All Students	Athletes	Four-year Average All Students	Athletes
Auburn	68	62	67	57
Bethune-Cookman	31	52	35	43
BYU	71	54	72	50
Brown	95	*	94	*
Dartmouth	95	*	94	*
Delaware State	30	54	29	39
Duke	93	88	93	89
Florida A&M	43	46	43	39
Georgetown	94	77	92	87
Georgia Tech	68	63	68	53
Howard	58	62	50	59
Loyola Marymount	70	73	70	68
UCLA	85	64	81	65
UMass Amherst	61	64	60	66
University of Connecticut	69	60	69	62
University of Georgia	70	60	67	64
University of Kentucky	58	48	56	45
Louisiana State	57	55	54	52
University of Miami (FL)	65	51	63	53
University of Michigan	84	82	83	73
UNC (Chapel Hill)	80	64	80	70
USC	76	56	73	61
Northwestern	93	87	92	89
North Carolina A&T	40	23	43	36
Notre Dame	95	92	94	87
Ohio State	59	60	56	59
Penn State	80	80	80	79
Rice	92	81	90	82
Rutgers	72	72	73	68
Syracuse	77	81	75	79
Stanford	93	84	92	87
Texas Tech	52	56	49	55
The Citadel	66	67	68	64
U.S. Air Force Academy	79	*	77	*
Vanderbilt	84	75	83	78
Wake Forest	87	79	87	76
Xavier	71	66	71	74
Yale	95	*	95	*

* Schools do not offer athletic scholarships

Chapter 4: Key Points

1. The negative influences of peer pressure and popular culture must be countered through positive imagery of present and historical Black males infused into the curriculum.

2. The negative influences of peer pressure and popular culture is further reduced through the 'web of protection' created by a variety of adults and organizations.

3. Parents should consciously limit their son's access to negative media images.

4. Teachers should engage Black males in critical-thinking discussions of current events and pop culture influences.

5. Adults should be proactive in influencing peer culture directly and indirectly influencing peers themselves.

6. Teachers should identify opportunities for culturally-relevant research papers and lessons.

7. Black males should be encouraged and supported in honors, academically gifted, and AP classes.

8. There is a direct link between lack of literacy and criminal incarceration.

9. An elementary–middle–high school collaboration is needed to provide early intervention and early identification of academically-gifted Black males.

10. Infuse values into lesson design and program expectations.

11. Identify supplemental programs and activities to reinforce values and personal attributes.

12. Design lessons around student's dreams and aspirations to develop their critical-thinking skills and to construct their kindergarten-through-college plan.

Chapter 5

Instruction

Research studies continually emphasize teachers' attitudes and dispositions toward poor achieving minority students in rural schools or urban depressed areas. For instance, Ferguson's extensive meta-analysis (1998) reveals that teachers, both Black and White, almost always have lower expectations for Black students than they do for White students. Arroyo, Road and Drew (1999) as well as The College Board (1999) reached a similar conclusion and go on to note that this way of behaving has an impact on the self-esteem and self-concept of minority students. Thus, the low self-expectations, coupled with teachers' low expectations of them, lead to low performance and achievement.

— *Perspectives on Teacher Education Reform*

Expectations

While recently at a bid whist party—one of the most common events for Black folks to get together—whether highly-educated or uneducated; a six-figure income or living below the poverty level; working in law enforcement or a career criminal; Ph.D. and high school dropout alike, all types of Black people get together to play cards and talk trash. Highly-educated Black folks can reclaim their roots if they can talk trash and play some cards. While the trash talking is customarily friendly, it can result in 'The Dozens.' Right in the middle of one of the hands of cards, a mother came through the kitchen with her daughter in tow, holding two books:

> *"Look at my baby, she was recognized in <u>Who's Who Among American High School Students</u> and she made <u>The National Honor Roll</u>. Tell them what you want to be and where you're going to college, honey. That's my baby."*

Nowhere is there a greater misunderstanding, miscommunication, and conflict between Black parents and classroom teachers than as it relates to the education of Black children. Black parents want to see their children succeed academically, however, they are less-likely than White parents to have a positive relationship with classroom teachers to ensure that this happens. Black children, who have a good teaching-learning style match and those who can compensate for any mismatches succeed, the others, through each grade level fall further and further behind. Black parents become increasingly frustrated and develop increasingly negative attitudes toward schools and classroom teachers.

Building the bridge between parents and teachers so they are talking about what to do to ensure that Black children are successful academically will do more to close the achievement gap and increase the societal success of Black children in general, and Black males in particular, than perhaps any other single initiative. Building such a bridge begins with understanding the roadblocks between teachers and Black parents and conceptualizing strategies to develop more effective communication and build stronger relationships. In so doing, teachers must keep in mind, as previously outlined in Chapter three, *Climate & Culture*, the communication and relationship may not be with a student's parents but with another influential adult, i.e., aunt, uncle, grandparent, older sibling, coach, pastor, or mentor.

Curriculum Night—Problems & Solutions

Schools and school teachers put a lot of time into preparing for and hosting curriculum night in elementary, middle, and high schools. Many Black parents don't attend curriculum nights. Teachers perceive this to mean that Black parents don't care about the education of their children.

While this can be the case, the reasons Black parents don't attend is oftentimes twofold:

- Firstly, Black parents (the majority of whom are single-moms) are already overloaded—several children in more than one school setting (i.e., elementary, middle, high school, and sometimes college), a full-time job working during the day for someone who doesn't appreciate them (and a full-time job working at home for children who oftentimes don't appreciate them), no one to baby sit, other children who need help with their homework, and the other issues which come with running a household. They just don't have the time, or want to make the time, to come to curriculum night.

- Secondly, curriculum night is often viewed as a waste of time. It's a teacher-directed lecture where teachers tell parents what they're going to teach and rarely provide parents with anything meaningful to ensure parents that their children are going to be successful within their classrooms.

To make curriculum night more productive for teachers and valuable for parents and students it should rise to the ranks of a school custom which celebrates student achievement and reinforces academic expectations. This can be accomplished by:

1. Having a brief awards presentation preceding the parent-teacher meetings. Use the presentation to highlight the range of academic recognition, awards, and programs offered by the school.

2. Display the academic awards, i.e., honor roll certificates, trophies, honor roll pins, and provide information regarding the academic clubs and programs.

3. Provide parents with sample grading rubrics and course syllabi as part of parent packages which provide all of the important information regarding the curriculum, recommended support materials, and support services.

4. Provide parents with sample kindergarten-through-college plans and how each grade level or subject area fits within the scope of such plans.

5. Provide parents with samples of student work within each of the grading categories, i.e., A, B, C, D, and F.

6. Use student hosts and hostesses to provide parents with information and to be ambassadors for the school.

7. Set up information tables with all of the important information appropriate to the school setting, i.e., elementary, middle, high

school, junior college, or college. (Information which students are responsible for taking home, but never reaches parents!)

8. Set up sign-up tables for parent involvement in PTA/PTSA, booster clubs, chaperones, photographers, stage designers, carpenters, concession stand workers, traffic workers, office support, mentors, and guest speakers.

9. Coaches should be in attendance to reinforce the importance of academic achievement.

10. Involve Black parents in planning and coordinating where possible.

11. Introduce your year-long series of parent seminars and book clubs dealing with raising Black males and developing college plans.

12. Set up display tables with samples and photographs of interdisciplinary units, field trips, guest speakers, and special events from the previous school year.

13. Set up television monitors with video tape and DVDs of student activities, school-wide events, and examples of classroom instruction.

14. Sell supplies, spirit wear, and display student artwork, research papers, models, and examples of how students are applying what they are learning through the curriculum.

Use these and other ideas to make curriculum night an event which showcases student talent, school activities, and builds school spirit and pride.

Grades

Grading methodology and grading practices must be constructed in ways that are student and parent-friendly. Grades not only provide an assessment mechanism but should provide a motivating factor in encouraging student effort as students set and pursue their own goals. Teachers must be willing to reassess grading methodology constructed in a way that all but assures that typical Black males cannot earn the highest academic grades. Both teachers and parents know 'typical' Black males, like males in general, are:

- Unorganized.

- Unmotivated to do homework, class work, or prepare for tests and quizzes.

- Given to lying, "Mama, I turned in my assignment, the teacher must have lost it ..." and "Ms. A, I left my assignment at home. My mama is going to bring it to school."

- Given to peer pressure or girl pressure, Black males will clown around in class, refuse to participate in classroom discussions, or otherwise deprive themselves of classroom participation grades.

In many situations, before the first parent-teacher conference, Black males have so many missed assignments and low test/quiz grades that A's are unheard of, B's are unlikely, C's are within reach, but D's or F's are probable.

Many teachers take the position that a student has 'earned his grade,' which oftentimes is an 'F.' Subsequently, the following statistics (as stated in the previous chapter) are entirely predictable:

- Boys receive approximately 70 percent of the D's and F's. Among students performing in the top fifth of high school grade ranges, 63 percent are girls.

- Boys make up two-thirds of the learning disabled and 90 percent of the behaviorally disabled, and nearly 100 percent of the most seriously disabled. Boys account for 80 percent of brain disorders.

- Boys constitute 90 percent of discipline problems in school and 80 percent of dropouts.

The reason this issue does not come to the forefront of the educational debate as it pertains to Black male achievement is that teachers who establish grading policies without taking into account student needs, developmental levels, student interests, and the overall goal, i.e., learning, have not internalized a mission to ensure that Black males achieve academically. The grading policy is established for the teacher not the student. Grades and grading practices punish rather than serve as a motivator. Black males, who understand establishing a goal of breaking forty-five seconds in the 400-meter, running ten seconds in the 100-meter, hitting a .300 batting average, or reaching a 90 percent free-throw percentage, are frequently unmotivated to put forth any real effort toward grades because they learn that no matter how hard they try, 'A's' are most frequently out of their reach.

These same young men are intrinsically driven to put forth effort when they 'believe' there exist the possibility of winning. However, many teachers take away any opportunity to win, i.e., get the best grade, with grading practices which punish them for getting a slow start. Subsequently, year after year of such grading practices cause more and more young men to put forth less and less effort and internalize their weaknesses, i.e., lack of organization, ineffective note-taking and study skills, and any inability to connect their learning-style to a teacher's teaching-style, as deficiencies. Their attitude becomes, "Why bother?"

Our younger son is currently an 'A' student, wants to be an 'A' student and fits the profile of what teachers consider an 'A' student. He is atypical. Our older son (a current high school junior) is a typical Black male and as such, does all of the wrong things, i.e., misplaces or doesn't do his homework unless my wife and I deprive him of something, doesn't prepare for tests and quizzes unless my wife and I force him to prepare, works well for teachers he likes and doesn't work at all for teachers whom he doesn't like, and, despite our best efforts, will typically have a lapse of concentration, and/or motivation, at some point during a grading period.

Despite his lack of motivation, lack of organization, and attempts at deception, we have largely been able to push him academically to a level which few Black males reach or even aspire toward. As a result of our prodding, pushing, and prayer—as a sophomore he scored a 560V and 570M in his first sitting for the SAT, and a 25 on the ACT. His GPA is currently 3.3 as the result of having been blessed to have teachers who care and parents who push. Those teachers whom my wife and I have successfully collaborated with have been willing to answer a question many teachers refuse to even ask:

What is in the best interest of students?

What's clearly in the best interest of Black males and their families is to:

- provide frequent opportunities to retake tests and resubmit homework until they reflect student ability levels and teacher/parent expectations ... AT FULL CREDIT!;

- create grading policies which don't penalize Black males for clearly predictable behaviors, i.e., late assignments, lack of test/quiz preparation, lack of classroom participation, sloppy work (at least, initially);

- tell parents 'exactly' what they can do to ensure the academic success of their sons—this means compensating for fully making up the grades for missed assignments and/or low test scores and providing opportunities for students to demonstrate knowledge through multiple areas of intelligence (e.g., visual/spatial, bodily/kinesthetic) which may not be demonstrated in quiz and test grades (i.e., verbal/linguistic, logical/mathematical); and

- not grade on a curve.

  "In my class I am going to award 3 A's, 6 B's, 12 C's, 6 D's, and 3 F's. You have to decide which group you are going to be in!"

Such a teacher may as well continue the discourse:

"I rarely award A's to Black males!"

Or, the teacher could simply write on the chalkboard the first day of class:

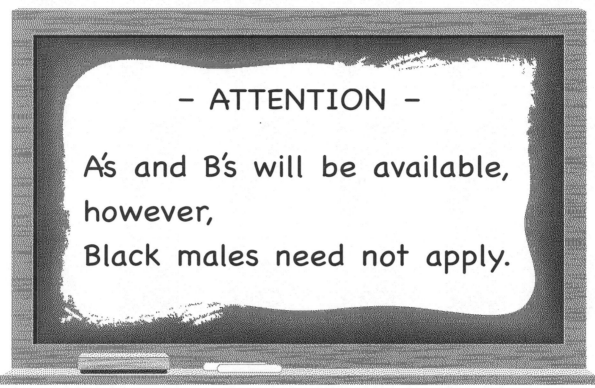

– ATTENTION –

A's and B's will be available, however,
Black males need not apply.

My wife and I typically set higher standards than our sons' teachers. If papers don't have the appropriate headings we make them redo the entire paper. If their math homework doesn't clearly show each step we make them redo the entire homework. If they don't earn an 'A' on a test of quiz we would prefer they retake the test again, and again, and again, if necessary until they earn an 'A.' Subsequently, my wife and I are able to get quality work from our sons and deepen levels of learning, both of which is in the best interest of both teachers and parents because the outcomes are reflected on end-of-grade exams and standardized tests.

Unfortunately, teachers who use grades as instruments for punishing students, either don't understand or simply don't care about the needs of families and students to ensure that all students have every opportunity to succeed and to stay motivated to do the course work throughout a grading period. Subsequently, teachers will make the argument that I am advocating students receive artificially inflated grades. This is not the case at all. Artificially inflated grades cripple Black children. It is in everyone's best interest for Black children to earn the highest grades by applying themselves to their course work, completing assignments, performing research, participating in classroom discussions, and deepening knowledge to the depths needed to convey what they know in a way that can be meaningfully assessed. There is no research which suggests that punishing students for their lack of organizational skills (or their lack of interest) by artificially deflating their grades is in their best interest or increases their proficiency.

Alphie Kohn, in *Punished by Rewards*, notes the importance of structuring an environment in which students can explore, make mistakes, acknowledge when they don't know, and risk failing without risk of ridicule from the teacher or their peers:

> *... a classroom that feels safe to students is one in which they are free to admit when they don't understand something and are able to ask for help. Ironically, grades and tests, punishments and rewards, are the enemies of safety; they therefore reduce the probability that students will speak up and that truly productive evaluation can take place.*

> *... just as adults who love their work will invariably do a better job than those goaded with artificial incentives, so children are more likely to be optimal learners if they are interested in what they are learning. Several studies have found a positive correlation between intrinsic motivation and academic achievement for children of different ages. Most of this work has been correlational, which means that we can't necessarily assume the child's motivation causes achievement to go up or down; indeed, there is reason to think that achievement may affect motivation, too. Still, at least one researcher has concluded there is a causal relationship: "reduced intrinsic motivation produces achievement deficits."*

> *When we look at how children view a particular assignment, the relationship is even more impressive. One group of researchers tried to sort out the factors that helped third and fourth graders remember what they had been reading. They found that how interested the students were in the passage was thirty times more important than how 'readable' the passage was ... there may be some disagreement about why interested learners are likely to be effective learners, but the fact itself is hard to dispute.*

Grades should not be reflective of:

- *how organized students are;*
- *how quickly students understood;*
- *how interested students were in the lesson;*
- *how quickly students can calculate;*
- *how effectively students were able to prioritize their time;*
- *how prepared students were for pop quizzes;*
- *how much academic support students had at home;*
- *how much exposure students have had;*
- *how much preexisting knowledge students had; or*
- *the student's ability to make a connection between his or her learning-style and the teacher's teaching-style.*

To the contrary:

- Student grades should reflect teacher effectiveness in ensuring each students' progress on a continuum.

This is not to suggest teachers *can* be effective with all students. This means teachers *want* to be effective with all students, and genuinely want to provide an opportunity for all students to excel. My wife and I love both of our sons but, despite our love, caring, and best efforts, we are not effective with them 100 percent of the time. However, whenever they "Don't get it" we accept partial responsibility:

1. Did we teach it in the best way in which it could have been taught?

2. Did we identify their intrinsic motivation as a means of inspiring them to learn what may simply have been uninteresting?

3. Were we successful at connecting our teaching-style to their learning-style?

4. Did we use the best examples, share the best stories, provide the best anecdotes, use the best parables, or provide the best illustrations?

Syllabus & Rubrics

As many teachers have experienced, and parents live with on a daily basis, many young men are unorganized, lack consistent academic focus, and consciously conspire to avoid the consequences of their lack of academic focus and performance. Parents play this game with their sons year after year:

Mother: "Mark, what do you have for homework?"

Mark: "We don't have any homework today."

Mother: "Mark, how can you never have any homework?"

Mark: "Mom, she never assigns homework."

At the teacher conference, which occurs nearly halfway through the grading period, Mark's mother discovers that Mark has a zero for nearly every homework assignment and homework is computed as 15 percent of Mark's overall grade! To avoid this nonsense, and to help young men like Mark, some of whom are placed on punishment by their parents from the midway point of the first grading period for the balance of the school year, consider the needs of such young men and their families.

Following is a list of some of the instructional practices which can increase parental support and the academic success of such students:

- A syllabus which clearly outlines teacher expectations, grading policies, dates that parents should expect to receive progress reports, how grades are computed, what extra credit opportunities will be available, how and when the teacher can be contacted, and the learning outcomes which should occur in the class.

- Study guides, sometimes called refrigerator sheets, which provide quick reference to specific units of study to be covered in the class which keep parents abreast of what their sons should know and provide a tool for reinforcing classroom instruction.

- List of supplies, resources, and supplemental materials needed to complete assignments and reinforce learning.

- Monthly or weekly calendar outlining lectures, homework, class work, projects, tests, and quizzes.

- Schedule of make-up assignments and quiz dates.

- Grading rubrics which clearly outline expectations in parent-friendly language and provide examples of assignments, projects, and tests within each graded category.

- Grading rubrics for class work, homework, and projects which allow students frequent opportunities for self-assessment.

- Classrooms where teachers maximize time-on-task through class structure and consistent routines.

- Teachers who have been exposed to or have developed instructional practices in such areas as:
  - gender-based instruction
  - . brain-compatible instruction
  - learning-styles

- multiple intelligences
- . interdisciplinary units
- alternative assessments
- diverse cooperative grouping arrangements (i.e., personality types, multiple intelligences, ability-levels, learning-styles, or gender-based)
- the ability to build relationships and bond with students

- Identifying before- and after-school tutorial assistance by tutors who represent diverse gender, age, cultural, and instructional styles.

In addition to instructional practices, many young men will benefit from being assigned to teachers who:

- Have effective cross-cultural, cross-gender, cross-socioeconomic communication skills.

- Are able to create supportive, collaborative, culturally-sensitive classroom cultures.

- Recognize the need to develop culturally-enriching and visually-reaffirming classrooms.

- Have an intrinsic desire to collaborate with colleagues, administrators, and parents to gather data and identify strategies which best meet student needs.

In the *Hope for Urban Education: A Study of Nine High-Performing, High-Poverty, Urban Elementary Schools*, a focus on instruction was identified as one of the most critical areas of focus shared by successful schools:

The quantity and quality of time spent on instructional leadership activities increased. Principals spent more time helping teachers attend to instructional issues and decreased the time teachers spent on distractions that diverted attention away from teaching and learning. Also, principals put other educators in positions that allowed them to provide instructional leadership. School leaders constantly challenged teachers and students to higher levels of academic attainment. They used data to identify, acknowledge, and celebrate strengths and to focus attention and resources on areas of need.

Educators aligned instruction to the standards and assessments required by the state or the school district. Teachers and administrators worked together to understand precisely what students were expected to know and be able to do. Then, they planned instruction to ensure that students would have an excellent chance to learn what was expected of them.

School leaders created opportunities for teachers to work, plan, and learn together around instructional issues. Time was structured to ensure that collaboration around instructional issues became an important part of the school day and the school week.

School leaders created additional time for instruction. In some cases, efforts focused on creating additional time for attention to critical instructional issues during the school day. In other cases, efforts focused on creating additional time beyond the regular school day.

Making Connections

There are so many subjects, variations in content from school district to school district, and from level to level of the same class within a school district, which parents oftentimes do not understand of how to make the connection between classroom content and practical application in a meaningful way.

Teachers are clearly in a better position to make connections and to provide parents with handouts, worksheets, supplemental materials, at-home suggestions, and ideas for making the connection in a meaningful way to deepen a student's levels of learning.

Making connections between instructional content and students requires that teachers:

1. Care enough about students to want to better understand their levels of pre-existing knowledge, levels of exposure, cultural frame of reference, interests, and aspirations.

2. Provide opportunities, either through classroom discussions, interest surveys, parent communication, or instructional lessons to better understand student reference points.

3. Avoid the inclination to make gender-, ethnic-, or socioeconomic-based assumptions about student interests, attitudes, beliefs, aspirations, and ability levels.

Some of the approaches teachers might use to better connect with students are:

*   Perform a pre-assessment of students as close as possible to the beginning of the year using multiple assessments, interest inventories, and parent or guardian surveys.

*   Use pre-assessment information for lesson design, establishing centers, and determining cooperative grouping methodology.

*   Use pre-assessment information for lesson design to ensure the best connection to learning-styles and multiple intelligences strengths.

*   Collaborate with colleagues to develop thematic and interdisciplinary units for major content areas.

*   Look for opportunities to make connections between content areas with student needs, i.e., character development, setting goals, identifying dreams and aspirations, developing stronger families, effectively resolving conflicts, or community empowerment.

*   Make use of illustrations whenever possible.

*   Make personal connections from your own experiences.

*   Make use of artifacts.

*   Make use of music, storytelling, skits, multi-media presentations, study trips, and guest speakers.

*   Align students in Multiple Intelligences groups and assign students roles based on their dominant areas of intelligence, i.e., bodily, musical, visual, verbal, or logical and allow students to contribute to a group project through their dominant intelligence.

- Provide frequent Multiple Intelligences opportunities for applying learning through illustrations, verbal presentations, storytelling, poetry, raps, musical presentations, model-building, skits, small group collaboration, PowerPoint presentations, multi-media presentations, and acting.

- Provide opportunities for students to translate content into a cultural frame of reference.

- Look for examples to relate instructional content to a broad range of sociocultural context.

When young men exhibit their extraordinary energy levels it is considered a deficiency in the classroom and they are labeled as hyperactive. The same energy and intensity on the football field or basketball court is valued and they are received throughout the school and community as heroes. When they speak loudly and play roughly at school, they are labeled as wild and coming from poor home environments. Outside of the school they are signed to contracts in professional wrestling, produce CDs, and receive leading roles in plays.

Our challenge is to avoid labels and identify ways of expanding their gifts, harnessing their energy, and helping them to value their uniqueness and to affirm their dreams. As uncommon as this is in classrooms, Black males find their refuge in athletic programs where they bond with coaches who celebrate their gifts, encourage their pursuit of excellence, and provide discipline and direction.

This dynamic need not be limited to coaches. Understanding that Black men have a rich tradition or oral communication, teachers can get up from behind their desks, walk around the classroom and solicit more verbal responses. High-spirited, high-energy discussions will have a better chance of capturing the attention of young men. If you've ever seen Black men speak professionally, you've noticed how they move their bodies and their hands communicating as much nonverbally as they do verbally. They raise and lower their voices for emphasis. They code switch between standard and non-Standard English. The truly good ones have the unique ability to identify with a cross-spectrum of people from young to old, rich to poor, uneducated to professional, using code switching for emphasis: "Y'all know what I mean?"

Challenge young men to develop a rap about history, math, and science. Setting aside one class period for "Rapping English, Poetry Math," and "Open Mic History" can turn, otherwise boring lessons into high energy discussions and platforms for young men to "show their stuff!" This merges the skills and talents they want to develop with the material the teacher wants to cover. Getting them to move from their seats to the front of the class to explain answers will help to keep them awake and focused, avoiding their becoming restless and disinterested. By developing a supportive and encouraging classroom environment, you will provide them with the opportunity to overcome shyness, enhance their public speaking abilities, and develop their presentation skills. Encouraging them to speak loudly and clearly will help them to better and more forcefully articulate their ideas, feelings, and opinions.

Janice Hale-Benson, in *Black Children: Their Roots, Culture, and Learning-styles,* refers to research performed by Akpan Ebsen:

"The African modes of child-rearing give rise to the development of humane attitudes and the care syndrome. Unlike Western child-rearing, African socialization emphasizes the closeness of man-to-man. Physical and psychological closeness is reinforced by encouragement of body contact between people."

Some of the techniques which can assist in making a better connection with Black male students are:

- Shaking student hands as they enter the classroom.

- Touching a student's shoulder or slapping a student on the back when he participates in a classroom discussion.

- Addressing students by their surname, i.e., Mr. Wynn, Mr. Kambon, Mr. Carreker, Mr. Jones, or Mr. McBride.

- Using positive body language.

- Moving around the room during discussions.

- Providing multiple examples, i.e., visual, verbal, stories, parables, anecdotes, and manipulatives.

- Providing multiple opportunities to 'discover' the answer to a question and providing multiple clues.

- Being consistent.

- Setting clear expectations, rules, and procedures.

- Avoiding confrontations and stepping outside of the classroom with students who are determined to engage in a confrontation.

- Getting to know each student's family.

- Developing seating patterns based on student needs rather than by the alphabet.

- Making frequent use of cooperative grouping.

- Avoiding auditorium-style setting arrangements.

- Creating a risk-free environment, i.e., no laughing, name-calling, or put-downs.

- Consciously avoiding negative language, sarcasm, and negative body language.

- Never threaten a student!

Chapter 5: Key Points

1. Make 'curriculum night' more celebratory and parent-friendly with parent input.

2. Ensure that grading methodology meets student-family needs and is used as an intrinsic motivator rather than as punishment.

3. Don't grade on a curve but establish policies which continually inspire students to complete work and catch up on missing or incomplete work throughout the grading period. Don't forget rewards!

4. Develop a clear syllabus, grading rubrics for tests and major projects, study guides, supplemental materials and all of the necessary information to assist parents in supporting their son's academic achievement.

5. Identify and advise parents of teachers with expertise in multiple intelligences, single-gender classrooms, brain-compatible instruction, learning-styles, and other special needs or instructional areas.

6. Use pre-assessment data for lesson design, to identify tutorial support, materials, and field trips to increase student knowledge and to provide the necessary level of exposure.

7. Utilize Multiple Intelligences grouping to create a collaborative learning environment where student's learn to value each other's intellectual gifts and abilities.

8. Provide frequent opportunities for oral presentations.

9. Learn how to bond with students.

Chapter 6

Assessment

*If there is no struggle, there is no progress. Those who profess to favor
freedom, and yet deprecate agitation, are men who want crops without
plowing up the ground. They want rain without thunder and lightning.
They want the ocean without the awful roar of its many waters. This
struggle may be a moral one; or it may be a physical one; or it may be
both moral and physical; but it must be a struggle. Power concedes nothing
without demand.*

— *Frederick Douglass*

The area of assessment is far too broad (i.e., authentic, portfolio, grades, standardized tests, and end-of-grade exams) to be covered in any depth. The book, *A High School Plan for Students with College-Bound Dreams,* addresses in sufficient detail the importance of focusing on and preparing for such exams as the SAT, SAT IIs, ACT, AP exams, standardized tests, and high school exit exams and provides worksheets for tracking student exam scores and progress. The area of concern to be explored here, as it relates to Black males, is course grades and the importance of establishing academic goals.

Focus & Identify Goals

Setting goals and assessing strategies is one of the most challenging areas for young men and their families. Some of the reasons are:

- It is difficult to overcome preexisting stereotypes to objectively assess classroom instruction. For example, when Black males are unsuccessful in the classroom the prevailing assumption is they don't care, they're innately lazy, or they lack the intellectual capacity to be successful.

On deeper study some of the many areas of assessment which could explain classroom failure of teachers and students are:

- mismatch of teaching- to learning-styles

- cross-generational, cross-gender, cross-cultural, or cross-socioeconomic communication breakdown

- lack of preexisting knowledge in the subject matter

- lack of higher-order or critical-thinking skills

- ineffective note-taking or test preparation skills

- instructional approach relies on least developed areas of intelligence (e.g., verbal and logical versus bodily and interpersonal)

- Overcoming preexisting stereotypes to objectively assess the lack of parental involvement. For example, as alluded to in the previous Chapter, when Black parents don't attend curriculum night, respond to teacher notes, or attend teacher-requested conferences the prevailing assumption is Black parents don't value academic achievement.

On deeper study some of the many areas of assessment which could explain lack of parental involvement are:

- parents' negative experiences as a student

- parents' negative experiences with teachers who used the parents' lack of formal education to degrade or speak condescendingly

- parents' negative experiences in teacher conferences which seldom affirmed anything positive about their child

- parents' experiences with teachers who rarely take any ownership of the academic failure of their child and imply subtilely, or overtly, that all failure is attributed to the child's attitude or lack of parental support

- parent overload, i.e., a single-parent with school children in elementary, middle, and high school while working two jobs

- parents who are embarrassed by their lack of formal education and their inability to provide at-home academic support

- parents who are embarrassed by their appearance

- parents who have a criminal background, outstanding warrants, or are afraid to go to the school

- There may be an unwillingness to assess the overall effectiveness of teacher-controlled practices.

For example:

- Are classroom seating arrangements conducive to reducing personal conflicts and enhancing learning?

- Do grading policies, i.e., homework, pop quizzes, or loss points for failure to include proper headings provide a successful motivator?

- Does grading methodology, i.e., opportunities to turn in late homework for full grade, or opportunities to retake any test (failed or otherwise), motivate or demotivate student effort?

- Measuring effectiveness of discipline practices.

  - Is blind implementation of zero-tolerance policies having the desired effect?

  - Are intervention strategies appropriate and timely in preventing or reducing conflicts?

  - Does out-of-school suspensions and/or in-school detention function as a contributor or detriment to academic achievement?

  - Are discipline infractions occurring at certain times of the day, times of the school year, in particular classrooms, or in particular locations at a predictable rate?

Schoolhouses do not teach themselves—piles of brick and mortar and machinery do not send out men. It is strengthened by long study and thought, that breathes the real breath of life into boys and girls and makes them human.

— W.E.B. DuBois

Real education means to inspire people to live more abundantly, to learn to begin with life as they find it and make it better.

— Carter G. Woodson

Our people have made the mistake of confusing the methods with the objectives. As long as we agree on objectives, we should never fall out with each other just because we believe in different methods or tactics or strategy ... We have to keep in mind at all times that we are not fighting for integration, nor are we fighting for separation. We are fighting for recognition as free humans in this society.

— Malcolm X

Grading Methodology as a Motivator

In the previous Chapter, I discussed grading methodology within the context of instruction, here, we will examine it within the context of assessment through strategies of how to use it as a motivator.

The scope and magnitude of a person's goals is rooted in their experience, self-confidence, and faith. When one has experienced the thrill of victory, the satisfaction and adulation of extraordinary achievement, or the praise and acknowledgment which accompanies winning, one has an undeniable advantage over those who have never had such experiences. Setting and achieving smaller goals gives a person confidence in their ability to set and to achieve larger goals.

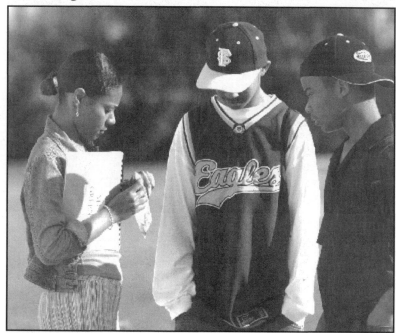

Many young men have never experienced winning academically; the exuberant feeling of having people pat you on the back and congratulate you on being the best; the personal sense of joy and fulfillment of having set a goal and achieved it is something many young men have never experienced in relation to academic achievement. They oftentimes live in households with few academic success stories, or worst, there is an academic success story they are reminded of daily as a means of further degrading or demeaning their lack of academic achievement.

For example, statements like:

- *"Why can't you be like your sister? I never have to remind her to do her homework."*

- *"Are you going to ever get an 'A?' Your sister is on the honor roll again."*

- *"What's wrong with you? You're stupid like your daddy."*

- *"I'm tired of getting called up to school. Why don't you just shut your mouth and do your work?"*

- *"If your school calls one more time, I am going to whip your butt!"*

Useni Eugene Perkins, in *Harvesting New Generations: The Positive Development of Black Youth,* quotes Booker T. Washington:

"The world should not pass judgment upon the Negro, and especially upon the Negro youth, too quickly or too harshly. The Negro boy has obstacles, discouragements, and temptations to battle with that are little known to those not situated as he is. When a white boy undertakes a task, it is taken for granted that he will succeed. On the other hand, people are usually surprised if the Negro boy does not fail. In a word, the Negro youth starts out with the presumption against him."

With the deck already stacked against Black males, we cannot allow anyone (including parents) to discourage them from setting extraordinary goals for themselves. Even the young man who has never received an 'A' on his report card must be considered an 'A' student on the first day of class.

"Class, on your desks you will find a paper with today's grade on it. Please place it into your binder and take it home to your parents. If your parents sign it and let me know the best way to get in touch with them in the event I need their help in ensuring you remain 'A' students it will count as your first extra credit grade."

A little boy walks up to the teacher. "Excuse me sir. You must have made a mistake. I ain't never been no 'A' student."

The teacher corrects the little boy's use of non-Standard English. "I haven't received an 'A' before?" The little boy responds, "You neither?"

The teacher goes on to explain to the little boy, "Young man, I'm an 'A' teacher and everyone in this classroom is an 'A' student. Since everyone is here today to learn, everyone of my students, including you, is an 'A' student today. If each student does what is expected of he or she throughout the balance of the grading period, then every student will be an 'A' student on the final day of the grading period as well. If you are not an 'A' student, then in some way I would have failed you as your teacher and I don't like to fail at anything."

The little boy stares at the teacher in disbelief. "Sir, if you're an 'A' teacher and I'm an 'A' student, then would you please call my mama after school today. She just isn't going to believe this. I just ain't never been no 'A', oh excuse me, I have never been an 'A' student before."

Thousands of Black parents, who are first generation college graduates, have experienced being told by teachers they were unable or incapable of becoming academic achievers, pursuing college-bound dreams, or had "unrealistic" aspirations toward certain professions. Many of them are the children of illiterate mothers and fathers who made sure they went to school, but who could offer little academic support after school. They know what their sons are capable of, yet, they find themselves frustrated with the low academic expectations of teachers and the constant undermining of their values and expectations by their son's peers.

Following my presentations I am often asked by teachers, "Aren't we setting these boys up for failure when we establish goals they can't possibly achieve? Can you really expect a boy who is below grade level to make it onto the honor roll in one year? Isn't it unreasonable to suggest to these children they can go to college? What's wrong with suggesting they pursue a more realistic goal like going to a trade school?" Anyone who would ask such questions doesn't understand the historical journey of the African people. Despite all of our problems and the apparently insurmountable obstacles confronting us, we have proven ourselves to be people of extraordinary resilience. We have endured terrible hardships and unspeakable cruelty, and, yet, we have survived and indeed thrived. Black men and women studied and taught themselves to read when it was forbidden and life-threatening to do so. They stood and spoke out against the treatment of Blacks, risking their lives to do so. The slave masters believed life for Blacks outside of slavery would be impossible. Racists behavioral scientists published pseudo-scholarly work claiming the Negro mind was limited genetically in the scope of its comprehension.

Don't worry about setting young men up for failure; set them up for success! Establish and affirm for them extraordinary goals. Despite their history of underachievement, there is no height Black males can't reach if they are encouraged, inspired, and lifted up toward their dreams. The job of teachers, parents, coaches, and counselors is not to determine what level of achievement is, or isn't possible for a young man, that's God's job. Our job is to encourage, inspire, enlighten, nurture, guide, and teach. God will determine their purpose, it is our job to determine their preparation.

What is in the best interest of the child?

Using this simple standard as the compass to guide the way, parents and teachers, can continually assess, evaluate, and challenge preexisting ideas and beliefs. Rules, consequences, rewards, and extrinsically motivating factors and strategies should undergo continual discussion, debate, adjustment, implementation, assessment, and reevaluation. This is not to suggest Black males be held to impossibly high standards. It is the continuing discussions and analysis which must be engaged in, always keeping in mind a future focus, "What type of men, husbands, fathers, employees, or entrepreneurs are we attempting to develop?"

Possible courses of action for classroom teachers:

- When papers don't have the proper heading, give them back and don't accept them until the heading is correct. Once the heading is corrected give full credit. Your strategy must be to force ownership of quality work not punish them to the point of it becoming a de-motivating strategy.

- Allow frequent opportunities to retake tests and quizzes to encourage continuing review of course content, deepening of knowledge, and the opportunity for before- after-school or tutorial support to inspire continually reaching for higher grades.

- Establish "Homework Make-up Days" where students who have completed and turned in all assignments have opportunities for enrichment, extra recess, movie day, or a field trip while students missing homework stay in class to complete the necessary work.

- Develop an effective communication mechanism with parents, coaches, tutors, or mentors to advise them of class work, missed homework, low test/quiz grades, or lack of quality classroom participation so they can reinforce your expectations.

- Review your grading methodology, homework policy, and policy for retaking tests within the simple context of, "Is this in the best interest of students?" Sometimes what is best for a teacher is not best for students. Students who have a history of low academic performance are in need of encouragement rather than punishment. Is the higher goal to get work done on time or to get the work done and the knowledge transferred? By the end of the K-12 process students should be academically proficient, organized, and prepared for success at the college-level. However, in the early years, academic proficiency has to have a higher priority than timeliness and organization. A homework assignment completed two weeks after the due date, yet a week before the exam, is in everyone's best interest.

Possible courses of action for parents or mentors:

- Meet with teachers to discuss the aforementioned ideas with the goal of developing common expectations and appropriate strategies which will nurture academic effort and encourage academic excellence.

- Make school and school work a priority, second only to God and family. What is on your son's back (i.e., what he's wearing) is never as important as what is in his head (i.e., what he's thinking)!

- Develop rewards and consequences within the context of educational expectations.

- When your son falls behind in his school work he may need to sacrifice his weekend to catch up. Despite his unwillingness to sacrifice 'his' time to catch up on 'his business' what you do will have long-range consequences and clearly communicate your expectations, or lack thereof, as it pertains to academic excellence.

Following are some of the strategies my wife and I utilize to reinforce our expectations:

- My wife and I have developed a ritual where we unplug and pack away video game systems at the beginning of the school year and we leave them packed away until the holiday or end of the school year.

- We also take all of the designer clothes and shoes out of our older son's closet until after the first progress report grades come home. He is able to use some of his grades to buy back articles of clothing.

- Our sons don't enjoy any weekend activities until all homework and projects are completed. The one exception is if they are up-to-date in all of their classes, they are able to participate in team sports where teammates depend on their contribution.

- We do not allow our sons to watch television from Sunday evening through Thursday evening unless they are up-to-date in every class, have all homework and projects completed, haven't had any assignments turned in late, and have completed all of their chores (as you may guess, they rarely earn the right to watch television during the week).

- Each of our sons begins the school year with a box containing everything required to successfully complete homework, i.e., dictionary, thesaurus, ruler, pens, pencils, pencil sharpener, three-hole-puncher, paper, colored pencils, and highlight markers.

- No telephone calls until all school work and homework have been completed.

- We e-mail teachers regularly, oftentimes daily.

- We post report cards and standardized test scores onto the refrigerator for everyone to see and to provide continually reinforcement of high expectations.

For more ideas and suggestions of how to create a home environment which promotes and reinforces academic achievement refer to the book, *Ten Steps to Helping Your Child Succeed in School.*

Parent–Teacher Communication

Parent–Teacher communication is key to paving the way toward higher academic achievement levels and the reinforcement of character, conduct, values, and guiding principles. Such communication is strengthened or weakened through the relationship between parents and teachers. The entire school community thrives or suffers as a result of the relationships between adult stakeholders, at the center of which, are parents and teachers. Thusly, Black males thrive or suffer as a result of the relationships between parents and teachers.

When confronted with low academic performance and disruptive behaviors in the classroom many teachers assume parents don't care about academic achievement and that we fail to appropriately and effectively discipline our children. I have sat in numerous parent-teacher conferences where I have received incredulous looks from teachers when I have told them the type of behaviors they are describing and experiencing in the classroom is unusual for our sons. On more than one occasion they have looked at my wife with an incredulous look, "Is he for real?" Teachers have been shocked to hear what's been said, in front of my children, in regards to our academic and behavior expectations. As has been the case since our sons have been in school, the only time their behavior has gotten out of control or when they have fallen behind academically, has been when their classroom teachers have been lax in communicating any problems to my wife and me.

Freeman Hrabowski, president of the University of Maryland Baltimore County, in *Beating the Odds: Raising Academically Successful African American Males,* notes:

In our work, we often hear African American parents expressing the hope and desire that their children will achieve at the highest levels academically. What we also hear from these parents, though, is that one rarely sees in the media examples of young Black males who are achieving academically, being rewarded for those achievements, and feeling good about being smart. Even among advantaged African American families, we find that young males are heavily influenced by the popular culture that discourages pride in high academic achievement, demands that young Black males present a hard veneer to the world, and provides numerous opportunities for these young males to become involved in a world of crime and drugs. In fact, the idea of this book originated from our concern about the frightening status of young African American males and the need to find effective, family-based, educational solutions to enhance their futures.

The ability for parents and teachers to reach agreement as to strategies and expectations is critical to the continuing academic success of Black males. These strategies must take into account the lack of academic support among peers, school-wide cultures which don't promote or reinforce academic achievement, and any past history of low teacher or parental expectations.

When our older son was in the fifth grade I pointed out to his teacher the Black males in her classroom who were academically capable of qualifying for the school's honor roll and volunteered to meet with her to discuss ways of motivating them to work harder and to take greater pride in submitting quality work. She rebuffed my efforts and told me that children should be allowed to fail so they would eventually grow to appreciate the importance of applying themselves.

We don't help young men by allowing them to develop poor study habits, low personal academic expectations, and dwell at the bottom of the academic achievement gap. When schools have academic recognition days, honor roll ceremonies, induction into the National Honor Society and there is a noticeable absence of Black males, we eventually find it is less noticeable they aren't participating as the entire school community comes to expect their absence. The end result of such a belief system was evident in the lack of Black males inducted into the National Junior Honor Society at the Middle School. As the guest speaker at the ceremony, I invited my older son to attend so that he would witness firsthand an induction group of nearly two hundred students with only one Black male.

> *I have come to a frightening conclusion: I am the decisive element in the classroom. It is my personal approach that creates the climate. It is my daily mood that makes the weather.*
>
> *As a teacher I possess tremendous power to make a child's life miserable or joyous. I can be a tool of torture or an instrument of inspiration. I can humiliate or humor, hurt or heal. In all situations, it is my response that dictates whether a crisis will be escalated or de-escalated and a child humanized or de-humanized.*
>
> *— Dr. Hiam Ginott*

Parents must consciously and purposefully attempt to identify the most nurturing classroom environments for their sons. The questions parents should raise are the same questions teachers should raise after reviewing their own data:

- Do Black males receive disproportionately lower grades than other students?

- Are they disproportionately referred to the office more than other students?

- Are their discipline infractions more punitively dealt with through suspensions and explusions than other students?

- Does the teacher make an effort to keep lines of communication open with parents and are parents informed of possible problem areas prior to discipline referrals or low and failing grades?

- Does the teacher encourage scheduling parent conferences in a manner most convenient for the parent or does the teacher offer alternative means of communication?

- Does the teacher recommend supplemental materials, tutors, or suggestions to deepen learning and enhance academic performance?

- Does the teacher provide a course syllabus which clearly outlines how grades are calculated, when assignments are due, how to best prepare for tests and quizzes, and in specific terms what is required to achieve success in his or her classroom?

- Does the teacher provide clear grading rubrics for major assignments which clearly outline expectations and how student performance will be objectively graded?

- Does the teacher provide clear and frequent opportunities to discuss a student's performance via pre-determined conference times, e-mail correspondence, before- after-school conference opportunities, or during regularly-scheduled planning times?

- Does the teacher appear to demonstrate a genuine interest in student success and is the teacher proactive in communicating ideas and suggestions for student success?

Chapter 6: Key Points

1. Gather classroom achievement data and engage in an ongoing assessment of classroom instruction.

2. Assess parental involvement and survey parents to better understand and meet parent needs.

3. Assess effectiveness of classroom management and identify where student-teacher, student-student, and classroom disruptions occur.

4. Use grading methodology to encourage excellence and to inspire students to submit quality work.

5. Collaborate with parents and mentors to ensure homework is completed and tests and quizzes are adequately prepared for.

6. Build strong parent-teacher relationships.

7. Consciously create a nurturing classroom environment.

8. Inspire students to set personal goals and lead them in developing the necessary kindergarten-through-college plans to achieve their goals.

Passion is not friendly. It is arrogant, superbly contemptuous of all that is not itself, and, as the very definition of passion implies the impluse to freedom, it has a mighty intimidating power. It contains a challenge. It contains an upspeakable hope.

— James Baldwin

Epilogue

Turn the Ships Around

Let it be known that we are looking for a brother who will turn the ships around.
A brother who will go into the crack house and turn the ships around.
A brother who will go to the places where it is open season on our children and turn the ships around.
A brother who will hear the screams of sisters beaten to death by the men who say they love them and turn the ships around.
A brother who will hear the whimper of our babies born with AIDS and turn the ships around.
A brother who will remember how freedom feels and turn the ships around.
A brother who will gather with the warriors and march down to the edge of the sea and turn the ships around, turn the ships around, turn the ships around, and this time, turn the ships around ...

— Pearl Cleage

The above referenced quote is taken from the book, *Deals with the Devil and Other Reasons to Riot*. Pearl Cleage describes the communication breakdown between Black women and Black men in dealing with some of the pressing issues of the Black community, families, and the rearing of Black children.

Brothers feel that we, their sisters, are giving mixed signals when it comes to the manhood thing. We want, they say, all the protection and safety offered by a strong man, but we are unwilling to accept the presence of the warrior's heart.

We, they say, are responsible for any confusion that exists on the manhood question; we are the ones, they say, that counsel caution instead of courage; diplomacy instead of defense.

They say that when the ships pulled up on the shores of Africa and slavers came ashore to look for us, we were the ones who held them back; the ones who told them that it might be dangerous to go down to the water's edge.

We were the ones, they say, who encouraged them to stay at home, telling them how worried we would be if they went down there with the other warriors to turn the ships around, assuring them that if they just sat here by the fire with us, the white folks would probably change their minds and go away all by themselves. They say that's the reason why they didn't turn the ships around. Because they thought we didn't want them to.

It has been my intent with each of the previous Chapters to provide clear strategies and solutions to many of the issues hindering the education of Black males. Turning the ships around will require that we, as advocates for Black males (i.e., parents, teachers, coaches, mentors) develop the courage to turn the ships around.

Fathers

Black males are desperately in need of fathers, or father figures who will teach them the lessons about manhood and fatherhood which only a father can teach. Black males learn more from watching what fathers do than from listening to what fathers say. Don't just "talk the talk," fathers must "walk the

walk." Among the most important lessons for fathers to teach young men is how to respect, protect, and cherish women. Whether their mother, grandmother, aunt, sister, girlfriend, wife, or teacher—young men must learn how not to verbally, emotionally, or physically abuse women. The first and lasting messages a Black male will receive will come from how he sees his father treating women. The mannerisms, language, tone of voice, and approach to resolving conflicts modeled by fathers will frame a young man's relationship with women for a lifetime.

Every opportunity a father has to spend time with his son should be treasured. Whether throwing a ball, taking in a movie, sharing a pizza, or sitting among older men sharing their wisdom and telling stories of days gone by—all of these moments should be viewed as opportunities to help a young man along his journey. These too, must be guided by a mission to assist in his development and a vision of the type of man he can become.

Women and Men

Black males learn to manipulate their moms against those men who would attempt to have a hand in raising them, albeit dads, step dads, grand dads, uncles, coaches, or boy friends. My wife has heard our sons say dad is mean, the football coach is mean, the track coach is mean, and their male teacher is mean.

"Mom, why is Dad so mean? He won't let me do anything."

"Mom, no matter what I do, the coach says I'm not doing it right. I don't want to play football anymore."

"Mom, coach wants me to run too many events at the track meet. I don't think I want to run track anymore."

"Mom, can you move me to another class, he's mean?"

"Mom, would you talk to Dad, I didn't do anything?"

Recognizing when a father or coach is being unfair or overdemanding versus having high expectations and stretching a young man toward reaching his potential can be difficult. There have been times when my wife has felt I was being overly harsh or had expectations which were unreasonably high. However, my wife and I have learned to privately discuss such issues and we both have learned to listen and to value each other's opinions. The compass which guides us is our shared mission of raising and preparing our boys for manhood and our vision of the types of men whom we are attempting to help our boys to become. As my wife and I work together in our attempts to identify the best strategies and most effective methods of discipline, we attempt to work with our sons' teachers and coaches in the same way. Through such discussions we have oftentimes adjusted strategies and revised our system of rewards and consequences. The question mothers, fathers, coaches, and teachers should ask is:

What is in the best interest of the child (or young man)?

Parents will have to be conscious of not becoming contributors to, or encouraging such counterproductive behaviors by:

- Allowing or excusing disrespectful behaviors toward adults.

- Taking sides with their sons against the other parent or against a teacher or coach. A disagreement between parents or between parents and teachers should be discussed privately between the adults involved.

- Allowing their sons to sloppily perform their chores and responsibilities, fail to complete class work, avoid homework, or simply refuse to go to work.

- Constantly excusing their son's behaviors.

In the case of single-moms, mothers must have a vision of the type of man she wants to nurture her son into becoming. Once the vision is clear, she must identify men who can positively influence the growth, development, and maturation of her son and actively try to provide opportunities for her son to interact with men whom she can trust to teach her son some of the important lessons of becoming a man and who will reinforce her moral and spiritual values.

My wife and I consciously try to settle our disagreements in private, develop strategies we both agree to, and continually seek God's divine guidance in raising our sons. My wife and I consciously work at limiting the instances in which our sons are able to manipulate us. However, despite our best efforts, they are smart! They know when one of us is distracted, likely to say 'yes' to something we normally would say 'no' to, or when we are simply in the mood to bend the rules a little. Our sons have attempted to play my wife and me against each other with their sneaky little schemes where they ask one parent for something the other parent has either said no to, or they know the parent is likely to say no. My younger son will walk pass my wife, through the entire house, come downstairs to my office and ask, "Dad can I have dessert?" My answer for him is always, "Go and ask you mother." I want him to know that I know what his mother would say, "No!" Other times my older son will say, "Dad, I finished all of my homework, can I go to the movies?" My answer to him is, "Leave your work on the table so I can check it and I'll get back to you." Then I go and speak to my wife to see if there are any other responsibilities which she has for him.

Women and men (albeit mothers and fathers, grandmothers and coaches, teachers and fathers, step parents or guardians, and/or teachers and principals) must be in agreement, share a common vision, and be willing to effectively communicate and collaborate in the social, emotional, spiritual, and intellectual maturation and development of young men.

Protecting Black Males

We must turn the ships around of those who would destroy Black males. While Black males need men in their lives, parents must take the time to get to know the people whom they are entrusting their sons to. Parents must become more discerning than to simply deliver their sons into the hands of teachers, coaches, programs, and peers without knowing the people, households, classrooms, or programs with whom their sons are spending their time. I believe my wife has the best attitude, "She doesn't trust anyone with our sons." While some may consider her attitude overly protective, there are too many Black males who don't have people looking after or out for them.

- *Abuse:* Abuse can occur anywhere and with anyone. Communicating with young men can be a difficult task. Oftentimes, they will begin a sentence but won't complete the thought. When pressured they will shut down completely, "That's alright" or "I don't want to talk about it." Keeping lines of communication open will require a great deal of patience and being aware of mood swings, depression, unprovoked anger, and any noticeable emotional changes following or subsequent to visits with relatives, friends, or other adults and even after they have been left with baby sitters. While we cannot always protect young men from physical abuse, we must be more watchful of the verbal abuse directed at them from parents, teachers, and coaches. Whenever we hear negative, dehumanizing, and humiliating language being directed toward young men, i.e., dummy, stupid, ignorant, fool, dumb ass, jack ass, or moron we must provide advocacy to help adults better understand the power of the language they are using and its ability to either uplift or destroy young men.

- *Coaches:* Get to know the coaches who recruit your sons. Research their programs, graduation rates, number of players who have discipline infractions, the standards of dress and behavior exhibited by their athletes, and the type of people whom coaches surround their athletes with (i.e., boosters, tutors, cheerleaders, or large donors). A coach who has the best interest of your son at heart should be able to articulate a clear vision of what will happen for your son while in his program. He should also be able to provide former athletes who can attest to his leadership and commitment to the emotional and social development of his athletes.

USA Today, January 27, 2005
Staff

A former high school coach told a federal jury Wednesday that he got offers of money, a job and free law school for his wife before he accepted a $150,000 payoff to steer his best player to sign with Alabama.

In testimony Tuesday in U.S. District Court, [Lynn] Lang said coaches at two other Southeastern Conference schools, Kentucky and Georgia, gave him money. He also testified that Tennessee, Mississippi, Michigan State and Arkansas offered money for [Albert] Means but never paid.

Lang added Memphis to the list of colleges that offered him a deal, testifying that then-coach Rip Scherer said he would arrange for Lang's wife to attend law school for free at the university.

Lang also told jurors Arkansas offered him either a coaching job at more than $80,000 a year or $150,000 in cash if he delivered Means and another player.

Means, who has not been accused of wrongdoing, previously testified he let Lang choose his college. Lang said he began shopping Means to various colleges in 1999 when he realized how many schools wanted him.

Lang, who made less than $30,000 at Trezevant [High School], said he kept upping the price until it reached $150,000.

- *Teachers:* Read the book, *Ten Steps to Helping Your Child Succeed in School,* and learn how to research and identify the best teachers for your son prior to his entering into the next grade level or a new school setting. If you are a teacher and you know there are ineffective teachers within your school who are destroying Black males in their classrooms, be an advocate and help the teachers to get better or help the young men to get out of their classrooms. "What would you do if it was your child?"

- *Mentors:* Meet the mentors before sending your son to a mentoring program and/or accompany your son to the first meeting. Get to know the mentors who will be working with your son and get their information, i.e., employer, home phone, and cell phone and find out how the program identifies mentors and whether or not they perform background checks.

- *Clergy:* Get your son involved in the right church with pastors and assistant pastors who are well known and have stellar reputations and make sure you know the pastor or assistant pastor who is working with your son.

- *Secluded, late night, or over night stays:* Be aware of where you son is, who he is with, and how to contact him. This includes sleep overs, late night tutoring sessions, field trips, overnight school-related trips, and out-of-town sporting events. Volunteer to be a chaperone until you have confidence in those persons who are responsible for caring for your son.

- *Sleep overs and camps:* In addition to what was previously stated, don't allow your sons to sleep over someone else's home or at an overnight camp unless you are absolutely sure your son is in a protective and caring environment. Don't allow him to spend the night with friends whose parents you don't personally know. Take the time to meet the parents and visit their home. Don't be weakened and give in due to his whining. The rule of thumb is, if he whines a lot, then he probably doesn't need to go anyway!

- *Girls:* Have candid conversations about girls: compromising situations to avoid; condoms; drugs; alcohol; cigarettes; how to avoid physical confrontations; how to recognize and avoid physical and emotional abuse; and how to adhere to a standard of behavior in the treatment of women which demonstrate a set of core or moral values beyond those which are popularized in film and music videos, and oftentimes encouraged by peers.

- *Gangs:* Don't assume that only certain types of young men join or are pressured into joining gangs. Learn about the gangs in your community and ways to avoid them.

- *Law Enforcement:* Teach Black males how to effectively respond to law enforcement—particularly, how to speak calmly, follow instructions, and keep any attitude to themselves.

- *Internet:* Locate computers in open areas, i.e., kitchen, den, family room, or your office. Keep computers out of rooms where young men can close the door and isolate themselves from the rest of the family. It's no longer enough to set up firewalls, passcodes, or to unplug the computer from the wall. Whatever measures you can think of to limit access, your son can probably figure out ten ways to get around whatever you've done.

- *Music and Music Videos:* Take away the headphones and force young men to play whatever music they want to listen to over the speakers so everyone can hear it. Pay attention to the messages which today's music and music videos are promoting (i.e., sex, degradation of women, infidelity) and ask yourself if these are the messages you believe young men should be exposed to each day, oftentimes for hours at a time.

- *Theater and Television Programming:* Go to the movies and sit with young men during their preferred television programming. Engage them in a discussion of the appropriateness of the behaviors and language of those being portrayed. Find out how their ideas, values, and beliefs are being influenced by the type of programming.

- *Video Games:* Unless a young man has completed all of his school work, is on or above grade level in reading, writing, science, and mathematics, has completed all of his household chores, and can talk to you about a good book he has read, there shouldn't be any time to play video games.

If he has truly earned video game time, carefully consider whether to allow your son to play the games which involve stealing cars, shooting people, or otherwise engaging in the type of activities or exhibiting the type of behaviors which we, as parents and teachers, are attempting to guide him away from.

- *Unsupervised Time:* One of the best ways to avoid predators and potentially dangerous situations is to maximize the amount of supervised and actively involved time. Filling his time with family activities, sports, community service, organized and supervised activities, hobbies, and special-interest areas such as art, music, martial arts, singing, building models, tutoring others, or coaching youth sports will substantially reduce idle time.

A Final Word ...

When I entered kindergarten, firmly rooted in my culture, I met a jolly teacher whose warm smile and tight hugs reminded me of my mother. This jolly old educator took me as I was, tattered clothes and nappy hair; full lips and broad nose; high energy and inquisitive mind. When I said, "I ain't got none," she told me, "I don't have any." The way she said it made it sound right although she never criticized me for saying it differently.

As I journeyed through school, I met other teachers who made me feel proud of myself. They never told me being Black was bad or my "Black English" was wrong. They just told me there was another way to speak so other people could understand me. When I came to school "Leanin'." With my pants hanging low and my shirt hanging out, they didn't tell me I was disgraceful, just that there was a standard of behavior and a code of conduct more befitting my royal heritage.

When they taught me math and science, they told me of the Africans who were the first great mathematicians, astrologers, scientists, and philosophers. When they taught me pride in myself, they told me of the strength, conviction, and principles of Booker T. Washington, George Washington Carver, Martin Luther King, Jr., Malcolm X, and Paul Robeson. They always told me I was capable of overcoming any obstacle; I would experience prejudice and ignorance, but I must never feel I was not entitled to the very best which life had to offer.

They always told me the homeless and helpless brothers were not always that way; there was a time when the world marveled at the architectural, intellectual, and artistic achievements of Africans; the beauty of African women and the strength, courage, and leadership of African men had inspired cultures throughout the world. They always told me I could become a great business leader; I could become an employer—not just an employee; I could shape the face of my community—not just wait for others to decide my fate.

Yes, beginning with that jolly old educator, I have been taught my lineage did not begin in the ghettos of America but at the beginning of civilization. I have been empowered with courage and confidence, cultural awareness and compassion, principles and conviction, diligence and determination. I have been loved and nurtured, disciplined and educated, taught self-respect and respect for others. Those who love me have placed me on the high road of life. I have been empowered to succeed!

Nathan and Julia Hare, in *Bringing the Black Boy to Manhood; The Passage*, state:

What we need, is some way to bring the Black boy to manhood, to highlight and sharpen the focus of the importance and significance of being a man. We must be in search of a way to give the Black boy a sense of becoming a man, a clearer sense of self and of purpose, responsibility to his roles as father and husband, a sacredness of self and others in the context of a more attentive family and community network of adult endorsement.

To understand the importance of "the passage," we must reflect culturally on the pre-colonial customs, rituals, and ceremonies of Africa. In Africa, there was a formal Rite of Passage for the young men of the tribe to make a ceremonial journey and accept the associated responsibilities of manhood. The Black community has no such community-wide program. There is no formal acknowledgment of, and associated responsibilities for, recognizing manhood.

Many young men undergo initiation rites when entering gangs. Is this the standard of manhood we want young Black men to be measured against? The gang code of conduct places them in direct opposition to the progress, prosperity, and development of the Black community. While hazing in athletic programs and college fraternities have come under intense scrutiny, we must continue to be every watchful of those initiation rites which have young men barking like dogs, walking, looking, and forced to behave in demoralizing and dehumanizing ways. No such practices represent the way through which young Black men should enter manhood?

So many young Black men have an overpowering, almost addictive, need to join a group or gang they are willing to do almost anything. A rite of passage program should elevate and edify young men to become men. Through a rite of passage, they should formally accept the responsibilities of manhood. They should be formally presented before the community and required to think, articulate, and display what it means to be a man. The transition from boyhood to manhood requires an awareness and acknowledgment of young Black men as representing the life-blood of the community. They are the future vanguards of our history, the fathers of our children, the leaders of our journey toward excellence in our schools, homes, churches, businesses, political offices, and communities. Even when such formal rites of passage programs are unavailable, a parent's continual reminder of the family's values, expectations, and vision can serve to lead a young man along his journey and push him toward excellence which will allow him to become what Tavis Smiley calls, "A Race Model."

The world will begin to see Black boys and Black men differently when they begin to see themselves differently. The world will begin to expect the best from Black men when they begin to expect the best from themselves. Perhaps more than any other race of people, future generations of Black men can stand as one of the Great Wonders of the World, having made the journey from hopelessness and despair to self-assurance and prosperity.

The *Rite of Passage* should become as common in our schools and homes as are pimples and puppy love. Our communities should come to bestow the same adulation on our young men who behave as men as we do upon athletes, entertainers, and movie stars. All young men should come to expect, and eagerly anticipate, their transition from boyhood to manhood and their ascension to the next generation of leadership within the Black community and throughout American society.

Attending to the growth and maturation of Black males requires that we never let our guard down. Black males are constantly in danger—sexual predators, media images, coaches who would exploit them, girls who would entrap them, teachers who won't teach them, law enforcement personnel who would imprison them, and other Black males who would kill them. Learn how to listen to young men and how to listen to those who advocate on their behalf. Oftentimes, it's not what's said but what remains unsaid. Listen to the words but learn how to read a person's actions. Finally, learn how to accept the pouting, whining, and complaining of young men as you establish boundaries, limit television time, and say 'No' to many of the things they want to do, places they want to go, and people whom they want to socialize with. While a son may rebel and may even say he hates you today, after he becomes the man whom God ordains him to become, he will love you for all you did to protect him.

To fully operationalize the strategies set forth in this book a collaboration between all of the adult stakeholders within a school community is needed to develop customs, rituals, awards, and ceremonies which motivate, inspire, reinforce, and celebrate Black male achievement. As a society we recognize and celebrate achievement in athletics and entertainment far above the levels of artistic, academic, community service, leadership, and citizenship. Each school community must recognize its capacity to develop awards, pins, trophies, jackets, sweaters, ribbons, plaques, certificates, and banners celebrating Black male achievement in ways which motivate and inspire young men to become all they can be and who God created them to be.

References

Accelerated Schools Project. (1995). *Accelerated Schools.* Stanford, CA: Stanford University.

Akbar, Na'im. (1991). *Visions for Black Men.* Nashville, TN: Winston-Derek.

Alston, III, J. & Richardson, B. (1991). *Story Power: Talking with Teens in Turbulent Times.* Stamford, CT: Longmeadow Press.

Bell, Janet Cheatham. (1986). *Famous Black Quotations.* Chicago, IL: Sabay.

Boyd, Todd. (2003). *Young, Black, Rich, and Famous.* New York, NY: Doubleday.

Brookover, W., Beady, C., Floor, P., Schweitzer, J., & Wisenbaker, J. (1979). *School Social Systems and Student Achievement: Schools Can Make a Difference.* South Hadley, MA: J.F. Bergin.

Brophy, J.E., & Good, T.L. (1974). *Teacher-Student Relationships: Causes and Consequences.* New York, NY: Holt, Rinehart, and Winston.

Canfield, Jack, & Hansen, Mark Victor. (1993). *Chicken Soup for the Soul.* Deerfield Beach, FL: Health Communications.

Carson, Ben with Murphey, Cecil. (1990). *Gifted Hands: The Ben Carson Story.* Washington, DC: Review and Herald.

Carter, Marlene. (2004). *Just Getting By: Middle Class African American Males Who Are Not Reaching Their Academic Potential.* University Press.

Children's Defense Fund. (May, 2004). *The Road to Dropping Out: Minority Students & Academic Factors Correlated with Failure to Complete High School.* Washington, DC.

Clarke, John Henrik. (1990). *Can African People Save Themselves?* Detroit, MI: Alkebulans.

Cleage, Pearl. (1987). *Deals with the Devil and Other Reasons to Riot.* New York, NY: Ballantine.

Cole, Johnnetta B. (1993). *Straight Talk with America's Sister President.* New York, NY: Doubleday.

Collins, Marva. (1992). *Ordinary Children, Extraordinary Teachers.* Norfolk, VA: Hampton Roads.

Collins, Marva & Tamarkin, Civia. (1982). *Marva Collins' Way.* New York, NY: G.P. Putnam's Sons.

Duncan, Thelma. *(PEP) Los Angeles Unified School District: Proficiency in English Program for Speaker's of 'Black English.'* Los Angeles, CA: Los Angeles Unified Schools.

Dunn, R., Dunn, K., & Treffinger, D. (1992). *Bringing out the Giftedness in your Child.* New York, NY: John Wiley & Sons.

Elliott, Jane. *A Lesson in Bigotry.* http://www.nwrel.org/cfc/newsletters/vol2_is6.asp

Enrollment in Public Elementary and Secondary Schools, by Race/Ethnicity and Locale. (Fall 1999). http://nces.ed.gov/surveys/ruraled/data/Race_Ethnicity.asp

Gardner, Howard. (1983). *Frames of Mind: The Theory of Multiple Intelligences.* New York, NY: Harper and Row.

Gurian, Michael. (2001). *Boys and Girls Learn Differently: A Guide for Teachers and Parents.* San Francisco, CA: Jossey-Bass.

Hale-Benson, Janice. (1986). *Black Children: Their Roots, Culture, and Learning-styles.* Baltimore, MD: Johns Hopkins University Press.

Hare, Julia & Hare, Nathan. (1985). *Bringing the Black Boy to Manhood: The Passage.* San Francisco, CA: Black Think Tank.

Harvard University. (2002). *The Impact of Racial and Ethnic Diversity on Educational Outcomes: Cambridge, MA School District.* Cambridge, MA: The Civil Rights Project.

Harvard University. (2004). *Brown at 50: King's Dream or Plessy's Nightmare?* Cambridge, MA: The Civil Rights Project.

Hilliard, A., Payton-Stewart, L., & Williams, L.O. (1990). *Infusion of African and African-American Content in the School Curriculum.* Morristown, PA: Aaron Press.

Holy Bible. King James Version. Nashville, TN: Winston Publishing.

Hood, Elizabeth F. (1973). *Educating Black Students: Some Basic Issues.* Detroit, MI: Detroit Educational Consultants.

Hrabowski III, F., Greif, G., & Maton, K. (1998). *Beating the Odds: Raising Academically Successful African American Males.* New York, NY: Oxford University Press.

Indiana Education Policy Center. (2000). *Minority Overrepresentation in Indiana's Special Education Programs.* Bloomington, IN: Indiana University.

Johnson & Johnson. (1988). *Motivating Minority Students: Strategies that Work*. Springfield, IL: Thomas Books.

Kennedy, Randall. (2002). *Nigger: The Strange Career of a Troublesome Word*. New York, NY: Vintage Books.

Kohn, Alfie. (1993). *Punished by Rewards*. New York, NY: Houghton Mifflin.

Kunjufu, Jawanza. (1989). *A Talk with Jawanza*. Chicago, IL: African-American Images.

Kunjufu, Jawanza. (1983). *Countering the Conspiracy to Destroy Black Boys, Volume I*. Chicago, IL: African-American Images.

Kunjufu, Jawanza. (1986). *Countering the Conspiracy to Destroy Black Boys, Volume II*. Chicago, IL: African-American Images.

Kunjufu, Jawanza. (1990). *Countering the Conspiracy to Destroy Black Boys, Volume III*. Chicago, IL: African-American Images.

Kunjufu, Jawanza. (1986). *Motivating and Preparing Black Youth to Work*. Chicago, IL: African-American Images.

Kuykendall, Crystal. (1991). Keynote Address: *The High Road to Life*. Atlanta, GA: Wholistic Institute.

Lein, L., Johnson, J.F., & Ragland, M. (1996). Successful Texas School-wide Programs: Research Study Results. Austin, TX: Charles A. Dana Center at the University of Texas at Austin.

Madhubuti, Haki. (1990). *Black Men: Obsolete, Single, Dangerous?* Chicago, IL: Third World Press.

Monroe, Lorraine. (1997). *Nothing's Impossible: Leadership Lessons from Inside and Outside the Classroom*. New York, NY: Random House.

Myers, Isabel Briggs & Myers, Peter. (1990). *Gifts Differing: Understanding Personality Type*. Palo Alto, CA: CPP Books.

National Center for Education Statistics. (1993-1994). *America's Teachers: Profile of a Profession*. U.S. Department of Education.

National Center for Education Statistics. (2001). *Educational Achievement and Black-White Inequality*. U.S. Department of Education.

National Center for Education Statistics. (2003). *Status and Trends in the Education of Blacks*. U.S. Department of Education.

National Center for Education Statistics. (1995). *The Condition of Education, 1994: The Educational Progress of Black Students.* U.S. Department of Education.

National Center for Education Statistics. (2001). *The Condition of Education, 2001.* U.S. Department of Education.

National Center for Learning Disabilities. (April 2003). *Minority Students in Special Education.* New York, NY: NCLD.

National Collegiate Athletic Association. (1997). *NCAA Research Report Characteristics of NCAA Division I Recruits in the 1994-95: Initial-Eligibility Clearinghouse (IEC).* Overland Park, KS: National Collegiate Athletic Association.

No Child Left Behind Act of 2001. (2001). Public Law print of PL 107-110. http://www.ed.gov/policy/elsec/leg/esea02/index.html

Organization for Economic Co-Operation and Development (OECD). (2000). *Reading for Change: Performance and Engagement Across Countries: Results from PISA 2000.* http://www.pisa.oecd.org/

Payne, Ruby K. (1998). *A Framework for Understanding Poverty.* Highlands, TX: RFT Publishing.

Perkins, Useni Eugene. (1990). *Harvesting New Generations: The Positive Development of Black Youth.* Chicago, IL: Third World Press.

Persell, C.H. (1977). *Education and Inequality: The Roots and Results of Stratification in America's Schools.* New York, NY: The Free Press.

Peters, Stephen G. (2001). *Inspired to Learn: Why We Must Give Children Hope.* Marietta, GA: Rising Sun Publishing.

Rothman, Robert. (2001). *Closing the Achievement Gap: How Schools Are Making It Happen.* The Journal of the Annenberg Challenge. Vol. 5, Number 5.

Robinson, Weaver, et. al. (1978). *Beyond Identify: Education and the Future Role of Black Americans.* Ann Arbor, MI: University Microfilms.

Simms, E., O'Neal, B., & Kowalski, C.J. (2004). *Perspectives on Teacher Education Reform: Unique Partnership Initiatives.* Orangeburg, SC: South Carolina State University.

Smiley, Tavis. (2001). *How to Make Black America Better.* New York, NY: Anchor Books.

Smith & Chunn. (1989). *Black Education: A Quest for Equity and Excellence.* New Brunswick, CT: Transaction Publishers.

Southern Illinois University. (2000). *A New Look at the Educational System and Its Impact on the African American Male.* Carbondale, IL: Southern Illinois University.

Star Plan: The Portland Blueprint: Success for Students at Risk. (1989). Portland, OR: Public Schools.

Tatum, Beverly Daniel. (1997). *Why Are All the Black Kids Sitting Together in the Cafeteria?* New York, NY: Basic Books.

Texas Education Agency. (1989). *Effective Schools Research and Dropout Reduction.* Austin, TX: Texas Education Agency.

USA Today. (January 27, 2005). *Ex-high school coach says colleges offered cash for top recruit.* USA Today.

U.S. Department of Commerce, Bureau of the Census. (2003). *Poverty in the United States: 2002.* U.S. Department of Commerce.

U.S. Department of Commerce, Bureau of the Census. (2002). *The Black Population in the United States: March 2002.* U.S. Department of Commerce.

U.S. Department of Education. (1999). *Hope for Urban Education: A Study of Nine High-Performing, High-Poverty, Urban Elementary Schools.* U.S. Department of Education.

U.S. Department of Education White Paper. (October 20, 1997). *Mathematics Equals Opportunity.* U.S. Department of Education.

U.S. Department of Justice. (12/31/03). *Summary Findings of Prison Statistics.* http://www.ojp.usdoj.gov/bjs/prisons.htm

University of Nebraska-Lincoln. (2000). *The Color of Discipline: Sources of Racial and Gender Disproportionality in School Punishment.* Policy research Report #SRS1.

West, Earle H. (1972). *The Black American and Education.* Columbus, OH: Merrill.

Woodson, Carter G. (1933). *The Mis-Education of the Negro.* Associated Publishers.

Wynn, Mychal. (2005). *A High School Plan for Students with College-Bound Dreams.* Marietta, GA: Rising Sun Publishing.

Wynn, Mychal. (2005). *A Middle School Plan for Students with College-Bound Dreams*. Marietta, GA: Rising Sun Publishing.

Wynn, Mychal. (1994). *Building Dreams: Helping Students Discover Their Potential: Teacher, Parent, Mentor Workbook*. Marietta, GA: Rising Sun Publishing.

Wynn, Mychal. (1990). *Don't Quit – Inspirational Poetry*. Marietta, GA: Rising Sun Publishing.

Wynn, Mychal. (2001). *Follow Your Dreams: Lessons That I Learned in School*. Marietta, GA: Rising Sun Publishing.

Wynn, Mychal. (2002). *Increasing Student Achievement: Volume I, Vision*. Marietta, GA: Rising Sun Publishing.

Wynn, Mychal. (2002). *Ten Steps to Helping Your Child Succeed in School*. Marietta, GA: Rising Sun Publishing.

Wynn, Mychal. (2003). *The Eagle Team: A Leadership Curriculum*. Marietta, GA: Rising Sun Publishing.

Wynn, Mychal. (1993). *The Eagles who Thought They were Chickens: A Tale of Discovery*. Marietta, GA: Rising Sun Publishing.

Wynn, Mychal. (1994). *The Eagles who Thought They were Chickens: Student Activity Book*. Marietta, GA: Rising Sun Publishing.

1. Edelman, Marian Wright. (2001). *What Can We Do?* Quoted from: *How to Make Black America Better (p. 122)*. New York, NY: Anchor Books.

2. Data taken from Bureau of Justice Statistics. *Prison Statistics: Summary Findings (12/31/04)*.

3. SOURCE: U.S. Department of Education, National Center for Education Statistics, National Assessment of Educational Progress, 2003. http://nces.ed.gov/nationsreportcard/

4. Looping refers to classrooms where students stay together with the classroom teacher for the next grade level, i.e., from 4th grade to 5th grade.

5. AAU (Amateur Athletic Union), USATF (United States of America Track and Field).

6. Quality points refer to the additional points awarded by some school districts for honors, academically gifted, and/or AP classes. The points

are awarded to a student's class grade thereby resulting in a higher grade point average. For example, a final class grade of '85' in a class which awards 7 quality points would result in a final grade of '92' being posted to the student's transcript resulting in a higher GPA.

7. U.S. Department of Education, National Center for Education Statistics, National Assessment of Educational Progress, 2003. http://nces.ed.gov/nationsreportcard/

8. *Ibid.*

9. *Ibid.*

10. Alexandeer, K., Entwisle, D., & Kabbani, N. (2001). *The Dropout Process in Life Course Perspective: Early Risk Factors at Home and at School, Teacher's College Record, Volume 103, Number 5 (p. 775).* October 2001. New York, NY: Teachers College, Columbia University.

Films/Video Materials

ABC News (Producer). (1970). *The Eye of the Storm.* New York, NY: ABC Merchandising, Inc., Film Library.

CBS (Producer). (1979). *Marva.* (From 60 Minutes.) New York, NY: Carousel Films, Inc.

Paramount Pictures (Distributor). (2005). *Coach Carter.*

Mentoring Programs

100 Black Men of America, Inc.: http://www.100blackmen.org/

Big Brother Big Sisters: http://www.bbbsa.org

Jack & Jill of American, Inc.: http://www.jack-and-jill.org/

National Urban League: http://www.nul.org/

Young Black Scholars: http://www.youngblackscholars.com/

Index

– Other books from Rising Sun Publishing –

A High School Plan for Students with College-Bound Dreams, [Wynn]
Item #6903 • [ISBN 1-880463-66-0] • $19.95

Easy-to-follow planning guide for high school students. Helps students to understand how grades, standardized tests, behavior, activities, classes, community service, essays, and the billions of available scholarship moneys can all be factored into a plan (beginning in the sixth grade!) that can pave the way into the college(s) of their choice. Provides worksheets for tracking grades, test scores, awards, and class schedules.

A Middle School Plan for Students with College-Bound Dreams [Wynn]
US Version • Item #6901 • [ISBN 1-880463-67-9] • $15.95
Bermudian Version • Item #6902 • [ISBN 1-880463-70-9] • $19.95

Easy-to-follow planning guide for middle school students. Outlines how to maximize the middle school experience and how to prepare students for high school success as a stepping stone to students' college-bound dreams. Provides worksheets for tracking grades, test scores, awards, and class schedules.

Building Dreams: Helping Students Discover Their Potential: Teacher, Parent, Mentor Workbook [Wynn]
Item #5802 • [ISBN 1-880463-42-3] • $15.95

Guides teachers, parents, and mentors through exercises for facilitating discussion and direction for a student or group of students. Mentors learn how to move beyond the rhetoric of lecturing to meaningful and relevant dialogue; dialogue that will facilitate bonding and that will help students focus on long-term outcomes.

Don't Quit [Wynn]
Item #5002 • [ISBN 1-880463-26-1] • $9.95

Mychal Wynn's critically-acclaimed book of poetry contains 26 poems of inspiration and affirmation. Each verse is complemented by an inspiring quotation.

Empowering African-American Males: Teaching, Parenting, and Mentoring Success Black Males [Wynn]
Book • Item #5101 • [ISBN 1-880463-69-5] • $24.95
Workbook • Item #5102 • [ISBN 1-880463-71-7] • $15.95

Black males are the most "at-risk" students in America's schools. They are the most likely to be placed into special education, drop out of school, be suspended, be the victims or perpetrators of violent crimes, or be incarcerated. This book outlines a clear, cohesive set of strategies to turn the tide of underachievement to personal empowerment. Provides national discipline and achievement statistics.

Enough is Enough: The Explosion in Los Angeles [Wynn]
Item #5701 • [ISBN 1-880463-34-2] • $9.95

Provides an introspective analysis of the problems strangling those who live in America's urban battle zones and moves the reader toward solutions to help urban America help itself before it's tool late.

Follow Your Dreams: Lessons That I Learned in School [Wynn]
Item #5003 • [ISBN 1-880463-51-2] • $7.95

All students are confronted with choices during their school-aged years, from kindergarten through college. Which group do I identify with? How seriously do I take my schoolwork? How important is it to establish goals? What are my dreams and aspirations? How can my time in school help me to achieve them?

Mychal Wynn shares his story about the lessons that he learned while grappling with such questions and how he became a high academic achiever along the road to discovering his dreams and aspirations.

This Order May Be Placed By Mail • FAX • Telephone • E-mail
Payment May Be Made By Money Order • Check • Credit Card • Purchase Order

Enter the item number, description, corresponding price, and quantity for each selection (e.g., #1501, Laminated Don't Quit poster, $3.50/ea.) and compute the total for that item. Shipping is 10% of the subtotal (i.e., subtotal of $200.00 x .10 = $20.00 shipping charges). **Allow two weeks for processing.**

Item #	Description (Please Print)	Unit Price	X Quantity	= Total
5101	Empowering African-American Males *Book*	$24.95		
5102	Empowering African-American Males *Workbook*	$ 15.95		
6903	A High School Plan...College-Bound Dreams	$ 19.95		
6901	A Middle School Plan...College-Bound Dreams	$15.95		
7201	Ten Steps to Helping Your Child Succeed in School	$ 9.95		
7901	Increasing Student Achievement: Volume I, Vision	$ 29.95		
5601	The Eagles who Thought They were Chickens: Bk	$ 4.95		
5603	Eagles: Student Activity Book	$ 5.95		
5602	Eagles: Teacher's Guide	$ 9.95		
5003	Follow Your Dreams	$ 7.95		

Method Of Payment
Do Not Send Cash • No C.O.D.s

❑ A check (payable to Rising Sun Publishing) is attached
❑ A purchase order is attached, P.O. # _____
Charge my: ❑ Visa ❑ Mastercard

_____
Account Number   Expiration Date

_____
Signature *(required for credit card purchases)*

SUBTOTAL	$	_____
Shipping (Subtotal x 10%)		_____
Add Handling		3.50
Georgia residents add 6% Sales Tax		_____
DATE: _____ TOTAL		_____

✉ Mail to:
RISING SUN PUBLISHING
P.O. Box 70906
Marietta, GA 30007-0906

RISING SUN
PUBLISHING

☎ Phone toll-free: **1.800.524.2813**
FAX: **1.770.587.0862**
e-mail: orderdesk@rspublishing.com
web site: http://www.rspublishing.com

Ship to *(Please Print)* [Must be same as billing address for credit card purchases]:
Name _____
_____
Address _____
City_____ State_____ Zip _____
Day Phone (_____) _____ Email : _____

Increasing Student Achievement: Volume I, Vision [Wynn]
Item #7901 • [ISBN 1-880463-10-5] • $29.95

This, the first volume of the Increasing Student Achievement series, outlines how a school community goes about the business of developing a clearly-defined commonly-shared vision that drives systemic and sustained efforts toward increasing student achievement.

Inspired to Learn: Why We Must Give Children Hope [Peters]
Item #8901 • [ISBN 1-880463-08-3] • $12.95

Stephen Peters, former middle school principal, not only outlines his vision for the children in our schools, he goes on to share how he and his staff turned their vision into operational strategies.

School Violence...Calming The Storm: A guide to creating a fight-free school environment [Dolan]
Item #7101 • [ISBN 1-880463-14-8] • $29.95

Outlines all of the components and provides everything that a classroom teacher or principal needs to create a fight-free school environment: *instructional lessons; charts; parent communication; letters to the community; classroom, cafeteria, school bus, and school-wide activities; a lesson on the human brain and what causes anger; sample newsletters; fight-free pledge cards; certificates, and more.*

Ten Steps to Helping Your Child Succeed in School: Volume I [Wynn]
Item #7201 • [ISBN 1-880463-50-4] • $9.95

Outlines easy-to-follow steps for parents and teachers to better understand children so that we can better direct them. The steps help parents and teachers to easily identify a child's personality types, learning-styles, Multiple Intelligences, best and worst learning situations, dreams and aspirations.

Test of Faith: A Personal Testimony of God's Grace, Mercy, and Omnipotent Power [Wynn]
Item #6001 • [ISBN 1-880463-09-1] • $9.95

"This book has become more than a recalling of my hospital experiences, it has become a testimony of the power of the human spirit; a testimony of the healing power of the Holy Spirit; and ultimately a personal testimony of my relationship with God, my belief in His anointing, and my trust in His power, grace, and mercy."

The Eagle Team: Leadership Curriculum [Wynn]

Student Guide • Item #7501 • [ISBN 1-880463-66-0] • $15.95
Facilitator's Guide Item • #7502 • [ISBN 1-880463-66-0] • $15.95

An effective intervention and leadership program designed to help unlock the passion within students by leading them through a series of units that will help them to discover their dreams and aspirations as they develop the leadership and academic skills to be recognized as leaders within their respective school communities.

The Eagles who Thought They were Chickens: A Tale of Discovery [Wynn]

Book • Item #5601 • [ISBN 1-880463-12-1] • $4.95
Teacher's Guide • Item #5602 • [ISBN 1-880463-18-0] • $9.95
Student Activity Book • Item #5603 • [ISBN 1-880463-19-9] • $5.95

Chronicles the journey of a great eagle, historically perched at the right hand of the great king in her native Africa, who is captured and taken aboard a slave ship, the eggs that are eventually hatched, and their struggles in the chicken yard where they are scorned and ridiculed for their differences. The story offers parallels to behaviors in classrooms and on school playgrounds where children are teased by schoolyard "chickens" and bullied by schoolyard "roosters."

To order or to inquire about staff development, parent seminars, or student presentations:
770.518.0369 • FAX 770.587.0862 • Toll free 1.800.524.2813
E-mail: info@rspublishing.com • Web site: www.rspublishing.com